Revisiting the Days of Genesis

Revisiting the Days of Genesis

*A Study of the Use of Time in Genesis 1–11
in Light of Its Ancient Near Eastern and Literary Context*

B. C. Hodge

WIPF & STOCK · Eugene, Oregon

REVISITING THE DAYS OF GENESIS
A Study of the Use of Time in Genesis 1–11 in Light of Its Ancient Near Eastern and Literary Context

Copyright © 2011 B. C. Hodge. All rights reserved. Except for brief quotations in critical publications or reviews, no part of this book may be reproduced in any manner without prior written permission from the publisher. Write: Permissions, Wipf and Stock Publishers, 199 W. 8th Ave., Suite 3, Eugene, OR 97401.

Wipf & Stock
An Imprint of Wipf and Stock Publishers
199 W. 8th Ave., Suite 3
Eugene, OR 97401
www.wipfandstock.com

ISBN 13: 978-1-60899-597-4

Manufactured in the U.S.A.

All Scripture has been translated from the original Hebrew or Greek except where noted otherwise.

For all of my professors and students

הנסתרת ליהוה אלהינו והנגלת לנו ולבנינו עד עולם

"The unrevealed things belong to YHWH our God, but the things revealed belong to us and to our children forever."

(Deut 29:29 = MT 29:28)

Contents

Preface ix
Acknowledgments xiii
Abbreviations xv
Introduction xix

1. Real Events and Their Ideological Presentations in Literature 1
2. Time References in Genesis 1–11 and Their History of Interpretation 16
3. The Seven Day Structure and the Cosmic Temple of Genesis 1 35
4. Does *běyōm* Mean "When" in Genesis 2:4b? 70
5. A New Look at the Punishment of the Primeval Couple 99
6. The Genealogies of the Two Seeds 120
7. The Days of the Deluge 133

Conclusion 155
Bibliography 159

Preface

SOME PRELIMINARY ISSUES I would like to discuss pertain to the reasons I wrote this book and my particular view of the composition of Genesis. I will discuss the latter first.

The state of source criticism has often been lamented in the academic field today largely due to disagreements over identifying the exact sources and dates of the particular traditions that make up the book of Genesis. It is my opinion that the old view that saw Genesis as a sloppy patchwork of varying sources must now be discarded.

One of the problems I think scholars are facing is the fact that traditions cannot always be sufficiently nailed down. For the purposes of the present study, therefore, I will simply assume that Genesis has an actual author, who I would identify as a single priestly writer (sometimes identified as R), who has used a mixture of various traditions, both inside and outside of Israel. He has taken material from the earlier Pg (*Priesterliche Grundschrift*), as well as J and E, which had already adopted a variety of ancient Near Eastern traditions as well. In short, the author has done what most authors do, i.e., taken the traditions of his world and crafted them into a masterfully coherent composition. For this reason, a literary analysis of the book is the most beneficial trajectory to take for our current study, as the traditions that have been assumed by the narrative now carry the theology that the author desires to convey.

So why write this book? I found it necessary to write this book in an effort to clarify some important issues concerning the time frames used by the Genesis author—a clarification needed both within the scholarly community and within the community of faith as a whole. In recent years, the primeval history in Genesis has been assaulted from every direction, but one of the worst hits it has taken, ironically, comes from the faith community. This is largely the case because it has been interpreted in a crude and violent manner against its literary purpose. Hence, what it was originally intended to communicate has largely been lost on its modern audience. The time periods used by the Genesis author, as well, have been almost completely misunderstood, even by scholars who see the primeval history as essentially a literary creation.

As a young Bible student, I found myself firmly in the literalistic camp that saw most of biblical scholarship with a skeptical eye, especially when it came to Genesis 1–11. My interpretation was largely held prisoner to an apologetic mindset that only saw biblical criticism as a tool to attack the Faith. As is often the case, when prejudice of an issue gives way to more reflection, my perception of this criticism became one of more friend than foe.

One of the interpretive deficiencies primarily in play in my own misunderstanding was that of misidentifying the purpose of the narrative in my earlier studies. I had always assumed that the purpose was to describe the event taking place within the narrative in exacting detail. Hence, my interpretive methods fell into a long history of interpretation that sought to make sense of the events through the text. Because of this tendency, any claim that suggested that the description of the event did not correspond exactly as to how that event unfolded was to claim that the Bible was mistaken, and therefore, not of God. After all, if God was there, and He was the one communicating the text through the author, then the text ought to depict the event accurately. What liberated my exegesis from this idea was to see that the purpose of the narrative was not to describe the event, but to use the event to convey a message in ancient mythic terms. In other words, the text was referring to an event, but was not describing that event in exact terms. It was conveying theology through an ancient language, which carried within its descriptions mythic imagery that formed epic genres that unfortunately only exist in our day in the form of fiction. Hence, if a single event was described in three different ways within the Bible, or even within the narrative itself, it had absolutely no implications for what the Bible was. One could perceive it as purely man made, a partnership, whether equal or hierarchical, between God and man, or that it dropped out of heaven on golden plates. It simply said nothing as to what it was because it was the theologizing of history that was at the heart of its primary message, and as such, exacting details were not only irrelevant to the narrative, but would have often gotten in the way of the text's purposes.

But there was an even more foundational issue that led to my misconstruing the nature of the author's literary purpose, and that is context. At this early stage in my career, context was that which immediately preceded and followed the particular pericope one was reading. What I soon learned, as my skills developed, was that context is the entire literary work interpreted within its conceptual world. Something is not just out of context when it is lifted from its immediate context, since contextual importance holds equally for both micro and macro domains of a text (i.e., a word in its morphological and lexical form, that word in its sentence, the sentence in a paragraph, the paragraph in a larger discourse, the larger discourse within a section or book, the book within its ancient setting and within the canon). The debate that has raged on, including the numerous misinterpretations of the text that currently prevail, is largely due to a failure to read the text within *all* of these contextual spheres. What is needed is for the reader to understand that language is not just a bunch of grammar and words, but cultural symbols that conjure up images in the individual's mind when placed within various types of literature. Hence, to learn Classical Hebrew in an attempt to understand a text must also include an education of the ancient Near Eastern world that it signifies with those linguistic symbols. Once a reader does this, he or she may also realize that critical methodologies, comparative material, and literary readings are no longer threats, but companions, to faith, since they provide important information in deciphering the linguistic context of the ancient Hebrew that was used to write the biblical text.

This will become important for the student of Genesis 1–11, as he or she will be faced with the decision to interpret time within that narrative as a precise measurement that corresponds to the actual event (i.e., an exacting detail) or as a literary element that contributes toward the theologizing of an event that, in a far greater degree than a literal chronology or factual detail, brings an individual closer to understanding his or her Maker.

Acknowledgments

I WOULD LIKE TO thank the kind library staff at Princeton Theological Seminary for their willingness to spend the time to help someone who would otherwise be lost in their massive stacks; and for the great discussions that we've had during the days I would spend there.

I would like to thank my professors for giving me a diligence to study the text in its original languages, and within the biblical world in which it speaks, so that we might hear it in ours. I pray that this volume will prove that your labor has not been in vain.

I would like to thank Gordon Arthur, who copyedited this manuscript. Any remaining imperfections are purely my own.

I'd like to thank Tina Campbell Owens for her hard work in typesetting this manuscript.

I would like to thank my mother, Michele Bonnée Nichols, who is always a constant support of my work, and the person through whom chaos was conquered on my behalf.

I would also like to thank my beautiful wife, Allison Marie Hodge, who organized my bibliography and put up with my mental absence as I occupied my mind with the present subject for the past seven months.

I would like to thank my children, Jonathan, Alexander, Peter, Lily, and Andrew, for being a continual reminder to me of God's victory over chaos through His gracious gift of life and preservation. You are evidence that the loving Creator lives and is still at work in the world today. As always, *Sola Dei Gloria*.

Abbreviations

ACCS	Ancient Christian Commentary on Scripture
AE	*The Adapa Epic*
AEL	*Ancient Egyptian Literature*
AH	*Atra-ḫasīs*
ANF	Ante-Nicene Fathers
ARAB	*Ancient Records of Assyria and Babylon*
ARI	*Assyrian Royal Inscriptions*
AV	Alphabetisches Verzeichnis der assyrischen und akkadischen Wörter der Cuneiform Inscriptions of Western Asia
BBR	*Bulletin for Biblical Research*
BDB	Brown-Driver-Briggs, *Hebrew and English Lexicon of the Old Testament*
BM	British Museum (London) Museumssignatur.
CAD	*The Assyrian Dictionary of the Oriental Institute of the University of Chicago*
CANE	*Civilizations of the Ancient Near East*
CC	*The Chaldean Cosmogony*
CDA	*A Concise Dictionary of Akkadian*
COS	*The Context of Scripture*
DCH	*Dictionary of Classical Hebrew*
DSS	Dead Sea Scrolls
EG	*The Eridu Genesis*
Ee	*Enūma eliš*

EN	*Enki and Ninmaḫ*
ETCSL	Electronic Text Corpus of Sumerian Literature
GBHS	*A Guide to Biblical Hebrew Syntax*
GE	*The Gilgamesh Epic*
GKC	*Gesenius' Hebrew Grammar*
HALOTSE	*Hebrew and Aramaic Lexicon of the Old Testament*, Study Edition
HS	*Hebrew Syntax*
IBHS	*Introduction to Biblical Hebrew Syntax*
JANES	*Journal of Ancient Near Eastern Studies*
JBL	*Journal of Biblical Literature*
JNSL	*Journal of Northwest Semitic Languages*
Jouön	*Grammar of Biblical Hebrew*
JSOT	*Journal for the Study of the Old Testament*
JSOTsup	*Journal for the Study of the Old Testament Supplement Series*
JTS	*Journal of Theological Studies*
KAR	*Keilschrifttexte aus Assur religiösen Inhalts*
KTU²	*The Cuneiform Alphabetic Texts from Ugarit, Ras Ibn Hani and Other Places.*
LHBOTS	Library of Hebrew Bible/Old Testament Studies
LXX	The Septuagint; specifically, the Greek translation of the Pentateuch
NIDOTTE	*New International Dictionary of Old Testament Theology and Exegesis*
NPNF¹	*Nicene and Post-Nicene Fathers*, Series 1
NPNF²	*Nicene and Post-Nicene Fathers*, Series 2
OG	The Greek translation of the Old Testament, with exception to the Pentateuch
PG	*Patrologiae Cursus Completus, Series Graeca*
PL	*Patrologiae Cursus Completus, Series Latina*

PGL	*Patristic Greek Lexicon*
SBH	*Syntax of Biblical Hebrew*
SH	*Song of the Hoe*
SJOT	*Scandinavian Journal of the Old Testament*
SKL	*Sumerian King List*
SP	Samaritan Pentateuch
TDOT	*Theological Dictionary of the Old Testament*
TLOT	*Theological Lexicon of the Old Testament*
UT	*Ugaritic Textbook*
VAT	Vorderasiatische Abteilung, Tontafeln, Staatliche Museen, Berlin: W: Herbert Weld Collection, Ashmolean Museum, Oxford University
VT	*Vetus Testamentum*
ZAW	*Die Zeitschrift für die Alttestamentliche Wissenschaft*

Introduction

THE TEXT OF GENESIS has perplexed readers, both ancient and modern, seemingly since the time it was first written. Is it myth? Is it history? Is it a combination of both? These questions have continued to resurface with scholars positing both literalistic and allegorical answers throughout its interpretive history.

In recent days, scholars have made comparisons, both valid and invalid, between the motifs, literary patterns, and genre of the book of Genesis with those of ancient Near Eastern cosmogonies, annals, epics, etc., and have found much fruit from the tree of this knowledge. As with any discipline, however, that knowledge must be used as a handmaid to that particular scholar's or school of thought's ultimate presuppositions and worldview. In one sense, therefore, all interpretation stems from usually hidden beliefs that the author does not make explicit in his use of the evidence. Because of this, any individual interpretation will always take on a polemical aspect to it in one way or another, where the scholar is attempting to support his or her theory with the data. In another sense, however, much can be gleaned from this theoretical pursuit in that new ways of seeing the text may aid the community of faith to understand how the text might be read in light of other presuppositions, most importantly, ancient ones.

Much caution is needed in this pursuit, however, for although scholars see themselves as explorers into new worlds, they are unquestionably, and many times unwittingly, carrying in the old world with them. This can be seen in numerous scholarly books and debates where scholars acknowledge their enslavement to their presuppositions, but then carry on as though anyone who does not conclude as they do must be held suspect of bias, since the evidence is, well . . . self evident. Any objectivism that fails to reckon with the subjective nature of analysis must be removed from the study of true scholars if they are to understand that their theories may be true, but are not beyond doubt in light of their own epistemological limitations.

For the person of faith, the all important question becomes one that concerns itself with where his or her presuppositions ought to be acquired. This question is mandatory for any thinking person of faith, as it is more than likely, if he or she has grown up in the Western world, that his or her presuppositions have merely been assumed from the philosophical naturalism that pervades academic study and Western thought in general.

In conjunction with this, the false dichotomy between what is natural and what is supernatural, often infused into the Western mind, takes center stage as one discusses the biblical text. This is evident in comments made by certain scholars implying that if the text is mythological then it is not true, and if true, it would not be mythological. The biblical writers surely would have seen no such distinction. To them, the mythological is a beautiful vehicle that is used to express what is true.

IS GENESIS LITERAL OR MYTHOLOGICAL?

This brings us to the question concerning the nature of the Genesis text, specifically, Genesis 1–11, since that is the text with which this study is concerned. It seems clear that the ancient Israelites, as well as many peoples in the ancient Near East, often clothed real people and events in mythological language in an effort to convey something ideological or theological in nature. The texts are often molded to meet the goal of an ideological or theological presentation rather than convey the exacting details of an historical event.

A good example of this can be seen in the Hebrew Synoptics (i.e., Samuel, Kings, and Chronicles). It is clear that the Chronicler has the actual text of Samuel-Kings in front of him, copying the text, making minor variations here and there, but also making larger emendations that fit the respective theology he wishes to communicate. Likewise, it is probable that the events portrayed in both Samuel and Chronicles concerning King David are subordinate to larger theological themes, and should be seen as literary rather than a literal record detailing the events.

On the other hand, a good example of the other extreme can be gleaned from this very phenomenon and its interpretation by modern scholarship. It was once believed, and still held dogmatically by some of its supporters, that because these texts are theological in nature, utilizing literary craft and genre to convey theology, the historical events and people they describe are fictional as well. A good example of this is the existence of David himself. Many scholars thought that David was but a mere character in the fiction that is biblical history. One reason for this is that we have two different accounts of the Davidic narratives found in Samuel-Kings and Chronicles. One of the most eye-opening studies of my school career was going through Abba Bendavid's *Parallels in the Bible*, a work that sets the texts side by side and highlights the differences in red. It is clear from the standpoint of anyone who looks at the evidence that the Chronicler not only knows of Samuel-Kings, but has a copy in front of him, and is deliberately making changes to the text that accord with the theological message he wishes to communicate. One of the greatest examples of this, known to most students of the Hebrew Bible, is found in 1 Chronicles 17:14, where the personal pronouns in 2 Samuel 7:16 are changed from the second person singular (i.e., "your") to first and third person singular (i.e., "my" and "his").[1] In the original account, God was promising to protect the Davidic throne forever. In the Chronicler's revision, God promises to protect His temple forever. This makes sense, since in the Chronicler's time the Davidic throne had been replaced by various foreign rulers who had been installed over ancient Palestine. God reigned through His temple, and it is through the temple that the Davidic line still had its throne. The Chronicler, therefore, combined the throne of God with the throne of David, perhaps, in the hope of messianic expectations that predate those of the DSS.

For many scholars, however, these changes meant one thing and one thing only: theology, not history, was the sole purpose of these stories. David, therefore, was seen to be an altogether fictional character, who was fabricated merely in an effort to give a theological identity and hope to an exiled and oppressed Israel. This has been a very popular theory in recent days, and one can easily see why it would be. If the text is primarily theological or ideological, then who is to say that it is not exclusively theological or ideological? The problem for this position came with the discovery of texts such as the Tel-Dan and Mesha inscriptions that recorded David as a literal person, who actually lived, was king over Israel, and had literal descendents (e.g., Omri). The power of presuppositions surfaced as the scholars, who supported the idea that David was merely

---

1. Bendavid, *Parallels*, 43; cf. Enns, *Inspiration*, 59–66.

a fictional character in a story, scrambled to make sense of the new texts, ultimately concluding that the reading of דוד ought to be interpreted as Dôd, an obscure and otherwise unattested god in Israelite religion, rather than David. Ultimately, however, historical skepticism, for the most part, has given way to the acknowledgement that a real person, who was really king over Israel, and may have participated in some real events, was being described literarily and utilized as a character in the biblical text in an effort to convey theology, i.e., what was viewed by the biblical authors as more important than a mere realist understanding of historical details.[2] For Christianity, of course, this use of real persons and events being molded in theological presentations has been part of its long history of interpretation in terms of the four Gospel accounts.

The fact that ancient writers sometimes used real people and events in their theological presentations does not mean that they always did this. It is very possible that characters that did not exist are also constructed for the purpose of communicating theology. It is simply a caution that one must take in noting that when archaeology has allowed us to discover whether a person or event was fact or fiction, it has many times concluded that the individual or event has some historical basis in reality.

But what of our text here in Genesis? Specifically speaking, the "primeval history," found in chapters 1–11, seems to have a large amount of ancient Near Eastern mythology that clothes the events and characters within the narrative. It is very possible, since the authors themselves were distant from these events, having no historical records beyond what is reported in ancient annals and epics, that they took what knowledge they had from these sources, and presented them as characters in a highly theological book. In fact, if this is the case, the real question here might simply be whether the ancient sources and traditions used by the author were based upon real people and events.[3]

Another consideration, of course, is that the main character in Genesis is none of the human characters presented at all, but rather God

2. Although some scholars, like Athas (*Tel Dan Inscription*, 271–81), take the phrase בית דוד, which appears as a reference to David's ancestral dynasty 24 times in the Hebrew Bible, as a toponym, i.e., the "city of David," which appears 44 times as a reference to Jerusalem. Of course, these are not mutually exclusive options, as the Davidic throne may also stand as a synecdoche for Jerusalem.

3. A good example of this is Gilgamesh, who was a highly fictionalized character in Mesopotamian epic stories based upon a well-known, historical king.

Himself, who takes center stage as the only constant presence throughout the story. Since God is the main character, one could possibly argue that the other human characters are composed literary pieces that make up the setting and merely fulfill the needs of the narrative in presenting a theology of its main character.

How, then, does this concept of history and theology specifically relate to Genesis 1–11, a text that often has been viewed as purely fabricated? After all, is not the consensus of modern scholarship to see it as a complete myth apart from history? But such a conclusion, as we have seen, stems from a failure to recognize the union of two genres in biblical literature: the symbolic combined with what is perceived as historical tradition. What would normally be classified as epic literature, a designation that at first seems appropriate for the primeval history of Genesis, is overly simplistic in its observation. Epic literature is a combination itself of legend and poetry. What is interesting about the Genesis text is that, despite the idea that poetry manifests itself in numerous forms,[4] it is absent of the type of parallelism and other poetic devices that often constitute ancient poetry.[5] Instead, a remnant of the type of poetic-prose found within epic literature has been combined with what represents history of a time unknown in the author's day, existing only in pieces of tradition. In essence, traditional material formed into an historical timeline makes up the structure utilized for the Genesis text's epic stories.[6] But even so, the author only utilizes certain elements believed to represent that history, rather than relating a detailed account of historical information that is known to him. This is common in the ancient world. Since information is not known to the authors, it is subject to alteration. Hence, the details found within the primeval history were often rewritten and emended in texts both inside and outside the canon.[7]

---

4. Kugel, *Biblical Poetry*, 49–63. See a brief critique of this idea in Polak, "Poetic Style and Parallelism," 16 n. 48.

5. I say this in consideration of the excellent argument, made by Polak (Ibid., 2–31), that the passage contains various elements found within poetry, resembling that of certain Psalms, that indicates the possibility that P's account was once a hymn.

6. See White (*Narration and Discourse*) for the argument that the text utilizes older traditions in order to build the message of the narrative.

7. Cf. the author's use of these traditions in the book of *Jubilees*. "The significance of this material from *Jubilees* is that it demonstrates the manner in which the writer has embellished the flood narrative for the purpose of tracing certain of the Jewish festivals and practices to the patriarchs. Festivals, according to him, begin with Noah.

The major primeval traditions found within the text specifically are as follows:

1. The victory of the primary and/or creator deity (often depicted as a warrior king) over elements of chaos, whether personified or not (Gen 1; all creation accounts, e.g., Ee and the *Bilingual Creation of the World by Marduk*);[8]

2. The creation of humans from clay (Gen 2; SH; VAT 17019; EN; Ee; AH);

3. The singling out of a particularly special human (either a king or a wise man) by deity for the purpose of making a covenant with him (Gen 2; AH; AE; GE; EG);

4. The opportunity to hold immortality, only to lose or reject it (Gen 2–3; AE; AH; GE);

5. A delineation of people who fuse primeval history with the beginnings of civilization (i.e., known history), linked together themselves by the event of a cataclysmic flood (Gen 4–11; SKL);

6. The flood itself as a divine judgment upon mankind (Gen 6–9; SKL; AH; GE; EG).[9]

These are all traditional elements that thrived in the ancient Near Eastern conception of primeval history. The scheme (creation-human

---

Exact dates have been supplied for each event of the flood in the effort to validate a religious calendar for which the writer is doing propaganda. An effort is made to demonstrate that Noah acts in keeping with the ritual prescriptions of the Law and that he is the transmitter of esoteric knowledge (*Jub.* 10:14; 12:27; 21:10). Elements of the story that do not fit his purpose, such as the sending out of the dove, have been omitted. Theological interpretations have been added: angels assemble the animals for the ark; Noah's post-flood sacrifice is an atonement; his drunkenness is in connection with a sacrifice; and God is to dwell in the tents of Shem" (Lewis, *Interpretation of Noah*, 32).

8. Beyond the theogonies, where gods battle with one another in the primordial quest for supremacy, Ee is the only account in the ancient Near East to actually have a *Chaoskampf* creation motif that personifies chaos as evil gods and demonic powers (Hodge, "Labor of the Gods"). By "creation" here I mean to refer to those accounts that exist as a cosmogony or anthropogony.

9. A good summary of some guidelines scholars use to determine what texts should be used, as well as a defense that P uses Mesopotamian traditions specifically, can be found in Sparks, "Priestly Mimesis," 625–48, see specifically 627–9 for a delineation of an appropriate methodology in determining what Sparks calls emulation. See also Coats, *Genesis*, 38; and Clark, "The Flood," 187–8.

successions of greater longevity-flood-human successions of shortening longevity) connects a reader's contemporary history to the unknown pre-history of humankind. The fact that humans were created by immortal beings, but still die is explained by the fact that humans were once given the opportunity to become immortal like the gods, but either refused or lost the opportunity to do so. The event pattern consisting of creation-fall-succession-flood-succession, in varying order, is not necessarily particular to the Bible in its basic structure.[10] What is distinct, however, is what the author of Genesis does with this pattern in an effort to convey a theology about God, His intentions with humanity, and His people's deliverance from chaos.

Hence, Genesis 1–11 is history, but not the type of history that the modern mind expects. Instead, it is a history of how God has acted in the world. It is a history of His role as Creator and Sustainer of His people. It is *Heilsgeschichte* "salvation history," a creation out of, and redemption from, chaos, rather than something that seeks to report details of each and every event of the early history of the world as they literally occurred, as if that was even desirable or possible to record in a concise narrative in the first place. Instead, Genesis relates to its reader something about God and His work in the world. Somewhat in accord with this interpretation is Westermann's observation that the creation narratives have a purpose to convey something to its present reader

---

10. In fact, Smith (*The Priestly Vision*, 155–6) attributes the similarity in structural motifs between Genesis 1–11 and SKL to the likelihood that the primeval history is, in fact, meant to provide an historical account. He states: "For all their considerable differences, the parallel between the Sumerian King List and Genesis 1–11 is useful for understanding Genesis 1 in its larger context and for a consideration of the related question as to whether it is a myth. The parallel has been noted, mostly for potential traces of shared traditions . . . Like Genesis 1, the King List begins with the heavens ('when kingship was lowered from heaven'). It also relates sequences of time down through the flood and into historical time. Like Genesis 1–11, it details preflood and postflood figures. Compared with the reigns of its postflood figures, the Sumerian King List provides much higher dates for the preflood figures. Both Genesis 1–11 and the Sumerian King List incorporate various sorts of traditional information. Both are also recognized as now being composite works . . . What is the upshot of this comparison for the question of Genesis 1 as a myth? No one calls the Sumerian King List a myth, yet within its historiographical framework it contains references to 'mythic events' . . . For all their differences, both the Sumerian King List and Genesis 1–11 allude to mythic events, but this does not make either one of them a myth. One might characterize them as mythic in the sense that both contain elements we would associate with myth; still, it would be stretching the point from a literary perspective to call them myths."

rather than something about origins.[11] Westermann clarifies, however, that the narratives are about the past in terms of their implications for the present. Christian Link concisely sums up Westermann's argument along these lines:

> Westermann connects this observation with the suggestion, which is in no way self-evident, that the creation stories do not have the meaning that might be attributed to them by a modern reader. That is, they should not be understood as saying something primarily about an event in the past; instead the primary motif is 'not a question about the origin but about the world and humanity under threat in the present.' The biblical declaration about the creation must be understood from the present, against the background of historical catastrophes; it puts the unsettling question of whether the future will bring about all that was promised in the very beginning. Thus, 'the link between the origin and present must be obvious', not only to the exegete who analyses ancient texts, but to the people living today, who are seeking a secure foundation for their being.[12]

I would suggest, however, that the author does wish to describe the creation event, albeit in theological rather than in literal terms. He is communicating God's work in the world, rather than attempting to relate the details of the event, an event about which he does not have the details in the first place. This *Heilsgeschichte*, not the details of what is a largely unknown history, existing in bits and pieces of legendary material, is what is important to the author and his readers, who are ever more concerned about survival and God's intentions toward them in a chaotic and hostile world.[13]

---

11. Westermann, *Genesis 1–11*, 603.
12. Link, "Providence," 266.
13. I do not wish to be accused of a false dichotomy in saying that the text, if symbolic, cannot describe reality. After all, most scholars agree that a cataclysmic flood occurred in ancient Mesopotamian history, and certainly, humans came from other humans who preceded them, so a genealogy, either in literal or symbolic form, may relate that succession. What is important for the community of faith to see, however, is the theological message of the biblical text in its literary and ancient Near Eastern context in order to understand that as the primary purpose of said text. What one wishes to believe about the nature of the events that these symbols represent cannot be concluded from the text itself, but is rooted instead in whatever presupposition sits enthroned in the readers mind.

If in fact these traditional pieces of material represent, rather than measure and detail the events they describe, and are molded in accordance with the larger theological purposes of the narrative, then it is very likely that the temporal language used within that narrative is also representative of the time of those events.[14] In other words, the author's use of time within the text is literary rather than literal.

Hence, it becomes important to look at the way temporal language is used within the primeval history in order to discover and contemplate the book's message, not as a vehicle to identify the exact details of the people or events that are being used to convey that message. It is my hope, therefore, that, regardless of one's belief concerning the people and events themselves, the author's intentions, in regard to his use of temporal language, will be more fully understood by the reader in an effort to discover the means by which narrative time contributes to the overall literary intentions of the work, and through this discovery, gain a richer and more rewarding theological understanding of this notoriously elusive text.

---

14. Something analogous to the representative use of time might be found in the modern use of the word "day," to represent one's entire young life, found in the phrase, "In my day, we had to walk to school in three feet of snow."

1

Real Events and Their Ideological Presentations in Literature

There has been no little amount of ink spilt over the question concerning the nature of "myth" and its relationship to the Hebrew Bible. Most definitions, however, confuse the mythic understanding of a person or event with the way that person or event is described in literature.¹ Instead, one must make a distinction between what the author may believe to be true in correspondence to his perception of reality, and what the author seeks to communicate, using the numerous literary images at his disposal, one of which is mythic language, in order to communicate his intended message. The time has now come for scholars to start thinking in terms of what can be known from a text. If the event of a text is lost, and all that is left is a literary description of that event, then the task of the scholar is to interpret the text rather than to seek the impenetrable psychology of its author. In other words, the question should not be, "What does the author believe about reality," but instead, "What is the author communicating in this text?" Specifically, the event and the author's actual cosmological and historical beliefs, while they may be assumed to have commonalities with other ancient beliefs, are lost in the past, or at the very least, are not usually communicated in detail through theological literature. All that remains is the literature, rich in symbolic description, i.e., language that has its origins in ancient culture and literature, but poor in its ability to relate precise descriptions of the author's beliefs, at least in terms of the Genesis narrative.²

1. For a brief survey of some of the proposed definitions, see Childs, *Myth and Reality*.

2. Most scholars would agree with Paas (*Creation and Judgement*, 81–2) that the ancient Israelites probably viewed the world as a flat disc with a dome stretching overhead. However, note that the netherworld that is geographically located under the earth is also called ארץ (Stadelmann, *The Hebrew Conception*, 128).

In other words, the text, filled with the symbolism common to literature and having a telic moral, is not concerned about capturing the event as it occurred, but about communicating something greater than a mere description to its audience.[3]

A good example of this can be found within our own mythic language. Imagine if I were to take my son to the top of the hill at dawn in order to enjoy the scenery with him. I turn to my son and say, "What a beautiful sunrise." My son replies, "Yes, it is very beautiful." What has taken place here is communication through myth, but not the type of communication that seeks to describe reality as I believe it. I don't really believe that the sun rises over the earth. Instead, my comment only seeks to describe reality in terms of a more aesthetically satisfying imagery, which is best expressed in mythic/romantic language rather than precise scientific language.

Regarding the author of Genesis, this becomes all the more difficult, as he, no doubt, has beliefs concerning the world that are not of our modern scientific understanding, but neither can we say exactly what they are from the text, since he is seeking to convey a theology through mythic/romantic language, not a literal description of events that uses precise language consisting in literal units that measure ancient time.[4]

---

3. In this regard, with some of the reservations voiced by Childs ("Critical Reflections," 3–9), and a few of my own, my view of the Genesis narrative is very similar to James Barr's ("The Literal, the Allegorical, and Modern Biblical Scholarship," 3–17). See also N. Wyatt's comments ("The Mythic Mind," 12): "Myths may contain elements of history just as history may contain elements of myth." Wyatt states that one must distinguish what he calls "sober history," i.e., history that consists of an "objective sequence of events (as far as objectivity is possible, though *our* subjectivity in apprehending them does not detract from *their* facticity" (Ibid.).

4. Other vehicles exist in the ancient world that allow the scholar to substantiate, with probable accuracy, the cosmology of the author (a solid work that considers these creation accounts within the larger view of ancient Near Eastern literature is Stadelmann, *The Hebrew Conception*, noted above— although I would take a cautionary approach in the use of texts that display a high amount of mythological language). To be sure, many of the people who read the myths really believed them; but it would be a mistake, in light of the sophistication of the literary achievement that is the text of Genesis, to impose without qualification the unsophisticated beliefs of the masses upon a particular author. To be sure, the ancient author's cosmology is nothing near our modern understanding of the universe, but ancient concepts varied in their cosmologies from people group to people group (cf., e.g., the concepts found in Genesis 1 differ from those found the more poetic Psalms in terms of their use or lack thereof of the *Chaoskampf* motif). It is also, therefore, important to study ancient Near Eastern documents that are more scientific in nature in an effort to understand that myth and

In Jeremy Hughes's description, myth is "fiction which is used to express truth."[5] This itself may be too simplistic, as the term "fiction" has multiple meanings and expressions as well. Hughes does qualify the statement, however, by stating that this fiction is historical, and is utilized "to express ideological beliefs."[6] In terms of chronology and the literary distinctions of Genesis 1–11, Hughes's observation holds the most explanatory power in my opinion. However, I would want to add a further qualification by stating that historical fiction is still a depiction of real events, not simply a story-like parable or fable that is constructed *ex nihilo* for the purpose of theological instruction. The real event is described in mythic terms. There is, therefore, a vast difference between a completely mythic view of Genesis 1–11 and a view that would ascribe the use of myth in these chapters to literary description (i.e., a form of symbolic language) within a highly theological presentation of what the author and his readers consider real people and events.

A good illustration of this can be found in the arts. The school of realists might sit in front of a beautiful scene and paint it in detail so that the painting, as much as possible, accurately records the scene. An impressionist or an abstract artist, however, would sit down in front of the scene and reorder the scenery in terms of color and shape, and perhaps, even bring into the scene what is not already there. These latter artists are seeking to use the scene to express a message, whereas the former artist is seeking simply to record the scene, as though he has taken a picture of it. This is a good way to see the language of myth versus the language of precision that our scientific age so unfortunately requires of any piece of literature that claims to communicate truth.

To the biblical authors, however, truth is beautiful, and it should be conveyed to its audience with all of the symbolism and excitement of mythic language. It would be easy, for instance, for the Psalmist to say that God is sovereign and rules over everything; but it is more poetic and resonates with his audience in a much more profound sense to say, "He makes the clouds His chariot; He walks upon the wings of the wind"

---

science may be distinguished as separate methods of analyzing the world or it may be combined with more scientific data in the mind of the ancient author. Cf. the highly technical astronomy employed in Mesopotamia as it is coupled with myth and superstition (Hunger and Pingree, *Astral Sciences in Mesopotamia*).

5. Hughes, *Secrets of the Times*, 3.
6. Ibid.

(Ps 104:3). This statement is meant to convey what is considered reality by the biblical author, but reality and precise language are not the same. In a similar style as that found in the Psalms, in Genesis, people, places, and events are all used to support very impressionist and abstract narratives that communicate theology to their religious audience.

To go back to the sunrise analogy, I am describing a real event in front of me. I am not making up the fact that there is a picturesque view created by the light of the sun in front of me. What I am refusing to do, however, is to describe it with scientifically accurate language. Not only would my son have no clue what I was saying if I chose to do so, but I would also be deliberately throwing away the beauty of what I wished to communicate to my son by saying, "What an interesting shift in the terrestrial axis that captures heliacal trailing within atmospheric visibility!" Instead, there is something greater, more genuine, and much cleverer in the statement, "What a beautiful sunrise!" than can be found in the dull precision of the realist (or should I say, "literalist"?).

My son might think that this newer, more scientifically precise language offered him an education, and thus was informative, but I would have stolen any aesthetic connection he might have had to enjoy the beauty of the scene. If I wanted him to have an accurate and precise understanding of the scene, then I would have failed to communicate that to him by using mythic language; but if my purpose was to communicate something that, in my estimation, is much more profound, then I would have failed by refusing to use mythic language in my description of the real event before me.

As with events that take place in the present, history, as an event in the past, must be presented from the perspective of the person retelling it. The event cannot be recreated, but it can be retold, and it often is retold in the service of an idea.

One of the great examples of this in the modern era is the recreation of historical events and persons in movies. The purpose of the movie is rarely intended to merely relate historical facts. Instead, it is usually the purpose of a movie, even one that is in the style of a documentary, to communicate a point in an aesthetically pleasing way to its audience. Events, as they occurred, are reordered and edited with additional information, conversations, and molding of the historical details to fit the message the director wishes to convey to his audience. No one perceives the director as disingenuous simply because he or she wishes to recast the event in terms of the message. It is expected, and even known that what is delivered may not be what actually happened in history, but instead may be often seen as more valuable than a more precise retelling of events would be. After all, huge crowds did not flock to libraries to study William Wallace in his historical context before the movie *Braveheart*, and it is doubtful that many did afterward. This is because the retelling of the event in terms of an important message is more powerful and enduring than a raw list of facts absent of an interpretation and meaning assigned to them.

At the same time, no one doubts that William Wallace was an actual person or that the movie was based on actual events that took place in reality; but everyone must agree that the person and events themselves have been radically altered to give greater meaning and significance to the director's contemporary audience.

Another example of an event described in mythic language would be something of the following: "That mighty Zeus, in a flash of lightening, razed cities to the ground and stormed the world to the top of Persis's mountain."

Here we have a campaign conducted by Alexander the Great that really happened in history, but described in almost completely mythic terms. One would not be able to recreate the event in detail from the mythic description. What is more, if the author does not know how an event took place, then all one has is the mythic description of what is vaguely thought to be known from other sources available to the author.

Specifically applying this to mythic or narrative time, an example might be found in the following summary of a greedy rich man's life:

> All that he had acquired brought him to the lap of luxury, but when the clock struck twelve and his life was required of him, his riches came to poverty. The security of his wealth he had befriended betrayed him at the third crow of the cock, and when night fell, the day did not return to him.

Each element of time used in the above narrative supports what the narrative intends to convey. The clock striking twelve is reminiscent of the Cinderella story where her riches turn back to rags at the stroke of midnight. The third crow of the cock is reminiscent of the betrayal committed by the Apostle Peter. The night conjures up imagery of the end of the day and the day not returning of death's finality. Each element essentially describes the death of the rich man in a very symbolic fashion. In this way, one can see temporal language as a part of the narrative, rather than a literal depiction of the time of the rich man's death. Furthermore, the allusions made by the text underscore the importance of knowing the culture within which a particular narrative speaks.

When we come to Genesis, it is important to understand that the author intended to convey a theology through history rather than absent from it. However, this does not mean that history is the primary objective of the narrative.

J. P. Fokkelman so succinctly states:

> We may say, in other words . . . that the stories from Genesis have the ontological status of the literary work of art. That is why these stories can be readily analyzed as works of fiction, so like the novel or the lyric in European literature . . . [However,] the narrative prose of the Old Testament is characterized by an "intentionality" which differs from that of the works of fiction of Western literature. It has a claim to two other sorts of truth, apart from that of fiction. Thus, no doubt, the listeners/readers were convinced that the people, relationships, and events had existed just as they were told. The patriarchs as they appear in Genesis signified to the Israelites their own national history. So the specific "fictionality" of OT prose may not be represented as opposed to what ancient Israel meant by historicity; rather it can be said to include that historicity . . . The narratives themselves, though, will have had a considerably subtler opinion of the historicity of what they told. The exact shaping power we find in Chapters I and II renders it highly probable that they were conscious of the fact that by shaping and by creating structures their own contribution was considerable, if not decisive. They felt perfectly justified in re-fashioning the raw "historical" material they had and in putting it into the service of a higher truth, mostly that of their faith.[7]

Hence, historicity and myth/cultural symbols work together for the theological purposes of the author's message. Of course, the question arises, "What do we mean when we say that the text of Genesis uses myth?"

---

7. Fokkelman, *Narrative Art in Genesis*, 7.

THE BIBLICAL USE OF CULTURAL SYMBOLS

Even though I have thus far used the term "myth" in terms of language, I prefer the phrase "cultural symbolism" over the term "myth" for numerous reasons. The primary reason is that the term "myth" is simply too often confused with a large number of definitions often associated with it.[8] For this reason, it is better not to use the term too often, to avoid misunderstanding. Another reason I reject it is that it just is not an accurate description of what is going on in the biblical texts.[9] The Bible uses mythic language, but mythic language is meant to convey reality, and not just a reality for the ancient reader, but what is to be considered reality for everyone. Myth itself often functions more like a fable in the ancient world that is often believed to be an accurate assessment of natural phenomena. It is meant to provide an etiological explanation of an observed event or describe that event in some way. Myth, therefore, is often employed to describe the reality of nature. Although many would assign this same sense of the word to the biblical authors, I think it is more accurate to say that they are not attempting to describe reality in terms of understanding cosmology/nature, but instead employing mythic language, that they very well may have believed otherwise, as a means to understanding theology.[10] In other words, the Bible uses what I would call mythic language, but not for the purpose of relating

---

8. Smith (*The Priestly Vision*, 159) states that whether a person assesses the nature of the text of Genesis 1, and by extension Genesis 1–11, to be myth "depends on what we mean by the word myth and what we think myths are really about."

9. Although with some reservations, I see valuable insights concerning the definitions of myth offered by Oswalt, *The Bible among the Myths*.

10. Consider the popular idea among scholars captured in Moberly's statement concerning the theology of Genesis 1: "For example, there is only one deity, not many; creation come from sovereign word and action, not from triumphing over others in combat; and there is no account of God, for example in battle or performing other actions, other than in relationship with the world—that is, there is a 'demythologizing' in relation to other ancient Near Eastern accounts. Although of course the sovereignty of the one God is present in Genesis 1 on any reckoning, it is an aspect of the text that receives particular emphasis in this kind of comparative reading" (*Theology of Genesis*, 52). According to Moberly, such a demythologizing needs to be understood "in relation to other ancient Near Eastern accounts." This is an important distinction, since Genesis 1 is not demythologized from all mythic language and concepts in general, but from polytheistic theogonies, debasing anthropogonies, and the idea of creation through the *Chaoskampf* motif found in Ee. The text, however, remains rich in symbolic language (e.g., chaotic waters, temple imagery, man as God's image, etc.).

the myth, but to communicate theological ideas.[11] Such a distinction is like night and day. I simply do not believe that there is any biblical text that attempts to teach cosmology, but every biblical text does intend to teach theology. In this regard, issues of inspiration come into play for the community of faith, as God is able to communicate theology in an aesthetically pleasing manner through the human author's cosmological beliefs without compromising the message being conveyed.

I realize that individual biblical texts are often ripped from their respective contexts by some scholars in an effort to give examples of the text literally supporting ancient cosmology; but I would caution such a one that the books of the Bible should not be left chopped up into little pieces, as some scholars have often carelessly done in the past. Whatever their tradition history may have been, the individual pieces of a text now function to support the larger literary argument of a biblical book, and a biblical book, the larger *Heilsgeschichte* argument of the canon. Whatever the individual use or meaning of a particular tradition may have been before it was included in the final form of the biblical text, it is to be rendered obsolete in so far as it is capable of contributing to the narrative, and therefore, suspect in its ability to render a sure contribution toward discovering its purpose in the present text. Hence, if a tradition was at one time intended to teach mythology within its original *Sitz im Leben*, that tradition is now enveloped by the biblical text, and

---

11. To illustrate this point, I would direct the reader to myths such as that found in 6:1–4, which gives little explanation and detail to a passing note. Yet, the myth is employed in order to convey something about the chaotic state of humans, a notion fitting to the text's literary purposes. Here, myth has been turned into language. It no longer functions as it normally does (i.e., to provide an etiology or description of a current phenomenon or legendary event) within the larger ancient Near Eastern culture. It now functions as a part of the larger narrative argument of the book. See the statement by Hendel ("Of Demigods and the Deluge," 24) that "though the story no longer serves the purpose it once did, it fits well enough into its new context as one of several illustrations of mankind's evil activity prior to the flood." He further concludes that "the story is a piece with the other narratives of the Primeval Cycle. It is a mythological fragment, displaced from its original traditional context and integrated by the Yahwist into the structural and thematic framework of the Primeval Cycle. The work of the Yahwist, I suggest, was conscious and complex; the myths that he used had resonances all their own" (Ibid., 25–26). Cf. also the biblical use of the legend of Enmeduranki's sage Utuabzu (= Enoch) that "looks like a meager remnant of the mythological story" (Borger, "*Bīt Mēseri*," 227) in Genesis 5:24 that contains even less and far more ambiguous information about the sage than what can be gleaned from Mesopotamian tradition (Ibid., 224–33).

works together with the rest of the text to accomplish the author's literary goals. In this sense, therefore, there is simply no biblical text that teaches ancient cosmology, just as there is no biblical text that teaches Hebrew grammar or ancient measurement tables; but every biblical text seems to be supported by the language and imagery of the world that assumes them.

LITERARY USES OF TIME IN SYMBOLIC NARRATIVE

The language of imagery and the cultural symbols that are used in ancient texts also include the use of temporal language that builds a setting for the culturally symbolic depiction of an event. As persons and events can be molded to fit the purposes of the author's message, the temporal language that belonged to that event may be molded as well. As conversations and imagery are added to a narrative to bring about what is needed to support the theology conveyed, so temporal elements, i.e., depictions of time, may also be added in order to accomplish that same goal.[12] Although many of the events, for the author, originally took place in real time, the temporal language that is employed for the purpose of setting and theology ought to be seen as connected to the larger language and purpose of the narrative. This should be done in place of seeing such language as independently placed within the narrative for informational purposes only, and this language is distinct from the symbolism used to communicate the author's message. Hence, time measurements, especially in the primeval period, are representations of something else. Either they are symbolic of the real time during which an event took place, or they represent an imagery that contributes to the argument of the text in some way. In this sense, temporal language is symbolic. It is time in culturally symbolic terms, or what Bervard Childs calls "mythic time."

Childs describes "mythic time" as follows:

> It transcends the modern categories of empirical time. Moreover, mythical time is in no sense an abstraction by which relations between temporal things are measured in terms of space as, for example, 'length of time'. Rather, it is substantialized as a concrete reality which is identical with its content . . . this scheme illustrates the mythical understanding of time as moving in a rhythm and being identified with its content.[13]

---

12. This is true of other elements, such as geography, in a narrative as well. See Beck, "Geography as Irony," 291–301.

13. Childs, *Myth and Reality*, 74–5.

The distinction I would propose here is that the use of time in richly symbolic narrative like myth is also "essentially timeless."[14] I will attempt to demonstrate in the following chapters that the use of time is not meant to be a temporal measurement, calculating either the duration of an event or at what point in time the event happened; but is instead a part of the symbolic language utilized by the author in an effort to complete the impressionistic or abstract picture he desired to create. The biblical authors are not realist painters. They are impressionists and abstract artists that seek to paint the historical picture in terms of a literary masterpiece that conveys a theological message, and will give their audience a greater understanding of God and His work in the world.

Hence, the much proclaimed objection that Genesis 1–11 is not a strict example of poetry, and therefore is not symbolic, has a base understanding of literature. There are numerous genres of literature that are very symbolic and yet not poetry. All literature, as stated above, is a picture that has been painted by an author. Symbolism, therefore, can be painted into any picture, regardless of the theme, the colors used, and the strokes that are made with the brush. The question, therefore, becomes, "How does one understand the intention of the artist in his conceptual context?" In this book specifically, my answer will seek to put flesh on the bones of the literary view of Scripture in terms of its analysis of temporal language and its function within the larger picture that has been painted by the author.

THE LITERALISTIC HERMENEUTIC AND ITS ASSUMPTIONS

The first assumption that needs to be removed from the preconceptions of the reader is that what is symbolic is not true. Peter Enns discusses the peculiarity in the alliance between what is perceived as modern liberal and modern conservative views of truth and the genre of Genesis.

> Taking the extrabiblical evidence into account, I question how much value there is in posing the choice of Genesis as either myth or history. This distinction seems to be a modern invention. It presupposes—without stating explicitly—that what is historical, in a modern sense of the word, is more real, of more value, more like something God would do, than myth. So, the argument goes, if Genesis is myth, then it is not "of God." Conversely, if Genesis

14. Ibid., 74.

is history, only then is it something worthy of the name "Bible." Again, it is interesting to me that both sides of the liberal/conservative debate share at least to a certain extent these kinds of assumptions. The liberal might answer, "Yes, it is myth, and this proves it is not inspired, and who cares anyway?" The conservative might answer, "Well, since we know that the Bible is God's word, we know it can't be myth." And so great effort is expended to drive as much distance as possible between the Bible and any ancient Near Eastern literature that poses problems.[15]

This assumption, held by "conservatives" and "liberals" alike, confuses what is being communicated and the vehicle through which that message might be conveyed. It is also a matter of understanding the purpose of the narrative. If one supposes that the narrative purpose is to describe an event in scientific terms (whether from ancient phenomenology or modern science) then it is less likely that suggestions of a symbolic text will be accepted in the religious community. If, however, the text's purposes are theological, which is the primary objective of all religious literature, then the forms of communication and genre used as the vehicle to convey that theological message becomes irrelevant to the question of truth. In essence, the language and genre of the text has to do with a completely different question than whether the theology being conveyed is true. If one studies Aesop's Fables, the symbolic imagery is evident even to the cursory reader; but whether or not the moral taught is valid is a completely different consideration to ponder. The two subjects are simply not related, as truth can be communicated in a variety of forms.

A good method of communicating the difference between these two categories is to use well-known fables. I, personally, would often use the story of "The Three Little Pigs" with a class of students. I would ask them whether they thought the story was true. They would usually laugh at the apparent absurdity of the question, as they boldly and dogmatically declared, "Of course not!" Certainly, in agreement with my students, most would not see the story as true. Pigs do not talk and build houses. Wolves do not attempt to blow houses down. But this is a woefully flawed misunderstanding of literature. I would then continue to ask the students whether they thought the author was attempting to

---

15. *Inspiration*, 49. See also Smith (*The Priestly Vision*, 157), who discusses two different approaches to the text and offers a third way that sees a value in both.

communicate that pigs really do talk and build houses, and that wolves really try to come along and blow houses down. Perhaps the author was mad, and really did think that animals talked? Perhaps he was trying to deceive his ignorant audience, who might believe him as he told it these falsehoods? The students, however, would soon realize that these suggestions were not plausible, and instead, the purpose of the author was to communicate something about life, and about building things in one's life that will stand against the difficulties—adversities that often materialize and threaten those things out of which the individual has constructed his or her life.

I would then point to the fact that this is a biblical idea. The Lord Jesus Christ says something very similar in terms of those who hear His words (Matt 7:24–27), as did Paul when speaking of what a person teaches (1 Cor 3:1–15). I would then ask the students whether what Jesus and Paul are teaching is true. They would, of course, say, "Yes." Finally, I would ask the question again, "Is the story, 'The Three Little Pigs,' true? Most would then say, "Yes."

It is this sort of understanding that needs to pervade the mind of the individual who reads literature, whether secular or sacred, but especially sacred, since what is communicated has more spiritual weight assigned to it by the faith community than what is perceived as merely human advice and wisdom. Once this is understood, the idea that what is symbolic equals what is not true can be discarded, and the individual will then be able to move forward in an effort to understand the sacred message more clearly. Ironically, then, what was in ignorance perceived as an attack upon the biblical text becomes the foundation for understanding it all the more.

The genuine attack upon the biblical text, however, is found when one fails to see its intended meaning because he or she is preoccupied with false assumptions of what constitutes "truth," as well as seeing all language in terms of scientific precision. The Bible is made up of every genre of literature (epic, historical narrative, legal, wisdom, poetry, prophetic, apocalyptic, epistolary, contractual, etc.) in order to communicate with God's people. To pretend that accurate communication can only come from a realist view of an act, event, or conversation, rather than taking upon the clothing of an impressionistic or abstract form of communication, is not only inaccurate, but seeks to hinder God's Word in a false form of piety. Distorting God's message to His people by taking what is meant to be symbolic in a literalistic fashion is about as pious as one who puts the Bible on a shelf because he does not wish to wrinkle the pages of such a holy book by reading it. God does not wish his readers to act as if the Bible is holy by defending positions that have deafened their ears to its actual message, but to treat it as holy by reading and seeking to understand the message in whatever form that message may have been communicated.

Finally, the assumption that the literalistic hermeneutic is the "plain reading" is only a modern illusion created by the Enlightenment-oriented reader who does not share the language and culture of the original recipients of the text. To give an example of this, what is meant by David being "a man after God's own heart" to a modern reader means that David had fuzzy feelings for God, hence creating an understanding of biblical religion as primarily one based on emotions that an individual has for God. Such a concept has led to all sorts of strange religious ideas, not to mention the modern concept of privatized religion. To the ancient reader, however, the phrase meant that David was the person of God's choice to be king, as opposed to Saul who was the people's choice. The term לב "heart" in the ancient Near East refers to the seat of the mind, and only rarely to the seat of emotion as it does in our modern context. In context, it is also clear that the contrast is between Saul, the people's king, and David, God's king (i.e., the king who was considered appropriate according to the people's thinking and the king that was considered appropriate according to God's thinking). All of this is simply to say that the "plain reading" of a text should be understood as the way the ancient reader would have read it, not the modern reader who has his or her own language and conceptual world, which inherently causes him or her to take what he reads out of context without him or her even knowing it.

Along the lines of misreading texts due to cultural distance, historical authors have often been concerned with issues that surfaced within their own life times rather than those issues that originally concerned the author of the biblical text. Hence, sometimes the wrong answers are received because the wrong questions are asked. One of the ways we find ourselves asking the wrong questions is when we ask a biblical text to address a modern philosophical claim. We then approach the text looking only to how it might answer that claim, and often become unaware of the question that particular text is really addressing. Although we give a great level of importance to our own questions, in a very many instances, the biblical text is more concerned with its questions than ours. In fact, it often seems completely unconcerned with the questions we wish were answered. Verses like Deuteronomy 29:29 provide the individual with some perspective in his or her larger understanding of the Bible's purpose (i.e., that the text is meant to give what is needed to God's people for the purpose of salvation and righteousness).

Occasionally, one's misunderstanding of the text stems from one's misunderstanding of language in general. As discussed before, it is often thought that if the text uses symbolic language, what it conveys is imprecise. This is then further extrapolated to mean that the text cannot answer modern questions at all. The flip side of this view is to see figurative language as untrue and conclude that everything in these passages, therefore, must be literal in order to be true. In short, the use of what is figurative is equated with what is loosely defined and the use of literal language is equated with what is precisely defined. Hence, if something is not precisely defined, it is not literal, and if it is not literal, it is not true.

But even the short example I mentioned before will show that this type of thinking is misguided. For instance, if, again, one were to imagine me asking my son, "What time does the terrestrial axis shift in order to capture heliacal trailing within atmospheric visibility?", although the most literally put, the question would be taken as incomprehensible to him, as well as to the average person. Whereas modern readers would like the Bible to have expressed its ideas in this type of modern scientific language, it does not. Instead, the Bible, like us, chooses clarity *via* symbolic language over scientific accuracy *via* technical language in an effort to communicate to its audience. Hence, the best communication is sometimes figurative or even mythological, not scientifically literal, so that those seeking to be clear would restate my question in mythological terms, "What time is sunrise?" This, of course, is mythological language. The sun doesn't rise as though the earth was a flat disk over which the sun moves. Much to the disappointment of some, the Bible uses common figurative and mythological, not scientific, language in order to communicate its message. While some may think this to be less precise, others would conclude that precision is in the eye of the beholder. An interpretive methodology of language that seeks mathematical precision rather than an aesthetic verbal image, in language that contributes to the imaginative theological picture, can only be described as literarily inept at best. As much as everyone remembers "word problems" posed in middle school math books, the pursuit to introduce mathematic and scientific precision with literature leaves something to be desired.[16]

Genesis is, of course, literature; and as such the reader ought to expect it to be filled with figurative and mythic imagery if it is worth reading. What makes Genesis better than just a piece of literature is the combined sacredness of its text and message, not its contribution toward modern cosmology. With this in mind, the text of Genesis 1 ought to be placed in its appropriate ancient and literary context when the modern reader asks questions concerning the nature of the days found therein.

---

16. It may be true that the language is also phenomenological to the ancient reader; but I am positing the use of mythological language in the text as a sophisticated literary language that must be divorced from the idea that the author is simply describing phenomena as he literally perceives it. What the author believes is a question that, in its own way, seeks to recreate the event (and something immaterial about the event at that). It is asking what the author was thinking to himself about the text he is writing. This is an absurdity, since what he was thinking cannot be ascertained by the modern scholar, absent of a time machine. One may surmise that the author believes what his world generally believes about these things, but that says nothing to his intended message within a literary document he is constructing. However, what the author communicates in that text is a question concerning the text itself. It is the latter with which the scholar must occupy his study.

2

Time References in Genesis 1–11 and Their History of Interpretation

UNFORTUNATELY, INSTEAD OF ASKING questions about the original intent of the narrative, historically, interpreters of Genesis 1–11 have been locked in a perpetual battlefield between those who attacked the literalness of this section of Scripture with the intention of undermining the message of the Bible in general, and those who used everything in their arsenal to defend the literal interpretation, believing this was the only way of saving the Faith. In other words, the literal interpretation has often stemmed from the perception that the faith is undermined by the erosion of the idea that the book of Genesis is literal. It is, after all, the book of foundations, both historically in one sense and ethically in another. Genesis provides information concerning the origins of God's interaction with humans, as well as displaying creation ethics, i.e., ethics that transcend culturally derived behavior due to their divine origins and approval. Hence, in times of greater philosophical persecution and infiltration, historical interpreters have often reacted by not giving an inch to those who attempted to use any breach in a believer's interpretation as a club with which to bludgeon the rest of that individual's faith.

Hellenistic ideas of cosmology and time challenged what were perceived to be biblical teachings concerning cosmology and the age of the earth. Literal postures were taken supposedly to ensure a greater faithfulness to the biblical text that did not compromise on a single *iota*.

It is clear, therefore, that the literalistic approach to the text is often a reaction against what is perceived as a corrosion of truth in general that restricts the language of the text so that it must correspond with the details as they occurred within the reality of the event described. In other words, if the interpretation of the text is limited by realism, then

Time References in Genesis 1–11 and Their History of Interpretation

any impressionist or abstract interpretations that seek to undermine the faith will be nipped in the bud.

However, it must be noted that the reverse is also true. There have been those in the history of interpretation, both ancient and modern, who sought to "protect" the text by allegorizing it in an effort to provide harmony between the Bible and contemporary origins theories. Augustine, in his *Confessions* is a great example of this. His wild allegorizing of the text has left many a reader bewildered and perplexed for centuries, but it is clear that these unbridled intellections were the result of an overreaction to Manichean polemics that sought to undermine the truthfulness of Christianity by arguing that the biblical creation accounts were absurd. Augustine's liberty with the text is a result of his first attempt to protect the text itself, and also to break down any wall that might hinder anyone with similar views to the Manicheans from coming to Christ.[1]

However, he does then seem to change his mind by the time he writes *De Genesi ad litteram*, where he concludes that the creation narratives actually describe the events as they occurred. He contends that if

---

1. He occasionally relates this concern: "It not infrequently happens that something about the earth, about the sky, about other elements of this world, about the motion and rotation or even the magnitude and distances of the stars, about definite eclipses of the sun and moon, about the passage of years and seasons, about the nature of animals, of fruits, of stones, and of other such things, may be known with the greatest certainty by reasoning or by experience, even by one who is not a Christian. It is too disgraceful and ruinous, though, and greatly to be avoided, that he should hear a Christian speaking so idiotically on these matters, and as if in accord with Christian writings, that he might say that he could scarcely keep from laughing when he saw how totally in error they are. In view of this and in keeping it in mind constantly while dealing with the book of Genesis, I have, insofar as I was able, explained in detail and set forth for consideration the meanings of obscure passages, taking care not to affirm rashly some one meaning to the prejudice of another and perhaps better explanation . . . With the scriptures it is a matter of treating about the faith. For that reason, as I have noted repeatedly, if anyone, not understanding the mode of divine eloquence, should find something about these matters in our books, or hear of the same from those books, of such a kind that it seems to be at variance with the perceptions of his own rational faculties, let him believe that these other things are in no way necessary to the admonitions or accounts or predictions of the scriptures. In short, it must be said that our authors knew the truth about the nature of the skies, but it was not the intention of the Spirit of God, who spoke through them, to teach men anything that would not be of use to them for their salvation" (*Gen. litt.* 1:19–20, IXX; 2:9). Also cf. his work entitled, *De Genesi contra Manichaeos*.

one does not understand how they can be literally true, the problem is in the interpreter rather than the narratives.[2]

Whether as the result of polemics, superficial hermeneutics, or an understanding of the text in its literary context, what cannot be said is that there is a standard, orthodox interpretation of the temporal language used in Genesis 1–11 that automatically excludes further investigation into the text. To advocate such a thing is not only to ignore history, but to deny the text any further voice to speak beyond the reader's cultural blinders, presuppositions, and fears in order to communicate to him a greater understanding of its theological message. The ultimate purpose of the sacred text has always been perceived in the church, by both allegorist and literalist alike, as that which reveals the *sacramenta fidei*. It is the revelation of those mysteries of the faith with which its message is occupied. Knowing that the converse is often claimed, however, we will now turn to questions concerning the historical interpretation of time as it is used in the Genesis text.

THE SECOND TEMPLE PERIOD

Nowhere is this idea taken to such an extreme as in the Book of Jubilees. The author of Jubilees clearly communicates that the two first books of the Pentateuch contain laws and regulations that all faithful believers are to follow, regardless of their cultural situation. It is also clear that the author believes that the infiltration of Hellenistic ideas that were becoming ever more prevalent in the mainstream of Jewish society were leading to an erosion of the faith, a collapse in devotion to God, and the corruption of idolatry. In fact, he believes this to such an extent that he attempts to argue that the solar calendar the Jews had traditionally used was the only heavenly ordained calendar, and hence, the lunar calendar was a later pagan invention.

Time according to the author of Jubilees is important because it dictates the days upon which Israel was to celebrate the festivals that stood at the center of the community's worship. To fiddle with the calendar is to set Israel on a path of disobedience, since it can no longer observe the festivals on the days upon which they were instructed by God to do so. Observing the festivals as God intended, including the

---

2. Kim, *Augustine's Changing Interpretations*, 103–7. Note also that Augustine found the text so perplexing that he reinterpreted it around five different times within his lifetime (Ibid., 163).

Time References in Genesis 1–11 and Their History of Interpretation

weekly observance of the Sabbath, can only occur if the true dates of their observances are known. Hence, the calendar was of utmost importance, and to compromise, in the mind of the author, was to compromise one's Jewish identity and covenantal relationship with God.

Here we see that the belief in a literal interpretation and adherence to what is perceived to be the biblical message concerning temporal language leads one further to believe that compromise of the literal interpretation suggests compromise of the biblical message in general. After all, if one does not literally believe what the Bible tells one about a time frame, why would he or she not compromise on other biblical teachings? There is, of course, more going on than just this slippery slope argument. The Jews had just undergone a brutal persecution under Antiochus Epiphanes, who attempted to wipe out Judaism by replacing its cultic observances with those that honored Zeus instead. Of course, the Hellenistic calendar was lunar, and thus, it follows logically that the author of Jubilees associated the dethroning of a biblical calendar or time period with an attempted destruction of the faith as a whole.

In conjunction with this idea, the Greeks believed that the world was very old. This conflicted with the view of the author of Jubilees, who believed that, based on the Genesis chronology, creation had begun relatively recently. Hence, when he comes to the six days of creation, it is no surprise that he interprets them literally, even to the point that he states that God Himself literally observed the Sabbath after His work week as an example for His people to follow.[3]

However, this literalistic hermeneutic does not come without the needed midrash to explain any contradictions that might be created by the clash of two supposedly literal statements within the text. For instance, where the Hebrew Bible states that God had finished all of His work on the seventh day, and all of His work was clearly finished on the sixth day, interpreters who wished to maintain a literalistic hermeneutic had to change the day upon which all things were finished to the sixth. Hence, the ancient versions, from the Samaritan Pentateuch to the Old Latin that influenced much of the early Western Church, mainly following the LXX text, changed Genesis 2:2a to read ἐν τῇ ἡμέρᾳ τῇ ἕκτῃ (i.e., ביום השישי) "on the sixth day" from the MT's ביום השביעי "on the seventh day."[4]

---

3. *Jub.* 2:17–20.
4. This is followed by Jubilees (2:1–4), and most likely the Qumran community, as

Similarly, the author of Jubilees had to maintain harmony between the six days of Genesis 1 and the one day of Genesis 2. The day of 2:4b was either seen as a figurative day or a day that represented a longer period of time. Hence, the Garden of Eden was created on the third day and man on the sixth, even though the text of Genesis 2 presents them both as being created on the same day.[5]

A natural result of the literalistic hermeneutic was, of course, the need to fill in the gaps of the text. It had to explain everything that didn't seem consistent in the way that the literal hermeneutic had understood it, and it needed to make sure that a foundational text like Genesis was consistent with the rest of sacred literature and the ancient interpreter's understanding of that literature.

Hence, in terms of the contradiction between the days of Genesis 1 and 2, the text was in need of some imaginative harmonization. James Kugel sums up:

> Early interpreters transformed the opening chapter of Genesis in several significant respects. The very first thing that God created was wisdom. When He said "Let there be light" God was referring to a special light unknown to human eyes. God created the angels, either on the first, the second, or the fifth day. God's words in Gen. 1:26, "Let us make man," were understood to mean that He had received aid or advice in creating man. Finally, some translations and retellings of the creation story differed from the traditional wording of Gen. 2:1[sic] by making it clear that the creation was entirely finished by the end of the sixth day.[6]

However, there were those, such as Philo of Alexandria, who were no longer threatened by a now familiar Hellenism, and thus, had little cause to reorder the Bible into a contemporary polemic. For instance, in Philo's view, the creation days merely reflect an order of God's creating, not literal days, as though such thing as a day existed without the sun during the first three acts of creation anyway.[7] Instead, he believed that

---

it was a major text read and accepted within the community (4Q216 5:2). What is interesting is that the community regularly gives evidence of the text type that anticipates the MT, but here, as in the rest of its tradition of the Genesis text, it shares its readings with that of the LXX instead (Brooke, "Genesis," 300).

5. *Jub.* 2:7–10, especially in 4Q216 6:3–4.

6. Kugel, *Traditions of the Bible*, 53.

7. "Creation cannot have taken place in six natural days, for days are measured by the sun's course, and the sun is but a portion of creation" (Philo 1929, xiii).

the term in Genesis 2:4b was the more literal in the sense that God had more likely created everything all at once.[8] This was not the most common view, however, as suspicion of Hellenistic corruption in both theology and practice sat at the back of the mind of Second Temple Jews, and often led them to fight for the literal chronology of the days in Genesis 1, especially because it pertained to the observing of Sabbath; but this interpretation did find support in other texts, such as Sirach 18:1: ὁ ζῶν εἰς τὸν αἰῶνα ἔκτισεν τὰ πάντα κοινῇ "He who is eternal created all things together."[9]

However, quite another story exists when contradictions are perceived within the text. In an effort to smooth out what is considered a rough patch in the text, authors will alter their strict views of the literal interpretation to include interpretations that allow for more symbolic concepts. For instance, when interpreting the "day" of Genesis 2:17, where the human couple will die if they eat the fruit of the tree of knowledge, some ancient exegetes argued that there is no contradiction between taking both texts as harmonious, since a thousand years is as one day to the Lord. Hence, as the author of Jubilees et al. state, Adam died within a day at the age of 930 years old.

PATRISTIC WRITERS

Most of the Patristic writers believed that Old Testament texts were to be interpreted as having either a literal or a symbolic meaning, and sometimes both. This gave rise to various disputes between those who supported allegorical interpretations of Genesis, both with a Christocentric focus and in general, and those who simply saw the texts as a literal description of events. One of the texts that informed both interpretations of the days is that of Psalm 89:4 (OG = MT 90:4): ὅτι χίλια ἔτη ἐν ὀφθαλμοῖς σου ὡς ἡ ἡμέρα ἡ ἐχθές ἥτις διῆλθεν, "because a thousand years in Your eyes are as yesterday that has gone by," interpreted in 2 Peter 3:8 as μία ἡμέρα παρὰ κυρίῳ ὡς χίλια ἔτη καὶ χίλια ἔτη ὡς ἡμέρα μία, "one day to the Lord is like a thousand years and a thousand years like one day." What this did was to allow an interpreter to see the two seemingly conflicting texts as complementary toward one another.

---

8. Philo, *On the Creation* 8; See also Kugel, *Traditions of the Bible*, 71–72. Philo's interpretation of the six days, therefore, is allegorical in nature (*On the Creation* 3).

9. However, cf. the NRSV translation, "He who lives forever created the whole universe."

If the six days in Genesis 1 conflicted with the one day in Genesis 2, then the one day could be taken as a longer period of time. Likewise, both texts could be perceived as longer periods of time, so that no further harmonizing was needed. In a similar way, if God said that Adam and Eve would die on the day that they ate the fruit, the idea that a day in God's eyes was equivalent to a thousand years provided the needed consistency within the passage.

Origen argued against the idea that the six days of creation are literal on the basis of Genesis 2:4a that stated the heavens and the earth had been created ᾗ ἡμέρᾳ "in the day."[10] He interpreted the days of Genesis 1 as symbolic, and the day of Genesis 2 as the more literal. In conjunction with others, he saw the world as less than ten thousand years old.[11]

By contrast, Cyprian suggested that the days referred to seven thousand years instead of literal days, and gave them allegorical explanations in the context of an apocalyptic discourse.[12]

> As the first seven days in the divine arrangement containing seven thousand of years, as the seven spirits and seven angels which stand and go in and out before the face of God, and the seven-branched lamp in the tabernacle of witness, and the seven golden candlesticks in the Apocalypse, and the seven columns in Solomon upon which Wisdom built her house, so here also the number seven of the brethren, embracing, in the quantity of their number, the seven churches, as likewise in the first book of Kings we read that the barren hath borne seven.[13]

It should be noted that the numerous interpreters, both ancient and modern, who seek to interpret the days as longer periods of time, whether a thousand years or an earth age each, are also seeking to interpret the text according to what they perceive it to signify directly. In their view, the word "day" cryptically refers to a thousand years. In this way, reading the text seriously, in their view, does not necessitate the idea that one must interpret the days as literal 24 hour periods of time that correspond objectively to reality, but may also include those views that saw the days as longer periods of time. This was possible due to the

---

10. See *Cels.* 6:50, 60.

11. Ibid. 1:20.

12. He also notes the symbolic use of the number seven as that which conveys complete perfection (*Fort.* 11:11).

13. Ibid.; *ANF* 5:503.

hermeneutic that allowed for a type of lexicography that saw the entire Bible as the context for a single word. Hence, two biblical texts that were associated with the same word (e.g., יוֹם) were combined, so that two distinct referents gained from those contexts could be combined into a single concept as well (e.g., a thousand years).

Irenaeus believed that the day was to be associated with the thousand year period of previous Second Temple thought. He thus concluded from the day mentioned in 2:17 that Adam and Eve died on the same day they were created.[14]

Likewise, Clement of Alexandria stated that Genesis 2:4 was placed in the text by God so that no one would think that creation literally occurred within time.

> That, then, we may be taught that the world was originated, and not suppose that God made it in time, prophecy adds: "This is the book of the generation: also of the things in them, when they were created in the day that God made heaven and earth." For the expression "when they were created" intimates an indefinite and dateless production.[15]

Here Clement argues that the infinitive in 2:4 indicates that there is no measurement of time that corresponds to a literal chronology of the creation event, since it took place before and during a period when there was no time.

Augustine also was unsure that the days of Genesis 1 should be taken in a literalistic fashion. Instead, he supposed that they existed in the text to convey a literary ordering of instantaneous creation events for the purpose of conveying distinction to the reader.[16]

> But simultaneously with time the world was made, if in the world's creation change and motion were created, as seems evident from the order of the first six or seven days. For in these days the morning and evening are counted, until, on the sixth day, all things which God then made were finished, and on the seventh the rest of God was mysteriously and sublimely signalized. What kind of days these were it is extremely difficult, or perhaps impossible for us to conceive, and how much more to say![17]

14. *Haer.* 5.23.2; *ANF*, 1:551–552.
15. *Strom.* 6.16; *ANF* 2:514.
16. cf. *Gen. man.* 1.9.15; FC 84:62–63.
17. *Civ.* 11.6.

It is well known that Augustine interpreted the days allegorically in his *Confessions*. Augustine's interpretation here is true allegory, not a literary reading of the text; but in his *De Genesi contra Manichaeos*, he clearly says that the days mentioned in the text are literal days, but that he is unsure of their nature.

However, many other Patristic writers, following in the steps of the author of Jubilees, believed that the days of Genesis 1 were to be taken in a literalistic fashion, even though most believed that the day of Genesis 2:17 was not to be interpreted in that manner. Lactantius believed that "God completed the world and this admirable work of nature in six days, as is contained in the secrets of Holy Scripture, and consecrated the seventh day, on which He rested from His works."[18]

Ephrem the Syrian, seeking to stay the hand of wild allegory, stated that the six days are to be taken as their plain meanings signify.

> So let no one think that there is anything allegorical in the works of the six days. No one can rightly say that the things pertaining to these days were symbolic, nor can one say that they were meaningless names or that other things were symbolized for us by their names. Rather, let us know in just what manner heaven and earth were created in the beginning. They were truly heaven and earth. There was no other thing signified by their names "heaven" and "earth." The rest of the works and things made that followed were not meaningless significations either, for the substances of their natures correspond to what their names signify.[19]

Basil stated:

> I know the laws of allegory, though less by myself than from the works of others. There are those truly, who do not admit the common sense of the Scriptures, for whom water is not water, but some other nature, who see in a plant, in a fish, what their fancy wishes, who change the nature of reptiles and of wild beasts to suit their allegories, like the interpreters of dreams who explain visions in sleep to make them serve their own ends. For me grass is grass; plant, fish, wild beast, domestic animal, I take all in the literal sense. "For I am not ashamed of the Gospel."[20]

---

18. cf. *Inst.* 7.14; *ANF* 7:211.
19. FC 91:74; ACCS 1:9.
20. *Hexaem.* 9:1; *NPNF*[2] 8:101.

He further argued:

> "And there was evening and there was morning: one day." And the evening and the morning were one day. Why does Scripture say "one day the first day"? Before speaking to us of the second, the third, and the fourth days, would it not have been more natural to call that one the first which began the series? If it therefore says 'one day,' it is from a wish to determine the measure of day and night, and to combine the time that they contain. Now twenty-four hours fill up the space of one day—we mean of a day and of a night; and if, at the time of the solstices, they have not both an equal length, the time marked by Scripture does not the less circumscribe their duration. It is as though it said: twenty-four hours measure the space of a day, or that, in reality a day is the time that the heavens starting from one point take to return there. Thus, every time that, in the revolution of the sun, evening and morning occupy the world, their periodical succession never exceeds the space of one day.[21]

Hence, both literal and allegorical interpretations existed in the early church, and although Christians disagreed with one another, they did not consider one another to be heretics on that basis, since, as Augustine so aptly put it, "these other things are in no way necessary to the admonitions or accounts or predictions of the scriptures."[22]

RABBIS AND SCHOLASTICS IN THE MIDDLE AGES

Rashi believed that the days were literal 24 hour periods of time, so much so, that he even speculated that the primeval light worked with the darkness to complete the day cycle before the sun was created.[23] Yet, he sees a theological connection between the term בראשית and Israel's religious and political history. He also interprets the first day in a theological manner, and says that יום אחד refers to the fact that God is בעולמו יחיד "the only One in the universe."[24] Rabbis, such as Maimonides, believed that Scripture and science should align, and therefore, the text of Genesis did not require a literal reading.[25] His work is another piece of

---

21. *Hexaem.* 2:8; *NPNF*² 8:64.
22. *Gen litt.* 2:9.
23. See Silberman, *Rashi's Commentary*, 3.
24. Isaiah et al., *Rashi's Commentary on Genesis*, 5.
25. *Guide of the Perplexed* 2.25.

evidence that indicates that those who believe the Bible to be threatened by the science of the day may retreat to an allegorical interpretation of the text just as well as a literal one.

Aquinas, however, interpreted the days as literal 24 hour periods of time. In the *Summa*, he explains the days as follows:

> *On the contrary*, It is written (Genesis 1), 'The evening and the morning were the second day . . . the third day,' and so on. But where there is a second and third there are more than one. There was not, therefore, only one day.
>
> *I answer that*, On this question Augustine differs from other expositors. His opinion is that all the days that are called seven, are one day represented in a sevenfold aspect (*Gen. AD lit.* iv, 22; *De Civ. Dei* xi, 9; *AD Orosium* xxvi); while others consider there were seven distinct days, not one only. Now, these two opinions, taken as explaining the literal text of Genesis, are certainly widely different.
>
> *Reply to Objection 7*. The words 'one day' are used when day is first instituted, to denote that one day is made up of twenty-four hours. Hence, by mentioning 'one', the measure of a natural day is fixed. Another reason may be to signify that a day is completed by the return of the sun to the point from which it commenced its course. And yet another, because at the completion of a week of seven days, the first day returns which is one with the eighth day. The three reasons assigned above are those given by Basil.[26]

What is interesting about Aquinas' observation is that he acknowledges a diversity of opinions have existed concerning the nature of the days, yet he makes no claim that one particular view is orthodox and one heretical. The days are, in fact, never made an issue until the time of the Westminster Confession, and even then, Reformed theologians have differed significantly over the interpretation of the text.

In the thirteenth century, Robert Grosseteste argued for an allegorical interpretation of the days in an effort to harmonize the biblical account with his view of creation. He stated that one "should know, then, that the six days draw attention [*designantur*] to the six ages of the world."[27] By this, he meant that each of the six days was representative of ages of the earth that followed creation, the first being the period

---

26. *Summa Theologica* 1.74.2.
27. *On the Six Days*, 258; and Grosseteste, *Hexaëmeron*, 253.

between Adam and Noah and the last starting from Christ to the end of the world.[28] Each of the periods also represents stages in human life and experience as well.[29]

THE REFORMERS

The Reformers largely held to a literal six day creation. Like some interpreters before them, they argued that this was the plain reading of the text, and such a reading was needed in light of the wild allegory displayed within many of the writings of the heretics. It was also needed to counter skeptics who sought to undermine the faith by attacking the literalness of the first chapters of Genesis. Although most moderns tend to think that the concept of evolution is a new one, the belief stems back a few millennia. Evolution, from a pagan standpoint, is how the world and its inhabitants came to develop from the creator god; and from an atheistic standpoint, it existed in advocates like Lucretius, who lived in Rome in the first century BCE.

Lucretius himself argued that all life evolved, without the aid of any gods, from simple to complex organisms, and therefore, the Patristic authors who later interacted with his poem concluded that his system implied the idea of God's making all things in the course of six days as nonsensical. His poem became well known in the Renaissance, and therefore to the Reformers, who were studied men of their age.

Hence, the Reformers sought to counter such ancient polemics against religion by stating that the plain reading of the text was the only genuine interpretation of that text, which to them, meant that Genesis 1–11 was to be taken as the historical account that they believed it to be. This meant that the temporal language used therein was to be interpreted as referring to actual measurements of time that characterized the duration of the events described. Hence, such skeptics were simply wrong in their theories of origins.

There may have been a perceived threat that lingered in the church through its history, or it may simply be the literalistic reading of the days that was passed down and functioned as a lens through which the Reformers saw the text that caused them to read the Genesis account this way.

28. *On the Six Days*, 258–60.
29. Ibid., 258–68.

It is true that those who sought to counter a perceived threat often fell back on the literal interpretation of the text, supposedly to protect what they perceived to be the message of that text. In other words, if the Bible described the duration of an event, and that duration did not take place in the same way in historical time, the Bible would be wrong.

Still others, like Augustine, sought allegorical interpretations, or what would be an early form of the Framework Theory[30] in an effort to do the same. Whatever the reasons (whether due to their commitment to the "plain reading" hermeneutic, coupled with the understanding that the text sought to describe the events to which it alluded,[31] or as a reaction against certain theories of cosmology[32]), the early Reformers seem to be unanimous about the subject.

In his commentary on Genesis, Luther argued specifically against Augustine's more allegorical approach, found within his earlier works. However, Luther was cautious to say that he was doing the best that he could in seeking to interpret the text of Genesis 1, and readily acknowledged that theologians did not agree with much else, beyond that the world had its beginning *ex nihilo*. Of course, they are no longer in agreement on this issue; but Luther's point was to stress humility in the area. As he sought to read the text for what he believed it said, he stated:

> Therefore, so far as this opinion of Augustine is concerned, we assert that Moses spoke in the literal sense, not allegorically or figuratively, i.e., that the world, with all its creatures, was created within six days, as the words read. If we do not comprehend the reason for this, let us remain pupils and leave the job of teacher to the Holy Spirit.[33]

His latter statement is in response to the question concerning how the first three "days" could be literal days when the sun and moon that measure and distinguish a day from other days/periods of time, did not

---

30. Something alluded to and dismissed by Luther ("Lectures on Genesis," 5).

31. The idea that the Bible is attempting to describe cosmology may reflect the relentless pursuit of the scholastics to make inquiries into the nature of the universe using both the Bible and Aristotelian philosophy. The Reformers did criticize the scholastics because of this, emphasizing the direct observation of nature as appropriate instead, but seem to have adopted the presupposition that cosmology can be gleaned from the text of Scripture.

32. Cf. Luther's reported reaction against the theorists of his day in his interpretation of the sun standing still in Joshua 10:12–14 (Tappert, "Table Talk," 358–9).

33. Pelikan, *Luther's Works* 1:5.

yet exist. Luther's point was that it is the duty of the Christian to trust in the Spirit that the literal words are true, and not seek to figure it out through human philosophy.[34]

The problem is that Luther here is asking the Christian to trust an interpretation of the text, not necessarily the text itself. If there is a contradiction between the fact that the days, and therefore those distinctions in time, had not yet been created and the use of those time distinctions in events that predate the creation of those very distinctions, then perhaps the text is asking the reader to look more closely at what it is really attempting to convey. It seems that Luther here, and perhaps other Reformers who follow him, are caught in the wind and waves of polemics that often afford little more than a narrow perspective to the interpreter.

However, there is another possibility to consider when it comes to biblical interpretation in the Reformed view, and that is that it had been indirectly influenced by later hermeneutics within post-Talmudic Judaism. As we have discussed before, Jewish hermeneutics were split, as were the Patristic views, between figurative and literal interpretations of texts like Genesis 1–2; but as arguments in favor of Christianity, whose claimed adherents had by and large oppressed the Jewish community, often came in the form of allegorizing hermeneutics, Judaism began to adopt a more rigidly literal hermeneutic to counter these claims. Such a transition took time, however, and was not finished until the Enlightenment period, but its mark is evident by the time of Calvin, a student of Hebrew and an avid reader of Jewish exegetes, especially Kimchi. In fact, because of his insistence on the "plain sense" of Scripture, as opposed to any symbolic meaning, he was accused by his critics of being a "Judaizer" who diminished the more spiritual meanings of the text by emphasizing the more historical-grammatical hermeneutic of the Rabbis.[35]

Likewise Calvin argued against the earlier interpretation of Philo and some of the Patristic writers concerning the six days of creation by stating:

---

34. Luther is unaware here that human philosophy is already at play when he interprets the days in the fashion that he does. The literal interpretation is no less interpretation than any other method employed.

35. Haroutunian, *Calvin: Genesis*, 10–11.

> Here the error of those is manifestly refuted, who maintain that the world was made in a moment. For it is too violent a cavil to contend that Moses distributes the work which God perfected at once into six days, for the mere purpose of conveying instruction. Let us rather conclude that God himself took *the space of six days*,[36] for the purpose of accommodating his works to the capacity of men.[37]

Of course, this interpretation is followed by the Westminster Confession in Article 4, where it is made into an important matter within the Christian faith:

> It pleased God the Father, Son, and Holy Ghost, for the manifestation of the glory of His eternal power, wisdom, and goodness, in the beginning, to create, or make of nothing, the world, and all things therein whether visible or invisible, in the space of six days; and all very good. (4:1)

A few years after the composition of the Westminster Confession, James Ussher wrote a series of works on the chronology of the world, where he concluded that the beginning of creation was to be dated at 4004 BCE. As we have seen, Ussher's conclusions are largely in agreement with much of the Christian world, both secular and sacred. James Barr summarizes his objection to seeing Ussher's chronology as a modern novelty.

> But this fact, in so far as it is known, is generally very ill understood. If people mention it at all, they mention it as if it made Ussher into a crank, in modern vulgar expression a crackpot, and as if Ussher in doing this was doing something peculiar or exceptional, something quite extraordinary which only a totally misguided person would undertake. If people so think, it only shows how little they appreciate the older religions and humanistic culture, and indeed, as I shall show, the older scientific culture, and how far removed the modern world is from that culture. For Ussher was in no way an exception in believing that he knew the year in which the world was created: such was entirely *normal* in his time and for a considerable period after him. Ussher was only

---

36. There is some debate concerning the meaning of the phrase sex dierum spatium, since this could signify that the "space" of six days had gaps in between it. However, it seems clear that Calvin and the Westminster Divines that followed him believed in a literal and successive six days of creation.

37. Calvin, *Genesis*, 78; and *Opera Exegetica*, 18.

one in a long series of scholars who concerned themselves with biblical chronology, and many of them were very great scholars, indeed they included some of the greatest minds of all time.[38]

As stated before, however, Reformed theologians since have differed dramatically over the interpretation of the days, not to mention the age of the earth.[39] More recent, scholars have begun to note the literary nature of the text, as well as the need for further study in determining what is being said therein. The chronologies, once taken by a large majority of interpreters as somewhat literal, began to be seen to be in conflict with what were considered more accurate chronologies of the world by scholarship.

Rasmus Rask summed up the consensus of early modern academia in his 1828 lecture:

> It would be in vain to deny what has been the result of the researches of all modern scholars relative to this subject, namely, that from the books of Moses no unbroken and unquestionable chronology is to be extracted—a proposition in which Bredow, Buttmann, Bauer, Vater, Rosenmüller, Gesenius, and others are unanimous.[40]

---

38. Barr, *Biblical Chronology*, 2.

39. William G. T. Shedd (*Dogmatic Theology*, 475–6) stated: "Respecting the length of the six creative days, speaking generally, for there was some difference of views, the patristic and mediaeval exegesis makes them to be long periods, not days of twenty-four hours. The latter interpretation has prevailed only in the modern church. Augustine, teaches (*ad literam*, IV.xxvii.) that the length of the six days is not determined by the length of our week-days." Herman Bavinck (*Our Reasonable Faith*, 170–3) concluded that the days should not be understood as regular days as we think of them. Charles Hodge (*Systematic Theology*, 570–1) is also a good example of someone whose interpretation stems from pure apologetic rather than an exegesis of the text itself. He was concerned that the text would lose credibility if taken literally. Hence, when discussing the word יוֹם in Genesis 1, he stated that "taking this account by itself, it would be most natural to understand the word in its ordinary sense; but if that sense brings the Mosaic account into conflict with facts, and another sense avoids such conflict, then it is obligatory on us to adopt that other." Likewise, B. B. Warfield (Alexander, *Rebuilding the Matrix*, 177; Livingstone and Noll, "B.B. Warfield," 283–94) said that he saw nothing in the text of Genesis 1 and 2 that would directly contradict the idea that evolution had occurred, and even went so far as to say that Calvin may have been a theistic evolutionist (Noll, *Princeton Theology*, 298). One may presume from this statement that Warfield did not take the days of Genesis 1 and 2 to be literal, nor did he seem to believe the traditional understanding of the genealogies as literal years recording the age of the earth.

40. Rask, *On the Longevity*, 2.

In essence, both Jews and Christians have had a long history of interpreting time references in Genesis 1–11 in terms of their harmonization or conflict with scientific or philosophical objections. If the author sought to protect the literal interpretation of time because he was of the opinion that the text intended to communicate the details of the event, he would simply dismiss scientific or philosophical objections as pagan speculation. If, on the other hand, the interpreter had a view of Scripture and science that demanded the two to be in agreement, that individual was more likely to interpret the time references as allegorical.[41]

THE SYMBOLIC VERSUS ALLEGORICAL INTERPRETATION

It goes without saying that a literary understanding of time references found within the primeval history did not fare well among twentieth century scholars. Those within modern scholarship have largely championed literalistic readings of the text, as though the ancient author intended to convey knowledge of the cosmos and the precise measurements of time it took to produce and destroy it. This kind of concordism speaks more to our presuppositions and worldview than it does of the text itself. No one reads *Moby Dick* and wonders whether Melville intended to say something about the psychology of whales. Yet, within its more recent history of interpretation, whether the individual scholar sought a polemic to undermine the integrity of the biblical text, or created another polemic in order to defend it, the time frames in Genesis have been, for the most part, seen as literal chronologies, life-spans, and mathematical measurements surrounding the events that are described within the narrative.[42]

---

41. There is, of course, the third group within the Concordist camp who seek to harmonize the text with current origins theories by interpreting the literal time references as referring to longer periods of time.

42. A Platonic dualism plagues the modern interpreter in that he or she sees physical and spiritual commitments in conflict. If something is to be known as true, it must be physically verifiable. If it is not, it is only mere speculation or belief, and in our modern context, belief is a matter of a subjective manufacturing of reality. Hence, what is true, to the modern interpreter, must be physically verifiable through empirical means. This has no less been true as it concerns the interpretation of temporal language within the Book of Genesis. One group sees the text as literal, and therefore a literal confirmation that God has directly worked in the world, and the other sees the text as allegorical, and often does not support any literal historical work of God in any direct and physical sense. The problem with this dichotomy is that the ancient author and reader would not have seen the text within these terms. Instead, as discussed before, a literal event is

But more than a simple apologetic might be at play. The attempt to harmonize texts, as though all of them were seeking to convey literal history, has been a tendency seen as early as the Second Temple Period. Its legacy continues through works such as Tatian's *Diatessaron*, which sought to eliminate all the variations and inconsistencies he saw in the texts of the four Gospels.

This type of interpretation, however, is not always driven by external influences, even though they have been a major force in the interpretation of Genesis; but it may be largely due to a failure to identify both the type of genre in which these texts are presented and the nature of literature in general. Often, the Bible has been thought to be a vehicle to communicate history in its narratives. Any interpretation that sees the narratives in a symbolic fashion, therefore, is assigned to the later allegorical imagination of the interpreter that has little resemblance to that which the original author of the text intended.

In fact, such thinking assumes *a priori* the nature of the biblical text and the usual purposes of literature, as well as confusing what is to be considered symbolism within literature and what is an allegorical use of literature. The former understands what is being communicated within its genre and its ancient Near Eastern and literary context. The latter does not usually take context into account. In this sense, the symbolic view of Genesis 1–11 should not be categorized as an allegorical interpretation, since its primary goal is to discover the ancient reader's "plain reading" of the text.

With this in mind, the reader will be more equipped to read the text of Genesis without the debilitating dichotomies that plague the literalistic and allegorical interpretations. The most faithful analysis to a symbolic portrayal of an event is to see that something real is being described in impressionistic and abstract terms. I believe this captures one strain of interpretation within the historic witness that sees temporal language as representing a real event, but signifying something other than mere measurements of time.

The real challenge for the interpreter of Genesis is to take caution in his motivations. Seeking to reconcile the text with modern notions of origins is misguided, and will ultimately lead to a further muddying of the text's message. If one feels he must "rule out" certain interpretations

---

being painted in non-literal terms in the same way that a literal scene in nature is being painted in a much more symbolic way but still retains its connections with reality.

simply because they do not accord with modern views of cosmology and anthropology, then that individual must also realize that he is engaged in an apology that will not allow the text to speak if it should go outside the boundaries of those purposes. I am not suggesting, of course, that one is capable of approaching the text with objectivity. As said before, such an animal does not exist within the finite human mind. However, I am suggesting that the text be allowed to join the conversation without the cage of those who seek to reconcile it to their particular theories of origins. There is a difference in giving the text a voice in the multifaceted complex that is human reason and drowning out the voice of the text with an *a priori* fortress of ideas. Otherwise, the text will simply be ignored and used as a stage upon which each may monologue his or her own preconceived message. Hence, this study will now turn to pursue the study of temporal language in its literary and ancient Near Eastern context for the purposes of giving voice to the ideas found therein.

3

The Seven Day Structure and the Cosmic Temple of Genesis 1

ONE OF THE MANY benefits of comparing ancient Near Eastern literature with the Bible is the fact that it can not only teach the modern interpreter how the text connects to its own culture, but it can also provide us with questions we normally would not ask of the text. A previously unasked question of the text can lead to a previously unknown answer, something the text always intended to convey, but buried under centuries of its interpreters' own concerns.

What the discovery of ancient Near Eastern texts has provided are the right questions that we have often failed to ask. Where contemporary culture is concerned about origins, ancient Near Eastern culture was primarily concerned with order and chaos, and whether or not the gods were powerful enough to hold the world and society together so that people might live in peace. It was concerned with the power that chaos seemed to have over the lives of people, and it wanted to know not only where refuge was to be found from it, but whether it would ultimately triumph in its quest to destroy humankind.

As many scholars have observed, from Jon Levenson's observations in his book, *Creation and the Persistence of Evil* to John Walton's recent release of *The Lost World of Genesis One*, the intended purpose of the text of Genesis 1 seeks to answer some of those concerns by presenting God as the sovereign deity who has constructed and now rests in His temple, in which He placed His representative image so that its multiplication might symbolize His complete control and victory over chaotic forces (i.e., states of being that prevented human life from existing and thriving upon the earth).[1]

---

1. Also see Levenson, "The Temple and the World," 275–98; Walton, "Equilibrium,"

It will be the purpose of this chapter to discuss the presentation of Genesis 1,[2] in its cultural and linguistic context, as the creation of God's cosmic temple, and simultaneous purification of the world from a chaotic state to an ordered one that can sustain human life.[3] Further, it will be my purpose to show, therefore, that the seven days in Genesis 1 are not primarily meant to convey a literal time period in which God made the world, but instead supports the symbolism of the text that conveys a complete process of temple building and purification from the chaotic state.

There are ten points that I think establish the idea that Genesis 1 should be viewed as the creation/purification of a temple. They are as follows:

1. In ANE cosmogonic texts temples/sacred places are made at creation.

2. The image/likeness (i.e., idol), which represents the deity is housed within the temple in order to convey the deity's sovereignty over a particular locale.

3. In the ANE, the deity rests in the temple as a symbol of his or her power over uncreation/chaotic land. God, therefore, rests on the seventh day, because it is ANE imagery representing the deity's sovereignty over the area in which his temple resides.

295; Weinfeld, "Sabbath, Temple," 501–12; Kearney, "Creation and Liturgy," 375–87; Wenham, "Sanctuary Symbolism," 403; and Arnold, *Genesis*, 48. Creation and temple are clearly linked in other creation texts within the Bible as well (Giere, *Glimpse of Day One*, 65–66). Thus, it is not unseemly to suggest the same connection exists, if not to a greater extent due to the prominence given to Genesis 1 by P (Mark S. Smith, *The Priestly Vision*, 117–38, see especially his conclusion on p. 137), in our current context as well.

2. In continuity with most of the scholarly world, what I mean by the phrase, "Genesis 1," is Genesis 1:1–2:4a.

3. It is not likely that the construction versus dedicatory dichotomy (i.e., form versus function) suggested by Walton (*The Lost World*, 38–46) is the correct way to see the Genesis narrative. Purification of the universe is occurring through the organization of the universe into the temple. This is actually not far from what Walton suggests, since his concern seems to be that of combating the idea that the concept of *creatio ex nihilo* is present in Genesis 1; but I would still suggest that construction of a local temple is made from material that exists. The issue is whether it already existed in the form that it does once God constructs His cosmic temple, and only functions need to be assigned to those forms, or the universe was made from pre-existing material and at that time assigned functions, as is more typical in cosmogonic texts. As we will see, however, reconstructing a literal chronology of events from the literary expressions in which they are clothed is misguided.

4. The text is structured in the seven day purification of the temple.
5. The word for the luminaries is that used of the lampstand in the tabernacle.
6. The text is meant to provide an *inclusio* with Exodus 32–40, which brings Israel from chaos to creation through the dividing of the waters, where it culminates in the ordering of the people with law and temple/tabernacle.
7. Genesis 1 is from the Priestly Source.
8. Seperation imagery of the cultus is used throughout the text.
9. The temple has the "word/command/law" at its center.
10. The *raqi$^{a\varsigma}$*, as a solid, temple ceiling that holds back the waters of chaos, represents the shelter of the temple from chaos.

1. TEMPLE/HOLY PLACE BUILT AT CREATION

Creation in the ancient Near East was primarily for the gods, not humans. It was meant to provide order to the gods and give them rest from chaos, whether chaos took form in a personal foe or impersonal state of being. This order and rest came to be symbolized in the creation of temples. If a god had a temple built, it meant that chaos had been subdued and the elements that were now ordered were capable of sustaining, not only a building project, but the presence of the god him or herself. Although this is altered by the Genesis account, the imagery used to symbolize God's complete subjection of the chaotic state is retained, and as we will see, the text also retains the idea that creation conveys something to the reader about God in the creation of His temple.

In the Hymn to the Ptah, we see that theogony is accompanied by the creation of cultic spaces and the images that are placed within them. These temples will identify the boundaries that define the dominion of the respective deity.

> ḫpr.n ḏd jrj tmw sḫpr nṯrw r ptḥ t3-tnn js pw
> msj nṯr pr.n ḫt nb jm.f m ḥtp ḏfw m
> nṯr ḥtp.t m ḫt nbt nfrt sw gmj s33
> ꜥ3 pḥtj.f r nṯrw sw ḥtp ptḥ m ḫt jrt.f
> ḫt nbt nṯr wḏ nb sk
> msj.n.f nṯrw jr(j).n.f nwwt grg.n.f sp3wt
> dj.n.f nṯrw ḥr ḥm.sn

srwd.n.f p3 ḥt.sn
grg.n.f ḥm.sn
stwt.n.f dt.sn r ḥtp jbw.sn
sw ʿq nṯrw m dt.sn
m ḫt nb m ʿ3t nb m jm nb ḫt nb rd ḥr
ḫwt.f ḫpr.n sn jm

> This it is said of Ptah: "He who made all and created the gods". And he is Ta-tenen, who gave birth to the gods, and from whom every thing came forth, foods, provisions, divine offerings, all good things. This it is recognized and understood that he is the mightiest of the gods. Thus Ptah was satisfied after he had made all things and all divine words.
> He gave birth to the gods, He made the towns,
> He established the nomes,
> He placed the gods in their shrines,
> He settled their offerings,
> He established their shrines,
> He made their bodies according to their whishes,
> Thus the gods entered into their bodies,
> Of every wood, every stone, every clay,
> Every thing that grows upon him
> in which they came to be.[4]

Egyptian literature often speaks of the "sacred mound" which is made at the time of creation for this very purpose. The rule of the god(s) over an area is represented by the existence of a sacred place/temple within that particular area.

The same can be said in Mesopotamian literature. In the most well known creation text, *Enūma eliš*, Marduk constructs a temple after he has split Tiamat and created the heavens and the earth from her corpse. In Tablet VI, he creates humans, and a temple in Babylon, his domain, is then made for him, from whence he and the gods under him may rule and rest.[5]

In Sumerian literature, the *Eridu Genesis* presents the establishing of cult places as the pinnacle of an ordered society, and chaos as its disorder in the flood. The ultimate ordering, of course, comes when people

---

4. The following translation is taken from *AEL* 1:54–55. Cf. also the translation by Allen, "The Memphite Theology," 21–23.

5. *COS* 1.111:401–2.

are preserved so that they might continue to order society into a livable habitat for both humans and gods.

> [. . .] im-ĝa₂-/ĝa₂\ [. . .]
> nam-lu₂-ulu₃-ĝu₁₀ ḫa-lam-ma-bi-a ga-ba-/ni-ib\-[. . .]
> ᵈnin-tur₅-ra niĝ₂-dim₂-dim₂-ma-ĝu₁₀ sig₁₀-[sig₁₀]-/bi\-[a] ga-ba-ni-ib-gi₄-gi₄
> uĝ₃ ki-ur₃-bi-ta ga-ba-ni-ib-gur-ru-ne
> iriki me-a-bi ḫe₂-em-mi-in-du₃ ĝissu-bi ni₂ ga-ba-ab-dub₂-bu
> iri me-a šeĝ¹²-bi ki kug-ga ḫe₂-em-mi-in-šub
> ki-eš-<bar> me-a ki kug-ga ḫe₂-em-mi-ni-ib-ri
> KUG? A niĝ₂ izi ten-na si mi-ni-in-si-sa₂
> ĝarza me maḫ šu mi-ni-ib-šu-du₇
> ki a im-ma-ab-dug₄ silim ga-mu-ni-in-ĝar

> . . . sets up . . . "I will . . . the perishing of my mankind;
> For Nintur, I will stop the annihilation of my creatures, and I will return the people from their dwelling grounds. Let them build many cities so that I can refresh myself in their shade.⁶ Let them lay the bricks of many cities in cult places, let them establish places of divination in cult places, and when the fire-quenching . . . is arranged, the divine rites and exalted powers are perfected and the earth is irrigated, I will establish well-being there."⁷

Hence, purification and the ordering of society in terms of cult services are instituted in order that divine rest/peace transpires there. The divine rest, of course, indicates the god's ability to relax due to the suppression of chaos, i.e., the reversal of uncultivated and uninhabitable land, and the establishment of order.

Coote and Ord comment on the nature of temple and creation in terms of the connection between the tabernacle and the cosmogony in Genesis 1.

> Creation in ancient texts means creation of the state and its social codes. At the heart of the state and its ordered way of life sit the temple and its cult. The temple is the prime focus of law and order in the state, and therefore the pinnacle of creation.⁸

---

6. See also the translation in *COS* (1.158:513): "May they [i.e., the Sumerian people] come and build cities and cult places, that I may cool myself in their shade."
7. Black, et al., "*The Flood Story.*"
8. Coote and Ord, *In the Beginning*, 95.

In *NBC* 11108, the projected temple is paired with the order (ME) instituted by Enlil over the land.⁹ Likewise, in the *Song of the Hoe*, after six temples are built (lines 35–58), measures are made to subdue chaotic, or "uncreated" land (lines 59–70).¹⁰

Likewise, in Ee, temples are made for the lower gods. Batto points out that "the gods in gratitude and in acknowledgement of Marduk's kingship built him a palace in Babylon from which to rule the universe."¹¹ They did this because their own temples were but mere reflections of his heavenly one. Thus, they were able to rest, knowing that "chaos had been completely subdued and there no longer existed any threat to the divine order."¹²

In the Ugaritic theogony, *Šḥr* and *Šlm*, also referred to as "Dusk and Dawn," creation is brought about from the sexual union between 'Ilu, the Creator deity in Ugaritic literature, and the Abyss.

9. me ᵈen.líl.lá.ke₄ kur.kur.ra šu nu.ù.du₇ [k]ù ᵈin.nin é.an.na.ke₄ nid[ba] nu'.ù'.túm' "The rule (ME) of Enlil over the land had not yet been completed, the [no]ble lady of An's temple had not yet received? food offerings]" (Kramer AV pl. 8; edition van Dijk and Kramer AV 125–33, collated with Horowitz, *Mesopotamian Cosmic*, 138). Also cf. the time of chaos when [i] šib.maḫ ᵈen.líl.lá nu.ù.ğál [š]u.luḫ.kù.ge šunu.ù.ma.du₇ "The Chief Priest of Enlil had not been brought into being, the purification rituals were not maintained." Setting society in order, something which can only take place with a culture centered on the temple, is an act of creation throughout the ancient Near East. In Egypt, the concept of Maat (i.e., the ordering element of society) is inherently linked to the creation event, both the primeval event and the contemporary reenactments (Karenga, *Maat*, 397–405).

10. Also cf. Ninĝirsu's reasoning that his temple ought to be built: "I will call up to heaven for humid winds so that plenty comes down to you from heaven and the land will thrive under your reign in abundance. Laying the foundations of my temple will bring immediate abundance: the great fields will grow rich for you, the levees and ditches will be full to the brim for you, the water will rise for you to heights never reached by the water before. Under you more oil than ever will be poured and more wool than ever will weighed in Sumer. "When you drive in my foundation pegs for me, when you really set to work for me on my house, I shall direct my steps to the mountains where the north wind dwells and make the man with enormous wings, the north wind, bring you wind from the mountains, the pure place, so that this will give vigour to the Land, and thus one man will be able to do as much work as two. At night the moonlight, at noon the sun will send plentiful light for you so the day will build the house for you and the night will make it rise for you." "I will bring ḫalub and neḫan trees up from the south, and cedar, cypress and zabalumwood together will be brought for you from the uplands. From the ebony mountains I will have ebony trees brought for you, in the mountains of stones I will have the great stones of the mountain ranges cut in slabs for you. On that day I will touch your arm with fire and you will know my sign" (Black et al., "Ninĝirsu's Temple," lines 282–305).

11. Batto, *Slaying the Dragon*, 35.

12. Ibid.

The Seven Day Structure and the Cosmic Temple of Genesis 1   41

[.] dd [.] <št> rgm l il ybl
aṯṯy il ylt mh ylt ilmy nʿmm [[agzry]]
agzrym bn ym ynqm b ap dd št špt
l arṣ špt l šmm w yʿrb b phm ʿṣr šmm
w dg b ym w ndd gzr [.] l <g>zr [.] yʿdb u ymn
u šmal b phm w l [.] tšbʿn y aṯt itraḫ
y bn ašld šu ʿdb tk mdbr qdš
ṯm tgrgr l abnm w l ʿṣm [13]

[The m]essage came to ʾIlu,
"ʾIlu's two wives have given birth!"
(ʾIlu asked:) "What did they bare?"
(The messengers replied: "They bore) the gracious gods!
The barrier gods, Sons of the sea,
Who suck the teats of the Lady's breasts.
One lip reaching to the earth,
One lip reaching to the heavens.
And there into their mouth (were placed)
The birds of the heavens,
And the fish in the sea.
And they stood
(Things) from one side to the other were put into their mouth,
but they were not satisfied.
O wives, whom I have betrothed,
O sons, whom I have begotten,
Arise, and prepare a sanctuary [*qdš*] in the midst of the wilderness,
Dwell there among the stones and the trees.

It seems clear, from numerous texts, that the creation of sacred space, in which the deity/deities may reside, is the pinnacle of order and conveys that the chaotic state has been reversed completely. Creation, i.e., the reversal of the disordered state of things is not complete until a temple, representing that the creator deity has complete rule over chaos, has been built. In Genesis 1, this takes upon the pattern as follows.

A   The earth is תֹהוּ "uninhabitable"—no house/temple for the image (v. 2aα).

B   The earth is בֹהוּ "uninhabited"—no image (v. 2aβ).[14]

---

13. KTU²1.23.30–34, 48–66. The restoration in the opening line is taken from Gibson, *Canaanite Myths*, 124–27.

14. בֹהוּ carries the idea of a particular place that is not inhabited by humans. Thus, the reversal of בֹהוּ is the creation of humans.

A′ God makes the earth/universe habitable—house/temple created (vv. 3–25).

B′ God makes the earth inhabited—image placed within temple (vv. 26–31).

Since order must be maintained if society is to be preserved through chaos, it was necessary to center the community's life on the temple, and that includes the community's stories that retell the creation of that community. Ancient cosmogonies, and therefore, society itself, saw the temple as central to the human existence, and apart from it, the community had no stability, would not have seen itself as having been created by deity, and would, therefore, have no sense of protection from the hostile forces of chaos that lurked around every corner.[15] The ideology of temple and society will become significant in the theology of Genesis, as humans are able to trust in God as their sovereign in a hostile world, knowing that He has overcome the forces of chaos and rests within His universal temple.

2. REPRESENTING DOMINION THROUGH AN IMAGE

However, as an ordered universe is incomplete and still subject to chaos without a temple, so is a temple without an image of deity. Hence, the image is that which represents sovereignty and the temple is simply that which houses the image.

This fact is easily obtained from examining "dominion" images without temples. These images, however, are usually royal images, as a king already has a physically visible palace in which he resides, rather than needing a temple *per se* in which to dwell. If an image is capable of representing the dominion of the one to whom it belongs, then it is not the temple, but the image the temple houses that is the essential component in representing the individual's sovereignty and order over that sphere.

An idol is a visible symbol which represents the dominion of the deity. It does not create dominion, but represents the sovereignty that already exists over a particular sphere of existence. The creation of human beings as God's image in Genesis 1, along with the command to multiply, fill up, and subdue the earth, expresses the divine desire to symbolize His

---

15. See Baines, "Palaces and Temples," 303.

The Seven Day Structure and the Cosmic Temple of Genesis 1 43

dominion by multiplying His images over the earthly domain as He cultivates through their labor created land over which He rules.

Despite the many attempts to interpret the image as a cognitive, moral, or spiritual likeness with God, the terminology is employed due to the temple imagery that is used within the pericope. Man is God's image who is then placed in God's temple to represent His victory over chaos, and humans are the ultimate symbol of victory, since it is their ability to now live in a peaceful world that hails the reversal of the chaotic state that once hindered their existence.

In Genesis 1:26–28, God makes human beings as His image and likeness.[16]

ויאמר אלהים נעשה אדם בצלמנו כדמותנו וירדו בדגת הים ובעוף
השמים ובבהמה ובכל הארץ ובכל הרמש הרמש על הארץ
ויברא אלהים את האדם בצלמו בצלם אלהים ברא אתו זכר ונקבה ברא
אתם
ויברך אתם אלהים ויאמר להם אלהים פרו ורבו ומלאו את הארץ
וכבשה ורדו בדגת הים ובעוף השמים ובכל היה הרמשת על הארץ

> Then God said, "Let Us make humankind as Our image, as Our likeness; and let them rule over the fish of the sea and over the birds of the sky and over the cattle and over all the earth, and over every creeping thing that creeps on the earth."
>
> So God created man as His own image, as the image of God He created him; male and female He created them.
>
> God blessed them; and God said to them, "Be fruitful and multiply, and fill the earth, and subdue it; and rule over the fish of the sea and over the birds of the sky and over every living thing that moves on the earth."

The two terms for "image" and "likeness" are found throughout the ANE to denote just this sort of sovereign imagery.[17] In the ninth cen-

---

16. I agree with Clines ("The Image of God," 80–85) here when, in taking the ב as *bêth essentiae*, he says that the text does not indicate that the "man *has* the image, nor is *in* the image, but that he *is* the image" (see also Jouön §133c) with some reservation. However, it should be noted that the prepositions ב and כ, added to the words דמות and צלם, may be intended to distinguish being כאלהים "like God" in 3:5 and "as" or "like" His image.

17. See Bird, "Male and Female," 342–3, who cites only a few examples of this expression, as well as the Egyptian evidence in Frankfort, *Kingship and the Gods*, 161: e.g., Amun would raise his *anḫ* toward the king and proclaim, "my beloved son receive my

tury Akkadian-Aramaic bilingual text from Tell el-Fakhariyeh, the two words are used interchangeably. The following Aramaic transliteration is taken from the published version of A. Abou-Assaf, P. Bordreuil, and A. R. Millard:[18]

> ... ṣlm hdysʿy
> mlk gwzn wzy ʾzrn lʾrmwddt krsʾh
> wlmʾrk ḥywh wlmʿn ʾmrt pmh ʾl ʾlhn wl ʾnšn
> tyṭb dmwtʾ zʾt ʿbd ʾl zy qdm hwtr qdm hdd
> ysb skn mrʾ ḥbwr ṣlmh šm
>
> ... Image of Hadd-yisʿī
> King of Guzan and of Sikan and of Azran for exalting and [?] his throne and for lengthening his life,
> And that the word of his mouth be good before the gods and the people.
> His likeness he made bigger than any before.
> Before Hadad, who dwells at Sikan, Lord of Habur, his image he
>   has erected.[19]

In both of these instances, an image and likeness is erected for the purpose of displaying the localized dominion of a king. In the latter inscription, the size of the image is meant to convey either the importance of the king and/or the expanse of his dominion. In Genesis 1:26–28, however, the expanse of God's dominion through His image, comes not from their size, but by their multiplication over the earth.

The phrase is also found within other Akkadian literature. The thirteenth century Assyrian Epic of Tukulti Ninurta displays this idea. The following is a transliteration and translation offered by D. Callender:[20]

> ina (AŠ) ši-mat ᵈNu-dím-mud ma-ni it-ti šīr (UZU) ilāni (DINGER. MEŠ) mi-na-a-šu ina (AŠ) purussê (EŠ.BAR) bēl mātāti (EN.KUR. KUR) ina (AŠ) ra-a-aṭ šas/turri (ŠÀ.TUR) ilāni (DINGER.MEŠ) ši-pi-ik-šu i-te-eš-ra šu-ú-ma ṣalam ᵈIllil (BE) da-ru-ú še-e-mu pi-i nišē (UKU.MEŠ) mi-lik māti (KUR) ú-šar-bi-šu-ma ᵈIllil (BE) ki-ma a-bi a-li-di ar-ki mār (DUMU) bu-uk-ri-šu

---

likeness [snnw]," an expression, although connected to the deification of the king, that indicates sovereignty.

18. *Tell Fekherye*, Lines 12–16.

19. Translation offered by Callender, *Adam in Myth and History*, 26–27.

20. Ibid., 27. His is an adaptation of Peter Machinist's translation found in "Literature as Politics," 455–82. See further Machinist's *The Epic of Tukulti-Ninurta*, 68–69; and W. G. Lambert, "Three Unpublished Fragments," 38–51.

The Seven Day Structure and the Cosmic Temple of Genesis 1   45

> By the fate (determined by) Nudimmud (=Ea) his [the king's] form (*mīnāšu*) is considered the flesh of the gods (*šīr ilāni*).
>
> By decision of the lord of the lands he was successfully cast into/poured through the channel of the womb of the gods.
>
> He alone is the eternal image of (*ṣalam*) of Enlil, attentive to the voice of the people, to the counsel of the land.
>
> Enlil raised him up like a natural father, after his first-born son (= Ninurta).

The king is once again caste as the image of the deity, a representative to creation of the god's dominion. The king was raised up specifically by the *bēl mātāti* "lord of the lands." It is his designation as Enlil's *ṣalam* that allows him to legitimize his special authority as king and representative of Enlil. His dominion is therefore Enlil's dominion.

Clines summarizes the ancient view in stating that "the image of god is associated very closely with rulerhood. The king as image of god is his representative. The king has been created by the god to be his image."[21]

Hence, the image in Genesis 1:26 is God's representative of His own dominion. However, the dominion of the humans should be seen, not merely as that of royalty, but instead as the cult image that is placed inside the temple. The connection of the ancient Near Eastern king that uses image terminology ought to be seen as gaining it's nuances from the cult image rather than vice versa. In fact, as J. Kutsko points out, that in Mesopotamian literature,[22] "the expression *ṣalam* / ALAM + DN (divine name) most often indicates the cult image of a god."[23] This may be, in fact, the reason why palace structures are often placed so close to temple structures.[24] The king is a living image. He accomplishes in his

---

21. Clines, "The Image of God," 85. This same terminology is utilized in VAT 17019 when it reports that the gods discuss "the creation of mankind" *ni-ib-ni-ma ṣa-lam* "Let us create an image." However, there is no explicit indication that the image here is anything other than a physical form, absent of any ambassadorial relationship with a particular god. Instead, as in other Mesopotamian creation accounts, humans are made to work for the lower gods, who once had been forced to work for their own food and shelter.

22. A Mesopotamian origin is the most likely source of this imagery. The proposal by Curtis (*Man as the Image*, 86–102, 113–19) and Ockinga (*Die Gottebenbildlichkeit*) that the image must be of Egyptian origin because of ancient Israel's later repulsion by idolatry, fails to consider the temple imagery in Genesis 1 and the linguistic elements used to distance man as God's actual likeness. For other objections to this proposal, see Kutsko, *Between Heaven and Earth*, 61–63.

23. Ibid., 58. Also see *CAD* Ṣ, 79 and *AHw* 1078b.

24. Baines, "Palaces and Temples," 313. Hence, the temples exterior was often decorated with the military victories of the king's campaigns because His victory and

reign over chaotic forces what the image in the temple represents of the deity's accomplishments over chaos in the world. Likewise, in Genesis 1, the two roles of cult image and king have been combined. The image inside the temple is the royal, living image. Therefore, as much as humans multiply and rule over creation, God displays His dominion over the chaos that once prevented those very humans from existing. The image, therefore, is about God's sovereignty over creation (i.e., the temple in which the image is placed). But divine images that represent the deity's reign do not appropriately exist out in the open. Usually, there is a need for houses to be built for such images. These houses are what we call temples.[25] Once the temple is built, the image can be placed inside, and the deity may rest as the established sovereign of that sphere.[26]

3. THE REST SIGNIFIES THE SUBJECTION OF ALL CHAOTIC AGENTS

Another indication that Genesis 1 is to be seen as the construction of a temple is the fact that God rests on the seventh day, the day after His victory over chaos is complete. In 2:2–3, the text reads:

---

dominion over chaotic forces on a microcosmic level represents the deity's victory and dominion over chaos on a macrocosmic level. The cultic and royal uses of the image are often, therefore, merged, as the symbolism of the palace and the temple were merged (Ibid., 315). See also Roaf ("Palaces and Temples," 427), who states that "sometimes temples and palaces were combined in a single structure." Also see Dever ("Palaces and Temples," 611–12) for the same combinations found in ancient Palestine.

25. I would make the distinction here between images that are meant to convey the deity's dominion over a household (hence, household idols) and images that are meant to display the deity's reign and protection over the entire town or state.

26. Further support that the image here is associated with the cult image in the temple may be found in the Mesopotamian *mis pī* ritual, where the cult image is given a "piece" of the deity's essence in order that it might come alive and represent his or her sovereignty over chaos within that specific sphere (cf. Schüle, "Made in the Image," 11–14; although I disagree with Schüle's conclusion that Genesis 2 is a response to, and a polemic against, Genesis 1—something not possible if J predates Pg, nor necessary, since the emphasis of an unfinished creation can be gleaned from the juxtaposition of the two accounts apart from this, i.e., Genesis 1: chaos subdued from the divine perspective, Genesis 2–3ff.: chaos continues within the perspective of human experience). Although this imagery does not appear in Genesis 1, it does make an appearance in Genesis 2, where the temple imagery is continued, although localized in J (Wenham, "Sanctuary Symbolism," 399–404). Also note that the "opening of the mouth" ritual was not only practiced in Mesopotamia but a form of it existed also in Egypt. See Lorton, "Theology of Cult Statues," 145–6; Fischer-Elfert, *Die Vision von der Statue*; and Robins, "Cult Statues," 1.

The Seven Day Structure and the Cosmic Temple of Genesis 1

ויכל אלהים ביום השביעי מלאכתו אשר עשה
וישבת ביום השביעי מכל מלאכתו אשר עשה
ויברך אלהים את יום השביעי ויקדש אתו
כי בו שבת מכל מלאכתו אשר ברא אלהים לעשות

On the seventh day God completed His work which He had done, And He rested on the seventh day from all His work which He had done. Then God blessed the seventh day and consecrated it, For in it He rested from all His work which God had created to make.[27]

Walton comments on the term שבת:

> The verb *šābat* describes a transition into the activity or inactivity of *nûḥa*. We know that when God rests (ceases, *šābat*) on the seventh day in Genesis 2, he also transitions into the condition of stability (*nûḥa*) because that is the terminology used in Exodus 20:11 ... His rest is also located in his "resting place" (*měnûḥa*) in Psalm 132, which also identifies it as the temple from which he rules. After creation, God takes up his rest and rules from his residence ... When the deity rests in the temple it means that he is taking command, that he is mounting to his throne to assume his rightful place and his proper role.[28]

The seventh day functioning as the signifier of sovereignty also provides an answer for the age old question as to how God completes His creation on the sixth day, but the Hebrew text states that He did not complete it until ביום השביעי "on the seventh day."

After Baal defeats Yam, his temple made and purified, he finishes his conquest and rests in his temple. This motif is common in the ancient Near East, and it mimics the actions of a human king, who after defeating his foes, may rest in his palace, having no more enemies to conquer.

---

27. This last phrase, "that God created to make," has often puzzled scholars; but it may in fact be an indication that God's intentions in creation are not over. Instead, the divine rest does not signify that God is finished creating, but rather that He has accomplished His goal of reversing chaos through the completion of His cosmic temple and that He is now in complete control of His creation. As the book will later indicate, even though God is the victor, chaos still exists within the universe, and is still in need of being completely expelled. Hence, creation itself is not complete.

28. Walton, *The Lost World*, 73–75. See Sarna's comments (*Genesis*, 15) that "God, through His creativity, has already established His sovereignty over space; the idea here is that He is sovereign over time as well."

ʿdr . l[ʿr] . ʿrm
ṯb . l pd[r . p]drm
ṯṯ . l ṯṯm . aḫd . ʿr
šbʿm . šbʿ . pdr
ṯmnym . bʿl . m[ḫṣ]
tšʿm . bʿl . mr[r]
b bt [ʿ]rb . bʿl . b qrb
bt . w yʿn . aliyn
bʿl [.]²⁹

He travelled [from city to] city;
he went from tow[n to to]wn
He seized sixty-six cities,
seventy-seven towns.
Eighty Baal [smote],
Ninety Baal [captured?].
Baal settled into his house,
into the midst of his palace!.³⁰

Nick Wyatt discusses this divine prototype as follows:

> Baal's tour of inspection would correspond to the royal progress of a king, at once an affirmation of his territorial authority, and the opportunity to quell local rebellions. The military action of a king is the earthly counterpart of the mythical action of the *Chaoskampf*. See Wyatt (1998a). Baal's tour is the paradigm of the kings.³¹

Completing the campaign against greater enemies, therefore, by touring local jurisdictions is a common practice. The king would then return to his palace and rest upon his throne as the victorious sovereign. Bernard Batto comments:

> But most important is the linking of divine rest (Gen. 2:1–3) with creation. As I have shown elsewhere, common to all versions of the Semitic Combat Myth is a motif of divine rest. After his victory over his archfoe, the chaos monster, the creator deity builds a palace (or temple) from which he rules the cosmos³² . . . As

---

29. KTU² 1.4.VII.7–15.

30. Wyatt, *Religious Texts*, 108. The connection between the house and temple are clear from the interchangeable uses of the terms that describe them. As Smith ("Like Deities, Like Temples," 5) notes, "house (*bt*) and palace (*hkl*) apply to both cosmic palace and terrestrial temple."

31. Ibid., fn. 150.

32. Of course, in Genesis 1, the temple is not made after creation, but the process of creation is described as the creation of the temple itself—whether we see that cre-

The Seven Day Structure and the Cosmic Temple of Genesis 1

the deity's home, this palace was also a place of leisure and rest. Indeed, the portrayal of the creator as resting after his victory over his foe is an ancient Near Eastern metaphor for that deity's status as the supreme ruler of heaven and earth. The deity can afford to lay down his weapons and relax because the enemy has been subdued and the deity's status as the divine sovereign is unchallenged.[33]

Batto further argues that the rest refers to God's resting as a display of sovereignty:

> Confirmation may be found in Psalm 8, which is generally acknowledged to have close affinities with the P creation account. Psalm 8:2 says of the Creator, "You build a fortress for your habitation, having silenced your adversaries, the foe and the avenger." The "fortress" is the temple-palace of Yahweh from which he rules. Behind Genesis 1:1–2:3 lies the same conception of the victorious divine warrior who retires to his palace to a leisurely kingship after subduing the foe.[34]

John Levenson concludes that the creation itself is a temple in which God rests, and thus displays His ultimate subjection of chaos.[35]

4. THE SEVEN DAY STRUCTURE REPRESENTS THE PURIFICATION OF SOMETHING, IN MANY CASES, THE PURIFICATION OF A TEMPLE

Although assigning concepts to the numerical symbols often can be a wildly speculative endeavor, it occasionally does have its roots in fact. The ancients did, in fact, see some numbers as symbolizing larger concepts than their mere numerical values might suggest. The number seven is one of those numbers that most scholars generally agree has a larger semantic significance.[36] This becomes important, since the cur-

---

ation as one of form with an emphasis on function or merely the dedication phase of the temple where the function is being assigned to an already existing universe (See Walton, *The Lost World*, 88–90).

33. Batto, *Slaying the Dragon*, 78.

34. Ibid., 79.

35. Levenson, *Creation and the Persistence of Evil*, 100–120. Cf. Schmidt's suggestion that the term יקדש refers to the arranging of a cultic event (Westermann, *Genesis 1–11*, 171).

36. Most of whom, such as Levenson (*Creation and the Persistence of Evil*, 66–68), simply follow the observations of Cassuto (*Genesis I*, 12–16). It is also clear even from

rent text under dispute makes more than a little use of the number, both in its underlying structure and in its grouping of the days of creation. It becomes a necessity, therefore, to pursue the number's general signification, as well as its specific application to the concept of the temple in the ancient Near East.

General Purification

The concepts of completeness and purification overlap semantically in the symbol of the number seven.[37] What is complete is perfect. What is imperfect is incomplete. In issues dealing with the holy and profane, what is perfect is unclean and what is perfect is pure, undefiled, clean. The concept of completeness can, therefore, remain in its general use when speaking of non-cultic contexts, or it can take upon itself the fuller idea of purification both in and outside the context of the cultus.

This double use is somewhat seen in the Ugaritic tale of Kirta. Kirta contains many examples of the number seven as a symbol of completeness. Kirta describes his loss of seven children in sevens in order to express the totality of his despair.[38] It is here that one sees the general use of completeness that the number seven represents.

He is then told by ʾIlu to wait seven days each time he attacks a city in order that his acceptability to the god might be complete.[39] This seven day period is connected with the preceding pericope which displays Kirta as bringing a sacrifice to ʾIlu in order to gain acceptance for his supplications.[40] In fact, it functions in a dream that the king has where ʾIlu is describing his acceptance of Kirta's sacrifice, and in return, giving him a gift. This acceptability is in a cultic context (i.e., Kirta is in ʾIlu's temple[41]).

---

texts, such as Leviticus 23, that the number is bound up with the proceedings of cultic festivities.

37. Thus, the sign in Sumerian for the number 7 can be translated as "all," indicating something as complete or whole (Horowitz, *Mesopotamian Cosmic*, 218).

38. KTU² 1.14.i.10. Cf. the statement "Keret saw his offspring, his offspring destroyed, quite ruined his dwelling and in its entirety was the family destroyed, and in its totality his succession" that follows the list of seven children (Wyatt, *Religious Texts*, 182–83).

39. Cf. 1 Sam 10:8. Fleming ("The Seven-Day Siege," 211–28) has shown that this seven-day siege pattern is associated with cultic ritual.

40. KTU² 1.14.iii.1–29.

41. KTU² 1.14.iii.26–29. For another interpretation of this, see Wyatt (*Religious Texts*, 195 fn. 91), who proposes that it may refer to Pabil's palace or even the towns governed by ʾIlu.

Danilu in the Epic of Aqhat also consecrates himself for seven days, even waiting an eighth day in order to show that he went beyond what was required for his supplication.

The circling of Jericho is accomplished in sevens as a precursor to the cleansing of the land that has been defiled by the Canaanites.[42]

The funeral for Saul and Jonathan consists of a fast for seven days, which signifies the time of mourning, a time for purification and renewal.[43]

Naaman is purified from his skin disease by dipping himself seven times in the Jordan river (2 Kings 5:9–14).

The earth is given rest from the wicked after seven days of waiting for the rain to fall. The structure is used to represent the purification of the defiled earth in the flood, and possibly retain the author's intended temple/chaos imagery (see chapter 7).

Seventy weeks (lit. "seventy sevens") is declared in Daniel 9:24 as the duration for Israel to be purified of its sins, after which the temple will be rebuilt (v. 25).

In essence, the ancient Israelite would have been less likely to understand the number seven, as it appears in sacred literature, as literal, and more likely to see the number as symbolically representing a real event as an occasion of purification. The number is used to such an extent in both ancient Israelite and ancient Near Eastern culture that even when it would be taken literally, it is likely that it would still retain some of the connotations of purification that it expresses in its more symbolic literary employment.

This use of the symbolism signified by the number is also evident in the fact that the six days of creation appear without the definite article. Hence, the pattern is a first day, a second day, a third day, a fourth day, a fifth day, and a sixth day. However, the seventh day appears with the definite article. What this does is mark the seventh day within the text as prominent. In other words, the seventh day is the climax of the seven days. Thus, the seventh day is indicating the end of an entire symbolic pericope that sets the seven days as a literary climb leading to a climax of purification.

---

42. Josh 6:4–21, especially v. 21.

43. 1 Sam 31:13. It may be purification, not only from the land being defiled by the dead, but also from the wicked acts of Saul.

Temple Purification

No little ink has been spilt over the years in an effort to discover the correct interpretation of the seven days of creation in Genesis 1. One thing that has been established, however, is that the heptadic structure of the narrative is intentional. It will be the purpose here to show that this pattern presents itself in the duty of purification, and the purification of the cosmic temple at that.[44]

Interpreting the seven day structure of Genesis 1 as purification of the God's cosmic temple is consistent with the purification of divine temples in ancient Near Eastern thought. In the Ugaritic *Ba'al Cycle* the temple/palace which is built for *Ba'al* is displayed as follows:

[ḫš .][45] *bhth . tbnn*
[ḫš .] *trmm . hklh* ...
tšt [.] *išt . b bhtm*
nb[l]*at . b hklm*
hn [.] *ym . w tn . tikl*
išt [.] *b bhtm . nblat*
*b hk*lm *. tlt . kb' ym*
*tik*l [*.* i]*št . b bhtm*
nblat [.] *b hklm*
ḫmš . tdt . ym . tikl
išt [. b] b*htm . nblat*
b [qrb . h]*klm . mk*
b šb' [.] y[mm] *. td . išt*
b . bhtm . n[bl]*at . b hklm*
sb . ksp . l rqm . ḥrṣ
nsb . l lbnt . šmḫ

---

44. The pattern is not common within cosmogonies, but it is common among temple building/purification texts. Cf. Psalm 104, which does not contain the heptadic structure, and yet, describes much of the details found in Genesis 1 (See Levenson, *Creation and the Persistence of Evil*, 57–59, esp. 59). If the idea of the number seven as perfection or completeness of creation was a part of this tradition, it would surely present itself in a poetic relay of the genre. (This is particularly the case because Psalm 104 is most likely a reflection of a larger tradition, having some resemblance to Egyptian texts [See Levenson's discussion of the Psalm's connection to the Hymn of Aten in Ibid., 60–65].) However, since a temple is not being described there, neither is the seven day purification, nor the heptadic pattern, utilized. In other words, there is evidence that the generic idea of purification found in the employment of the number seven is often conveyed in temple building. There is absolutely no evidence of this idea being applied to creation itself.

45. Gibson (*Canaanite Myths*, 62), followed by Wyatt (*Religious Texts*, 105) makes this suggested reconstruction. However, KTU² suggests a reading of i[lm] in line 16 and makes no suggestion for line 17.

aliyn . b'l . <b>hty bnt
dt . ksp . hkly [.] dtm
ḫrṣ 'dbt . bht[h . b']l [46]

[Quickly,] his palace was built,
[Quickly,] his temple was raised . . .
Fire was set in the palace,
Flames in the temple.
Behold, the fire consumed in the palace
A day and a second,
the flames in the temple.
The fire consumed the palace
A third, a fourth day,
The flames in the temple.
The fire consumed [in] the palace
A fifth and a sixth day,
The flames in [the midst of the] temple.
Then on the seventh day[47]
The fire escaped from the palace,
The flames from the temple.
The silver had turned into plates,
The gold had been turned into bricks.
Mightiest Ba'al did rejoice,
"I have built my palace of sliver,
My temple of gold."[48]

The seven day sequence can be isolated as follows: a day and a second, a third and fourth day, a fifth and a sixth day, on a/the seventh

---

46. KTU² 1.4.VI.16-17, 22-38.

47. Due to the fact that no vowels appear in Ugaritic, the article is typically absent from definite words in poetic/epic literature, and the text is broken and difficult to read here, it is impossible to determine with any certainty whether the phrase *bš'.] y*[mm] is definite as the climax of the seven day sequence or simply indefinite as the preceding list of days. It is more likely that the definite article was not in the original text, since there is only enough space for the 'ayin (i.e., ◁) and the "Trennungskeil" (i.e., the word divider). However, there is no Trennungskeil between the ordinal and the modified day on the fourth day, which may indicate that these words may be sometimes taken as a unit. Still, it is difficult to imagine the *he* in Ugaritic, a horizontal sign consisting of three wedges, fitting into the space provided together with the large wedge, the "Winkelhaken," which represents the 'ayin. There is a discrepancy in the sources. Where KTU² has the text broken only at the Trennungskeil and the doubled *mêm* on *ymm*, the cuneiform text provided by de Moor and Spronk presents the text broken also at the 'ayin (*A Cuneiform Anthology*, 26).

48. Translation mine.

day." Compared to Genesis 1, the sequence is almost identical: one day, a second day, a third day, a fourth day, a fifth day, a sixth day, on the seventh day. The significance is found in the opening of the sequence with an indefinite cardinal for the first day,[49] a sequence of indefinite days for the next five days,[50] and the use of the *b*/ב preposition for the seventh day, emphasizing it as the climax of the sequence.[51] The temple then serves as Baʿal's throne upon which he sits to rest once he conquers his enemies. The rest serves as a message that the god is now in complete control over his domain.

The seven day structure is also seen in the earlier Sumerian literature. The Gudea Inscription presents the temple as being purified seven times before it is ready for the deity to dwell within it.[52]

The number seven, as a symbol for temple purification, is clear from numerous biblical texts as well. Likewise, the consecration of its priests and its altar takes seven days in Exodus 29.

> The holy garments of Aaron shall be for his sons after him, that in them they may be anointed and ordained. For *seven days* the one of his sons who is priest in his stead shall put them on when he enters the tent of meeting to minister in the holy place . . . Thus you shall do to Aaron and to his sons, according to all that I have commanded you; you shall consecrate them[53] through seven days. Each day you shall offer a bull as a sin offering for atonement, and you shall purify the altar when you make atonement for it, and you shall anoint it to consecrate it. For seven days you shall make atonement for the altar and consecrate it; then the altar shall be most holy, [and] whatever touches the altar shall be holy . . . I will consecrate the tent of meeting and the altar; I will also consecrate Aaron and his sons to minister as priests to Me. I will dwell among the sons of Israel and will be their God. (vv. 29–30, 35–37, 44–45)

---

49. Although, it must be admitted that a noun in the singular is one of the common ways of opening an ordinal sequence in Ugaritic, and possibly Hebrew as well. See Sivan, *A Grammar of Ugaritic*, 93.

50. Even though it is true that most of the ordinals cannot be distinguished orthographically from the cardinals in Ugaritic (Segert, *Grammar of Ugaritic*, 54), *rbʿ* "fourth" and *ṯdṯ* "sixth" are distinct (*UT* 7.38).

51. Gordon calls what happens "on the seventh day" in this type of sequence the "climactic variation of refrain" (Ibid., fn. 1).

52. Gudea Cylinder B, col. XVIII.19, Statue B, col. VII.30. See also Kramer, "The Temple in Sumerian," 6.

53. Lit. "you will complete their hand."

The Seven Day Structure and the Cosmic Temple of Genesis 1

In 1 Kings 8–9, Solomon consecrates the temple twice as much as usual in an effort to display its holiness.

ויעש שלמה בעת ההיא את החג וכל ישראל עמו קהל גדול מלבוא אמת
עד נחל מחרים לפני יהוה אלהינו שבעת ימים ושבעת ימים ארבעה עשר
יום
ביום השמיני שלח את העם ויברכו את המלך וילכו לאהליהם שמחים
וטובי לב על כל הטובה אשר עשה יהוה לדוד עבדו ולישראל עמו
ויהי ככלות שלמה לבנות את בית יהוה ואת בית המלך ואת כל חשק
שלמה אשר חפץ לעשות
וירא יהוה אל שלמה שנית כאשר נראה אליו בגבעון
ויאמר יהוה אליו שמעתי את תפלתך ואת תחנתך אשר התחננתה לפני
הקדשתי את הבית הזה אשר בנתה לשום שמי שם עד עולם והיו עיני
ולבי שם כל הימים

> *So Solomon observed the feast at that time, and all Israel with him, a great assembly from the entrance of Hamath to the brook of Egypt, before the Lord our God, for seven days and seven days, a fourteen day [period]. On the eighth day he sent the people away and they blessed the king. Then they went to their tents joyful and glad of heart for all the goodness that the Lord had shown to David His servant and to Israel His people. Now it came about when Solomon had finished building the house of the Lord, and the king's house, and all that Solomon desired to do, that the Lord appeared to Solomon a second time, as He had appeared to him at Gibeon. The Lord said to him, "I have heard your prayer and your supplication, which you have made before Me; I have consecrated this house which you have built by putting My name there forever, and My eyes and My heart will be there perpetually." (8:65–9:3 NASB)*

The consecration of the temple, therefore, is signified by the sacred actions that take place in the duration of seven days.[54] As Levenson sums up:

> [The narrative] is at pains to tell us that this took place in the seventh month, indeed during Tabernacles, the seven-day feast in the seventh month. The parallel text in Chronicles depicts the dedication of the first temple in two sets of seven-day festivals, the first for the altar and the second for the Feast of Tabernacles, which apparently served as the general temple-dedication festival. The speech that Solomon makes on that occasion is structured in seven specific petitions. Indeed, the construction of the temple is said to have taken seven years, and this too betrays a

---

54. For a more thorough discussion of temple building, see Hurowitz, *An Exalted House*, 330–31.

more general Near Eastern mythos . . . In Loren Fisher's words, "If these temples were constructed in terms of 'seven', it is really no wonder that the creation poem of Gen. i is inserted in a seven-day framework. One must speak of ordering the cosmos in terms of seven even as the construction of the microcosm must be according to the sacred number." In any event, Solomon's dedication of his temple during the seven-day Festival of Tabernacles was hardly idiosyncratic.[55]

5. THE WORD FOR THE LUMINARIES IS THAT USED OF THE LIGHTS IN THE TABERNACLE

Light and darkness, day and night, constitute important elements for the symbolism of creation and chaos that the temple represents to the people among whom it resides. In Egyptian literature, the model of creation from chaos in the form of light from darkness is exemplified in the daily ritual of the priests of the sun god, Reʿ. As G. Robins notes:

> For instance, when the priest entered the sanctuary, which was the darkest part of the temple, he lit a torch so that he could see. On a cosmic level, the light dispelled the enemies of the sun god, Re, who were embodied in the darkness . . . The temple itself, the setting for the ritual performance, formed an image of the cosmos, both at the moment when the created world came into being, and at night when it was sunk into darkness in the absence of the sun.[56]

Although, Genesis 1 is absent of personified versions of chaos, the picture of light in the temple as a representation of creation out of chaos, and the deity's ultimate victory over chaotic elements cannot be overlooked. Creation and temple are linked in the ancient Near Eastern mind, and the roles that light and darkness play, especially in the form of the sun and the moon that are said לממשלת "to guard" the day and night in an effort to provide order to creation by maintaining the ceiling of the world/temple that holds back the waters of chaos, and by supporting the cultic calendar in Genesis 1:14-16, symbolizes this theme well.[57]

---

55. Levenson, *Creation and the Persistence of Evil*, 78–79.

56. Robins, "Cult Statues," 8.

57. Cf. the statement ᵈŠamaš i-na i-šid šamêᵉ "Shamash, who is upon the foundation of heaven" in line 19 of Tablet V of *Enūma eliš*. The sun is assigned to that station in order to guard the cross blockage set up to hold back the waters of chaos, as well as to

The word used in 1:14–16 is מָאוֹר, a cognate of the more familiar אוֹר "light," is the word used to describe the light of the tabernacle lamp. Four of the 17 uses of the word in the Hebrew Bible appear in Genesis 1:14–16. Another nine refer to the light produced by the lamp in the tabernacle. Two more refer to the luminaries in the heavens (Ps 74:16; Ezek 32:8). It is used once to refer to the presence of God in Psalm 90:8, a psalm traditionally attributed to Moses.[58] Finally, it is used generically to refer to the light that comes from the eyes in Proverbs 15:30.

Light produced from tabernacle lamp	Light produced by the sun and moon	Light produced by God's presence	Light of the Eyes
Exod 25:6; 27:20; 35:8, 14, 28; 39:37; Lev 24:2; Num 4:9, 16	Gen 1:13–16; Ps 74:16; Ezek 32:8	Ps 90:8[58]	Prov 15:30

Although some might consider this a polemical move against polytheistic religion, since the words for sun and moon (i.e., שׁמשׁ and ירח) are also used as the actual names for the deities who are designated by those terms, it is more likely that the primary intent of the author's use of the terms is meant to designate the presence of God in the temple. The cultic use of the lamp in the tabernacle functions as a representation of God's presence. In that regard, Psalm 90:8 is really an extension of these uses. Hence, any polemic, if one exists here at all, may be secondary.

The cosmological uses each identify the light that is produced by a particular luminary. Each of these is in the context of either the creation of the cosmic lights, or the dowsing of that light in the context of judgment. It is probable that the cultic and cosmological distinction func-

---

provide light to the world, also dispelling the darkness that characterizes chaos.

58. A cognate in Job 18:18, מְאוֹר "light," is contrasted with the darkness of the uninhabitable chaos of the netherworld/death. It is possible that this may offer another instance of the term if the pointing is emended. The emendation of Song 4:9 followed by HALOTSE (539) and DCH (5:117), as another possible appearance of the term within the Hebrew Bible, however, is not convincing. See Pope (*Song of Songs*, 481–2), who anticipates these emendations and rejects them based on solid grounds.

59. Cf. the literature in the DSS that associates the light with attributes of God and His presence, i.e., glory, spirit, wonder, blessing, everlastingness, etc. (*DCH* 5:117).

tions according to the typical language used by the Bible to present the tabernacle/temple as a microcosm of the ordered world. Setting apart the exception found in Proverbs 15:30,[60] the above categories, therefore, are not separate referents that divide the term, but instead one and the same designation representing God's presence in His temple both day and night.[61]

It is also possible that the designations of the luminaries in Genesis 1 as greater and lesser lights may mimic the greater and lesser lights in the tabernacle (i.e., the greater lampstand/light that gives light to the tabernacle during the day, and the lesser light that governs it by night).[62]

6. THE PASSAGE IS MEANT TO PROVIDE AN *INCLUSIO* WITH EXODUS 24–40

It has been observed many times that the pattern in the book of Genesis is followed by the narrative in the book of Exodus. There are elements of chaos that hinder the ability for human life to come about and thrive (Gen 1:2; 2:5; Exod 1:8–22). There are acts of God that counter chaos through divine decrees (Gen 1:3–31; Exod 5–15), the last of which is God dividing the waters so that His created people might enter on dry land. Finally, there is the establishing of the moral order, given to humans for the purpose of further establishing order (Gen 1:28; 2:16; Exod 20–23).

---

60. Even here, the concept has to do with life versus death, since the light of the eyes has to do with life, vitality and health (*TDOT* 1:158). In Proverbs, light is associated with the life given from wisdom, which often represents the Law or its practical applications in Biblical context (Ibid., 162). These associations would make sense in the context, since this light of the eyes makes the heart glad and the good news, with which it parallels, puts fatness on the bones. There is, therefore, a sense in which the term is connected to the law (i.e., wisdom) and the eyes (i.e., the lamps of the body's temple) in Proverbs. The law that is at the center of the temple in ancient Israelite thought is, therefore, situated in the mind, the body is seen as the temple that contains it, and the prosperity and order it brings surrounds the individual's life and health. Still, this use is far enough removed from the others that it should be considered to have a distinct referential nuance.

61. The cosmic lights governing day and night have some parallel with the light provided by the lamp in the temple as well, as priests would not only make sacrifices during both day and night, but maintain the temple services, such as keeping the fire from going out. For an argument toward the concept of a temple nightlife, see Edersheim, *The Temple*, 107–8, as well as Propp's suggestion that the lamp itself may have had to have been continually attended (*Exodus 19–40*, 429).

62. Cole, *Exodus*, 198; followed by Propp, *Exodus 19–40*, 428.

However, the most interesting parallel is found in the creation of the tabernacle itself. Before the command to build the tabernacle is received, Moses, Aaron and his sons (i.e., the high priest and priests) must wait on the mountain (i.e., a prototype for the tabernacle) for six days while the presence of God rests upon the mountain.[63] On the seventh day, God gives command to build the tabernacle.[64] It is important then to observe that the acts of God in the book of Exodus that precede the building of the sanctuary are creative acts. Once the sanctuary is built (35–40), the beginning of the story of God's people commences. Once God has completed the temple/tabernacle through divine command, He has established order with His people, signifying His complete victory over the chaotic forces in Egypt, and His people may now prosper if they remain in harmony with this creation through obedience to their sovereign.

The *inclusio*,[65] then, is that the opening chapter of the Genesis narrative contains the building of a temple at creation in order to convey God's sovereignty over the previous chaotic state, and the last chapters of Exodus convey the same through the construction and completion of His tabernacle (i.e., a portable temple).[66]

Scholars have noted for some time now that the word patterns surrounding the completion of the tabernacle mimics that of the declaration concerning God's completion of His creation. Westermann sums up this evidence:

> The last example, Ex 40:33, shows at the same time that there was a fixed form of speech at hand to P. Chapter 40 closes the erection of the "tent of meeting" which Moses had been ordered to erect in ch. 25 after the Sinai theophany. The ceremony is solemnly

---

63. This is not only the numerical pattern that is given in the command concerning Moses needing to wait until he enters into God's presence (24:16), but it is also related again to the Israelites as Moses gives them instructions concerning their six day work week and their rest on the seventh as it pertains to their building the tabernacle (35:2).

64. "Let them build a sanctuary for Me that I may dwell among them" (25:8).

65. Walton, *The Lost World*, 89.

66. It is very possible that John saw the purpose of the Genesis account and wrote his book of in order to create one big *inclusio* that governs the old and new covenants by employing the imagery of God creating the new heavens and new earth by expelling chaotic forces through Word and Temple. In essence, the concern there is the same as it is in Genesis, namely, that chaos is destroyed at the erection of a temple that conveys God's sovereign power over said chaos. It may be for this reason that the early church decided to position the Apocalypse as the last book of the canon.

closed by the appearance of כבוד יהוה in the cloud, 40:33. The sentence "so Moses finished the work" is a clear echo of Gen 2:2 (W.H. Schmidt points out that the preceding passage, Ex 39:32–43, offers some parallels to Gen 1: 39:32a to 2:1f,; 39:43a to 1:31; 39:43b to 2:3a). The same phrase "and he finished" occurs too in the Priestly writing in Gen 49:33; 17:22; Lev 16:20; Num 4:15; 7:1; 16:31. The quite unnecessary relative sentence "which he had made," . . . should evoke the recollection of the Sabbath command," W.H. Schmidt, p. 156. The phrase is rooted in the reason for the command, Ex 20:9; Deut 5:13f.; Ex 31:14; 35:2. It occurs three times in the short passage Gen 2:1–3.[67]

Joseph Blenkinsopp concludes, "What P seems to have done is emphasize the building of the sanctuary . . . as the climax of creation."[68]

Kenton Sparks also repeats the important point that "this narrative account of the tabernacle's creation is conceptually similar to the *logos* creation of the cosmos in P's seven-day creation week."[69] Hence, the theme of *creation by command* to build the tabernacle/temple and *creation by making* found in the execution of the construction of the tabernacle/temple also helps explain the contrast between *creatio via fiat* and *creatio via activitat* in Genesis 1, where God commands something to come into existence and then He proceeds to make it.[70]

7. GENESIS 1 IS PRIESTLY

Although specifics of the original sources used by the author may be in dispute, there is no question that the first chapter of Genesis comes from a cultic context. The Priestly source (or P or Pg) uses language that characterizes the cultus in general. It uses the term אלהים instead of the name יהוה collocated with a personalized form of אלהים, as is common in later texts that tend to depersonalize God and remove language characteristic of His imminence in order to replace it with more transcendent language.

It uses terms such as זכר and נקבה in order to identify the man and the woman rather than the more relational איש and אשה. These

---

67. Westermann, *Genesis 1–11*, 170.
68. Blenkinsopp, "The Structure of P," 286.
69. Sparks, "Priestly Mimesis," 638.
70. Also cf. the use of the term רוח as it is applied to the ordering of creation and the tabernacle. For more on this parallel, see Coote and Ord, *In the Beginning*, 95–96.

terms of classification are often used in contexts that indicate the procreative purpose of the male and female distinction. The terms are only used again in a conjunctive collocation in P's flood account to identify the procreative purpose of coupling animals together in the ark (6:19; 7:3, 9, 16). These same terms are contrasted in texts like Leviticus 18:22 in reference to the sexual act (cf. Gen 1:27–28).

The purpose of the lamps of the sun and the moon are to designate signs and seasons of the cultic festivals. Schmidt observed that "the heavenly lights are to serve as signs, in particular to fix cultic observances and the calendar."[71] Observing time for the purpose of festival was the duty of the temple. It has been suggested often that the rituals that exalt the gods at certain times each month or year may be in view, although altered to some degree, in this statement.[72] Hence, the fourth day (i.e., the day that describes the activity and observance of cultic festivals) is marked as especially important by its length of detail to describe it within the larger pericope.[73] The priestly calendar that starts here, as one would expect, ends with the completion of creation on the seventh day Sabbath, completing also the picture of the cultic calendar.[74]

The text also uses separation language that characterizes the levitical/holiness ideal of separating and making distinctions between two elements rather than mixing them, which leads to the next point we will discuss. All of these elements have come together to suggest to scholars

---

71. Schmidt, *Die Schöpfungsgeschichte*, 114 as translated by John Scullion in Claus Westermann, *Genesis 1–11*, 130. See also Vogels, "The Cultic Calendars," 163–80; and Rudolph, "Festivals," 23–40.

72. See, for example, Weinfeld, "Sabbath, Temple," 502–12, who is followed by Walton, *The Lost World*, 90–91; also Wiseman, *Creation Revealed*, 33. Although Kidner calls this a "hypothesis slenderly based" (*Genesis*, 54), it seems likely in light of the wide attestation of these events found within ancient Near Eastern culture. See also Lorton ("Theology of Cult Statues," 145–6) who notes the same in Egyptian rituals. Indeed, if the seven day creation is meant to convey God's supremacy over chaos, then the re-enactment of God's enthronement is not only found in the appointed festivals, but also on the last day of each and every work week.

73. Guillaume, *Land and Calendar*, 38–39. Interestingly, *Enūma eliš*, which contains some remnants of cultic terminology in relation to the temples that are built at creation, was cited on the fourth day of the Akitu Festival in the neo-Babylonian period (Tigchelaar, "'Lights Serving as Signs,'" 34–36).

74. Guillaume, *Land and Calendar*, 40–45. However, Guillaume's idea that Genesis 1 is more of a "sabbatogony" than a cosmogony (Ibid., 42) fails to understand the Sabbath symbol as subordinate to the larger temple imagery employed.

that "in short, Genesis 1 is a priestly narrative of the divine construction of the universe informed by priestly ritualistic concerns."[75]

8. SEPERATION IMAGERY OF THE CULTUS IS USED THROUGHOUT THE TEXT

The text's use of separation imagery would have been immediately identified as something that belongs to the priest and the temple. Although it is true that separation imagery comes from numerous cosmogonic texts in the ancient Near East, it must also be noted that these texts themselves are products of the temple priests in their respective cultures. The idea, therefore, that separation imagery does not necessarily belong to the priestly class due to this observation cannot be appropriately sustained.

In Genesis 1:4, 6–7, 14 and 18, explicit separation is made with the use of הבדיל the Hiphil form of בדל, and in vv. 9–10, 11–12, 21, 24–26, there is essentially separation *via* grouping of creation from either a gathering of waters from land or a distinction of species from one another למינה(ו) "according to their kind."

These divisions are clearly seen in other priestly texts surrounding the tabernacle in Leviticus 10:10; 11:47; and 20:24–26 in regard to בדל and 11:13–31 in regard to למינה(ו). As J. Milgrom comments:

> The making of distinctions (*lĕhabdîl*) is the essence of the priestly function. Ezekiel scores the priests of his time precisely on this point: "Her priests have violated (*ḥāmĕsû*) my teaching: they have desecrated what is sacred to me, they have not distinguished (*hibdîlû*) between the sacred and the common, they have not taught the difference between the unclean and clean . . . I am desecrated in their midst" (Ezek 22:26). The failure of the priests to distinguish between the sacred and common has resulted in the desecration of God's name. It constitutes *ḥāmās* 'violence', the very sin for which God brought a flood on mankind (Gen 6:11, 13), and for which Ezekiel's countrymen face destruction (Ezek 7:23; 9:9).[76]

Separation in the Levitical texts is necessary for the purity required for God's presence to dwell within the community. In summary, the language of Genesis 1 shared with that of the Priestly writings consists of separation, dividing animals according to their species, technical lan-

---

75. Smith, *The Priestly Vision*, 127.
76. Milgrom, *Leviticus 1–16*, 615.

guage of the male and female (once again, an identification of species or kinds), the description of the lights in the tabernacle, references to cultic festival days, and references to the Sabbath.[77] The language of the cultus, therefore, is fitting in Genesis 1, since the universe will be a temple in which God will dwell and rest.

9. THE TEMPLE HAS THE "WORD/COMMAND/LAW" AT ITS CENTER

It is possible that the reason why creation in Genesis 1 is *via fiat* is because the center of the temple in the Hebrew Bible are the Ten Commandments (Deut 4–5). Creation is connected in some way to torah and command. As in the Exodus, God's decrees bring about the subjection of chaos, and as such, are placed within the ark of the covenant within the tabernacle/temple in order to convey God's sovereign control and exaltation over His created order. If God's decrees set the world in order, then it is certainly fitting that they are placed within the temple that symbolizes that order.

Indeed, the Ten Commandments are contrasted with the golden calf icon in Exodus 24–40, being placed in the middle of the narrative, between the instructions to build the tabernacle and the carrying out of those instructions. It will be God's Word that represents Him in the tabernacle rather than the image of the calf. If this imagery is present in Genesis 1, it takes more of a structural role, since the image there are the humans created within His cosmic temple.

Therefore, the strange break from the common means through which a god creates *via activitat* can be explained best this way. Hence, the tension between God speaking (vv. 3, 6, 9, 11, 14, 20, 24, 26) and God making (vv. 7, 16, 25, 26) is resolved if the reader understands the symbols employed. Creation through making is a part of the conventional framework of ANE cosmogony, but the author weaves the *fiat* framework together with the former in order to display the temple imagery.[78]

77. Although one might be inclined to note the use of אלהים over יהוה, since this distinctive language belongs to Priestly literature that precedes the burning bush theophany, it exists here primarily to convey issues of transcendence as opposed to imminence (i.e., the standpoint from the divine perspective—all things are under God's rule—vs. the standpoint from the human perspective—chaos and order exist in the world in which YHWH walks). However, it is still clearly to be attributed to Pg, and contributes nicely to the author's view of theodicy.

78. Although divine *fiat* is occasionally the chosen method of creation in Egyptian

10. THE *raqîă* AS A SOLID, TEMPLE CEILING THAT HOLDS BACK THE WATERS OF CHAOS, REPRESENTS THE SHELTER OF THE TEMPLE FROM CHAOS

That the temple functions as a microcosm of the created universe is clear from the numerous depictions of the heavens and earth found on temple walls and ceilings in the ancient Near East.[79] The reason for this is because the temple represents, as stated before, the ultimate symbol of divine control over chaos that has come about through the deity's ordering of the world. The temple, therefore, represents the sovereignty of the deity and the comfort and shelter from chaos provided by the god or gods of that temple.[80] As the deity dwells within and has complete rule over his or her temple, so the average person could also trust that he or she had control over the designated sphere within which that temple resided.

This depiction carries over to our present text in Genesis 1 as well. The term רָקִיעַ, often translated as "expanse," appears 15 times in the Hebrew Bible (almost half of which are to be found in Genesis 1 alone), and is a solid vault made of metal.[81]

---

cosmogonic texts, specifically in the case of texts which place Ptah as primary creator, it is not the same concept (use of magic vs. authority to command), nor is creation *via* the magical word alone the common methodology employed by a creator god in the ancient Near East.

79. For a concise summary of cosmic depictions upon temple walls and ceilings, see Walton, *The Lost World*, 78–86. For Egyptian temples, see Baines, "Palaces and Temples," 312–13. For the cherubs, noted also by Eichrodt (*Ezekiel*, 55) see . Although see the discussion in van der Toorn et al. (*Deities and Demons*, 189–92). It is clear that the Biblical use of this imagery is oriented more toward the temple than toward popular use (see Keel and Uehlinger, *Images of God*, 154–8). See also Greenberg (*Ezekiel 1-20*, 54), who sees the imagery of cherubs in Ezekiel as referring to the images on the ark of the covenant, which is often represented as God's throne. Here, however, the entire temple, with God situated upon the ceiling, functions as the divine throne.

80. Cf. Assurbanipal's dedicatory description of a temple in Nippur that was destroyed and did not retain its function: "the foundation of which is placed in the breast of the ocean," i.e., the waters of chaos have overwhelmed it (*ARAB* 2:390).

81. *TDOT* 13:649; *HALOT SE* 1290. The traditional Egyptian "expanse" that divides the waters is found within the idea of the cosmic egg/bubble that is a protective sacred sphere from which the waters are held at bay. One Mesopotamian tradition of the "expanse" (largely found within Ee) is created from the dead body of Tiamat. The upper waters are made into heaven, and the lower are then gathered together to form land below.

The word for heaven in Akkadian is *šamû*, which itself is a compound of the two words *ša mû* "of/from the waters." This same etymology explains the common Semitic term evidenced in the Aramaic שְׁמַיָּא, Arabic *šamaʾu* and Hebrew שָׁמַיִם (cf. Akkadian

The Seven Day Structure and the Cosmic Temple of Genesis 1   65

It most likely then refers to the ceiling of the temple where the sun, moon and stars are depicted.[82] In fact, God is symbolized as sitting on top of it precisely to depict both the world as His temple and His exalted supremacy over His domain. This fact is illuminated by the context in which the word appears, where the glory or sovereignty of God is emphasized (Ps 19:1; 150:1–2).

The relation of the רקיע to God's temple is furthered by Psalm 150:1, where the text states הללו יה בקדשו הללוהו ברקיע עזו

---

uncontracted forms *šamāʾū* and *šamāmū*, from the original form **šamāwūʿ*. The *mêm* at the end of the word may be a reflection of the popular 1st Millennium synonym *šamāmū* (as well as the synonym *māmu* for *mû*) from which *šmm* was made into the dual *šāmayim* (the dual also makes sense in the context of Gen 1, as it explains the comment in vv. 6–7 that the waters were divided into two sections, above and below the *rāqîă* ("temple ceiling," outside of which is chaos and inside gathered and ordered groups of created elements).

In Ee, Marduk also sets up a *parku* "cross-blockage," which is related to the term *pariktu* "cross-wall," or "barrier," in order to keep the section of Tiamat, from which he creates the heavens, from crashing down. He further assigns a *maṣṣaru* "watchman," which is the term used for the luminaries. He tightens the *šigaru* "bolt" (*CAD Š*, 409-10) on the right and the left, which may allude to a concept that the support of the barrier was made of wood (See *CDA* 371, where the word is used for a wooden clamp, a neck-stock for captives, and a door lock); and he *ištakan elāti* "sets in place that which is above" (although this may refer to the zenith, the most common way of referring to the zenith is the collocation *elât šamê*, lit. "the upper part of heaven,"). Cf. the concept in some Mesopotamian texts where the lower heavens are thought to be made of jasper upon which the stars have been etched by Marduk (Horowitz, *Mesopotamian Cosmic*, 13–15). Also cf. Exod 24:10, where God is said to stand upon a jewel that is as pure as that of the sky.

Hoffmeier ("Some Thoughts on Genesis 1 & 2," 45) points out a fascinating parallel between the *rāqîăʿ* in Gen 1 and the *bj3* "metal" vault of the sky in Egyptian cosmogonies. He alludes to a Pyramid Text where "the resurrected king takes possession of the sky and splits or separates (*pšn*) the metal (*bi3*)." The sky (*pt*) itself is depicted as a vault (⌒), which keeps the upper waters from the lower waters. Hence, as stated before, even the word for those cosmic waters (*nw/mw*) is given the determinate for both the vault and its waters which are held back by it (⌒̿). He comments on the more common view that "some sort of poles or staves sustain the heaven over earth." See further his article (Ibid.) for attestation of terminology associated with the poles in both Egyptian and Biblical literature. Cf. especially Ps 104:2b-3a, "Stretching out heaven like a tent-curtain, He lays the beams of his upper chambers in the waters."

82. Westermann seems to unknowingly pick up on this as he states, "We must remember that among the traditional material that came down to P was the idea of creation as separation or division and the image of the heavens as a solid vault over the earth, something like a bell or a tent or a *roof*" (*Genesis 1–11*, 115, emphasis added).

בִּרְקִיעַ עֻזּוֹ "Praise YHWH! Praise Him in His sanctuary! Praise Him in the רקיע of His power."[83] In Ezekiel 1, the cherubim are depicted under the רקיע that is over their heads.[84] The cherubs represent the presence of God in His temple. His throne is set above the רקיע, expressing His complete sovereignty over the universe that the temple represents. In 10:1, this same scene has a man clothed in priestly linens enter and take coals from the incense altar to spread over the city. The passage continues:

> Now the cherubim were standing on the right side of the temple when the man entered, and the cloud filled the inner court. Then the glory of the Lord went up from the cherub to the threshold of the temple, and the temple was filled with the cloud and the court was filled with the brightness of the glory of the Lord. Moreover, the sound of the wings of the cherubim was heard as far as the outer court, like the voice of God Almighty when He speaks. (vv. 3–5)

Westermann concludes that the term refers to something made of solid metal, but then seems confused as to how the imagery of the heavens as a solid metal vault and the waters outside of it correspond;[85] but it should be noted to what each piece of imagery refers. The temple is clearly in view, and the רקיע is clearly its ceiling, with luminaries and sky-bearing creatures with wings depicted thereon (Gen 1:15, 17[86]; Dan 12:3).[87] Again, the ancient reader would have made this connection immediately; but it has been lost on the modern reader who is thinking

---

83. Cf. Ps 63:3: "Thus, I have envisioned You in the sanctuary to see Your power and Your glory." See also the inscription of Tiglath-pileser, where he describes his completion of the temples of Anu and Adad, and declares that he decorated its interior like that of heaven (*ARI* 2:18).

84. Cf. Kutsko's observation (*Between Heaven and Earth*, 83) that the divine epithet יֹשֵׁב הַכְּרֻבִים, "that is, the God who sits enthroned above the cherubim (1 Sam 4:4; 2 Sam 6:2)" is used to characterize the Jerusalem temple in 2 Kings 19:14–15.

85. Claus Westermann, *Genesis 1–11*, 117.

86. The בְּ preposition in vv. 15 and 17 ought to be translated as "on" rather than "in," since the luminaries in ancient Near Eastern thought are depicted on the cosmic ceiling, which is not expressed as an open chasm, but a solid metal surface.

87. *TDOT* 13:649–50. See also Baines ("Palaces and Temples," 313), who states of temples in the New Kingdom that "the top of each wall, and especially the ceiling, symbolizes the sky, parts of it bearing patterns of stars or more detailed astronomical representations, and parts, solar motifs indicating the passage of the sun through the temple."

The Seven Day Structure and the Cosmic Temple of Genesis 1

of Genesis 1 in terms of literal descriptions of the universe, as would be the norm in the realist construction of a modern cosmology. The רקיע "temple ceiling" of Genesis 1 reflects on a macrocosmic scale what the literal temple ceiling does on a microcosmic one, i.e., that chaos (here the waters of chaos) are kept at bay by the presence of the deity (*via* His image) within His temple. As the enclosure of a temple keeps out the chaos, and is the ultimate symbol of an ordered society, so also does the vault of the sky keep the waters of chaos outside of the ordered creation in order that life may thrive under God's protection.[88]

THE THEOLOGICAL FUNCTION OF GENESIS 1 WITHIN THE GENESIS NARRATIVE

There will be, without doubt, resistance to seeing the text in this manner. The literalistic hermeneutic has largely taken over much of Biblical studies in a day when a great erosion of the historic faith can be observed. Such suggestions are not quickly received in the heated furnace of logomachy that exists around the interpretation of Genesis 1. Clarifications, therefore, will be needed as the debate continues.

One objection and support for the literal view is founded on the basis that the seven days found in Exodus 20:9–11 are seven literal working days that belong to the week; but this would be to give credence to the false assumption that if two objects are placed in an analogy with one another, and one object is literal, then both objects must be literal. Nothing could be further from the truth. Analogies from fiction are applied continually, in all cultures, to real events that occur in life. Making an analogy between the seven days of creation in a figurative narrative and the seven days of the week in a more literal law code does not, therefore, cause the distinction between the genres to dissolve. In other

---

88. Cf. the statement in Dorman and Bryan (*Sacred Space*, xv): "The assertion that 'architectural space articulates the social order (Tuan 1977, 116) is amply confirmed by the architectonic forms and plan of the Egyptian temple, which represent the emergent creation, as well as by the varying degrees of public, priestly, and royal access to the temple itself (O'Connor 1991; Arnold 1992, 40–58; Schafer 1997, 2–9; Gundlach 2001). Social and cosmic order are here jointly stratified and glorified, and in the observance of religious ritual within such a context, space and time thereby fuse: 'the past reaches right into the present, and the two can not be separated' (Bradley 1993, 2; see also Schafer 1997, 2)." Also see Baines ("Palaces and Temples," 313), who describes the care taken in the construction of the temple roof in order that rain water might be drained away from the temple rather than have it accumulate and leak through the ceiling, thus entering the temple and losing the desired imagery.

words, there is no reason to maintain that a literal connotation must be assigned to both constituent parts of an analogy.

To return to the illustration of "Three Little Pigs," mentioned at the beginning of this book, one does not mean to imply the literalness of this fictional story if he were to say, "You shall build your house out of brick rather than straw in the same way that the prudent pig built his house out of brick instead of straw." Instead, the familiar symbolic story plays an analogous role in the literal command.

Another example of this might be found in the statement, "But like Isildur, the Nazis fell to ruin due to their lust of power." The fictional reference to Isildur does not make the literal reference to the Nazis also fictional. This is common practice. We do not equate the two elements of an analogy in terms of their literalness or lack thereof. In fact, the two elements of an analogy usually only overlap *via* a partial similarity with one another (i.e., they may only share a single, similar characteristic between them). We may be aware of which is which from other sources—whether one or both elements of the analogy are literal or symbolic—but this information is not usually gained from the analogy itself. Therefore, no such warrant exists to bind the use of such analogies to the strictly literal. Since this is the case, the objection that argues that the days in Genesis 1 must be literal days, because the days to which they are compared in the Book of Exodus are literal, is baseless.

CONCLUSION

The seven days of Genesis 1 are representative of a concept, not a measurement of literal temporal units. This is not to say that they are representative of longer or shorter periods of time, as they are not representative of time at all. Instead, they represent the consecration of what is ordered as a temple in an effort to convey a theological concept about God, humans, and the universe in which they reside. They, therefore, represent a sacred event, not the time period of that event. This is done so as to contribute to the larger picture of the universe as God's temple through which He represents His sovereign rule over all creation. The area that His temple covers, the multiplication of His image, and His resting on the seventh day express both the limitless boundaries, as well as the absoluteness, of His rule.

This fact will become significant for the theology of the book in that it will display God as master over both order and chaos, good and evil, creation and destruction, in the procreation and preservation of His covenant people. Genesis will ultimately end where it began, i.e., with God creating what is טוב good/order out of what is רע evil/chaos (50:20).[89] Rather than contribute to the erosion of the faith in our modern day, the theology of the passage instead supports the faith. It aids in our understanding of who God is, who we are, and the nature of good and evil around us. But what does a literal chronology give to us? How does it transform God's people? How does it give hope to those who are suffering, and depart wisdom and trust in God to those who are in the depths of chaos? Whether the literal is preserved with the symbolic or just the symbolic remains, It is my hope that literal timelines will soon take the backseat to the truly divine intent of Genesis 1.

---

89. In Genesis 50:20, the terms appear as טבה and רעה, but the concept remains the same, and the intended *inclusio* is obvious. What was meant to destroy life and order through agents of chaos was used by God to create order and preserve human life. Hence, although chaos existed in the universe, as in Genesis 1, God, as Creator, is able to construct out of it what He desires, and thus, rule over it completely.

4

Does *bĕyôm* Mean "When" in Genesis 2:4b?

THE TERM בְּיוֹם, EMPLOYED in Genesis 2:4b, has often posed a problem for the literal view of Genesis 1 in that it seems to describe God creating everything "on a day." Exegetes, past and present, however, have often sought to solve this problem by either suggesting that the seven days of Genesis 1 were not literal days, or that the term בְּיוֹם denotes a longer period of time than a day.

Luther stated that "'on the day' is to be understood in the sense of indefinite time, as if he were saying: 'At that time the condition of all things was most delightful.'"[1]

S. R. Driver assumed that the word is "compressing often what may have been actually a period of some length into a 'day' for the purpose of presenting it vividly and forcibly," citing Jeremiah 11:4 and 34:13 as examples.[2] John Skinner argued that the indefiniteness of the time refer-

---

1. Pelikan, *Luther's Works*, 1:83.

2. Driver, *Genesis*, 37. Both of these texts, however, refer to the literal day YHWH delivered Israel from Egypt to worship God on Sinai, which signifies the culmination of the act of YHWH's deliverance of the Israelites from their slavery in Egypt (Exod 3:12; 12:31; especially see 6:5–8, where YHWH has only brought them out of Egypt when He לְקַחְתִּי "takes" them as His people, i.e., when He makes a covenant with them at Sinai). Until the day that God met with Israel at Sinai, the Israelites had not yet been brought out of their slavery in Egypt. They had to break that allegiance by forming a new one with God. Hence, the covenant is perceived by Jeremiah to have been given to Israel on the specific day they had been delivered (cf. Exodus 13:3, where the same phrase is used to describe a literal day that Israel is to observe in future generations [vv. 4–10]). This is confirmed by the flow of the narrative. Where "brought them out of the land of Egypt" may first seem to refer to the day they leave their houses, cross the יַם סוּף, or even encamp at Sinai, Israel at this point has not yet been brought out מִכּוּר הַבַּרְזֶל "from the furnace," i.e., their enslavement (Lundbom, *Jeremiah 1–20*, 621). See McKane (*Jeremiah*, 237) for the view that Israel was already bound to the covenant at the time of their deliverance from Egypt, which McKane seems to view as equivalent to their departure.

ent in the term is explained by the word יוֹם that "often covers a space of time," and thus, should be translated as "when."[3]

Further muddying the semantic waters is the fact that it was often taken for granted that, since Genesis 1 detailed the divine acts of creation as taking place in seven days, the day in 2:4b must refer to a larger period of time. As we will pursue in this chapter, such an assertion fails to vindicate itself in light of lexical analysis and a proper understanding of the days in Genesis 1.

THE ASSUMED MEANING

There are three main factors that have gone into interpreting the term בְּיוֹם as adverbial.[4] The first is the Akkadian cognate *inūma/enūma*, which was once thought to be made up of the words *ina* "in" and *ūmu* "day," which literally means "in the day." The word in Akkadian texts is used as a temporal circumstantial meaning "when," or "at the time," and thus provides a parallel to the Hebrew term.[5] It is upon this etymological foundation that E. A. Speiser concluded that the term בְּיוֹם means "at the time when" due to its parallel use at the opening of Ee,[6] followed by the even more confident assertion by Westermann, who concluded that the term in 2:4b "corresponds exactly to the opening words of Enuma Elish."[7]

An issue arises, however, in that the words that make up *inūma* are not *ina* + *ūmu*, but instead *īnu* + *ma*.[8] Even if the morphological data were correct, the word *īnu* by itself means "when" or "at the time,"[9] and it is within this word, not within the word *ūmu* that the circumstantial is

---

3. Skinner, *Genesis*, 54. He also cites Jeremiah 4:11, discussed below, together with Exodus 6:28 and 32:34, both of which clearly refer to a specific day.

4. We might also suggest a fourth reason: scholars in their current languages use the term "day" to express a long period of time (e.g., "He was quite a jokester in his day"). The problem, of course, is that the term יוֹם in construct to a person's name does not exist in the Hebrew Bible. Instead, if one wanted to designate a period of an individual's life, he or she would use the plural construct יְמֵי "days of" in order to convey this idea (Brin, "The Formula X-יְמֵי and X-יוֹם, 183–96).

5. *CAD* I/J, 159–61.

6. Speiser, *Genesis*, 15.

7. Westermann, *Genesis 1–11*, 198.

8. It is clear that a distinction was made between the words. Cf. the use of the two words side by side in the example cited by *CAD* I/J, 153c: *i-na i-nu-um Anum ṣīri*.

9. *CAD* I/J, 152–53. The circumstantial is morphologically derived from *ina* + *um*, which gives it its distinct use from the preposition by itself.

found. If this variation carries with it the adverbial connotation, then the linguist does not necessarily have a parallel with the Hebrew ב, which by itself carries no such meaning.[10]

However, the word may be the victim of an etymological misidentification itself. It is the word *inūmī* that is made up of the constituents *ina* + *ūmī*. Tikva Zadok summarizes the evidence this way:

> Scholars have pointed out that the particles *inu* and *inūma*, as well as *inūmī*, originated from different sources, even though their meaning is identical. *Inu* was probably formed from *ina* "in, within", coupled with the locative-adverbial ending *-um*, which occasionally became *-u* as early as Old Babylonian times, whereas *inūma* originated from *inu* together with enclitic *-ma*. On the other hand, *inūmī* has its origin in *in(a)+ūmī* "on the day(s) when)."[11]

Hence, since the circumstantial particles in texts such as Ee and *Atraḫasīs* is *inūma* (appearing in its secondary form as *enūma*), and not *inūmī*, there simply is no etymological parallel between the use in Ee and ביום. Although Zadok notes that scholars have taken these terms as carrying essentially the same meaning, it remains to be seen whether the employment of the term *inūmī* in Akkadian texts is primarily meant to denote a particular day upon which something occurred or began to occur.[12]

Finally, even if the terms were found to be etymologically connected, this does not automatically warrant a semantic connection. The term must be determined by the literary contexts in which it appears within the particular language in which it developed. This would especially be the case if the Hebrew expression evolved separately from its East Semitic cognate.

James Barr so aptly placed etymological analysis in its proper place by stating that the historical use of a word may not demonstrate similarity, but distinction in use.

---

10. Cf. the entry in *CAD* (Ibid.): "Since the derivation of *īnu* from *ina* seems to be excluded by the frequent writings as *ēnu*, and since it seems unwarranted to consider *īnu* the conjunctional use of a substantive *īnu*, 'time,' which is not attested elsewhere in Akk., *īnu* and its numerous derived forms as adverbs, conjunctions and prepositions are considered here as belonging to a deictic element *īn* or *ēn* (see also the corresponding *ān* in *anūmišu*, etc.). From an early period on, *inūma*, *inūmišu*, etc. were interpreted as derived from *ina* plus *ūmu*, as variants and rare writings show."

11. Zadok, "The Use of Subordinating Particles *Inūmī/Inu/Inūma*," 21.

12. The term almost exclusively appears in royal inscriptions (Ibid.), and may in fact refer to a particular day. See the examples in Zadok's article (Ibid., 24).

But this history itself will often demonstrate that the word has moved far from the sense which belonged to its etymological source. The main point is that the etymology of a word is not a statement about its meaning but about its history; it is only as a historical statement that it can be responsibly asserted, and it is quite wrong to suppose that the etymology of a word is necessarily a guide either to its 'proper' meaning in a later period or to its actual meaning in that period.[13]

Likewise, the suggestion that the term בְּיוֹם mimics *enūma/īnūma*, found in *Enūma eliš* and *Atra-ḫasīs*,[14] which causes *ūma* to manifest itself with weakened semantic boundaries, is equally an etymological claim.[15]

For these reasons the phrase must be evaluated in its own contexts apart from seeking a parallel with its suggested Akkadian cognate. Its meaning is to be derived utilizing a synchronic methodology and only then can observations between its use here in Gen 2 and in Mesopotamian creation accounts, such as in *Enūma eliš* and *Atra-ḫasīs*, be brought into play in order to suggest any similarities or differences.

THE ARGUMENT FROM GENESIS 1

It is not surprising that the term בְּיוֹם has been widely misunderstood due to the author's juxtaposition of it with the seven days of creation in Genesis 1. In the popular *Theological Dictionary of the Old Testament*, Sandviken M. Sæbø argues the following:

> The meaning "day" is more or less weakened when a prepositional phrase with *yôm* (or occasionally *yᵉmê*) is itself lined with a verb. The most important usage of this type is *bᵉyôm* with an infinitive (almost 70 times) as a general indication of time or a temporal conjunction meaning "when," although the basic meaning "day" need not be totally absent (cf. the important passage Gen. 2:4b following the seven-day schema of creation).[16]

Sæbø considers Genesis 2:4b to be an important verse that demonstrates the theory that בְּיוֹם + infinitive weakens the literal meaning of the word to some extent. It does this because, it is assumed, the seven lit-

---

13. Barr, *Semantics*, 109.
14. Westermann, *Genesis 1–11*, 198.
15. Cf. Speiser (*Genesis*, 15), who accepts that בְּיוֹם is borrowed from Ee without discussion.
16. *TDOT* 6:15.

eral days of Genesis 1 conflict with the otherwise understood one day of Genesis 2. Hence, it is often cited by lexicons and grammars as a prime example illustrating that the word יום conveys a longer period of time than that of a single day.[17]

However, it has been shown that the seven day schema in Genesis 1 is not a literal time period, but a time period that conveys the cleansing of the cosmic temple. It is literary rather than literal. If this is the case, then the term in the very verse under dispute cannot be used against the backdrop of Genesis 1 in order to vindicate the default position. Hence, the word must be evaluated apart from its apparent conflict with the seven days of Genesis 1.

THE ARGUMENT FROM APPARENT USES

Other scholars, however, have sought to demonstrate the term's expanded use by its apparent overlap with longer periods of time, not only in the creation narratives of Genesis 1 and 2, but also in other texts as well.

DCH cites one verse (Gen 6:5) that supposedly supports the idea that יום itself can mean "time." The verse states: "And YHWH saw that the evil of man was great on the earth, and that every intent of the thoughts of his mind was only evil [כל היום] all the day."

However, the word clearly means "day" here, as in the phrase, "He would sit around all day long." It is, of course, perfectly acceptable for translators to replace the literal rendering with glosses such as "continually," or "all the time." However, what cannot be conceded is the idea that the phrase means a generic period of time here. The time is specifically stated. There was no break in the day (a gnomic use of day) when they ceased to form their thoughts for the purpose of chaos.

Two arguments for the expanded use of ביום may be found in Numbers 3:1 and 2 Samuel 22:1 (// Psalm 18:1). Numbers 3:1 is an introductory statement, much like that found in Genesis 2:4a, stating that what follows is a record of births.

> Now these are תולדת of Aaron and Moses at the time when the Lord spoke with Moses on Mount Sinai. These then are the names of the sons of Aaron: Nadab the firstborn, and Abihu, Eleazar and Ithamar. These are the names of the sons of Aaron, the anointed

---

17. E.g., *HALOTSE* 401; *TLOT* 529; *NIDOTTE* 2:420.

priests, whom he ordained to serve as priests. But Nadab and Abihu died before the Lord when they offered strange fire before the Lord in the wilderness of Sinai; and they had no children. So Eleazar and Ithamar served as priests in the lifetime of their father Aaron.

Some argue here that the ביום is parallel to all of these events at Sinai. However, there are two problems with taking this passage as evidence of an expanded use of the term. The first problem is that if one were to take the תולדות as births that occurred simultaneous to YHWH speaking to Moses at Sinai, one would first have to argue that דבר יהוה את משה ביום refers to the entire wilderness encampment, during which time, Aaron spawned and raised four children who then took over the priesthood within that same period. This, of course, is not possible, since at this period in Numbers, the Israelites have not been at Sinai that long, nor has the forty year sentence been carried out, nor would there have been enough time during their encampment at Sinai for Aaron to have and raise these children. This fact alone negates the idea that the phrase is simultaneous with the birth and upbringing of the children. Furthermore, the one who wishes to take the phrase as simultaneous with the births of Aaron's sons must take the word תולדות as a reference to the birth events of the children rather than the event of the recording of the children. The former, as discussed before, is impossible. Hence, the latter interpretation is the only viable option. The phrase, therefore, refers not to the entire begetting of Aaron's line, but rather to the day in which the genealogy was recorded on Sinai. It therefore refers to a literal day.

Finally, the reader must take note that this refers to the "birth records" of both Aaron and Moses, yet Moses' genealogy is not mentioned. This fact gives added evidence that the text is simply referring to a record that was made on that particular day rather than events concerning the birth of Moses' children, as the children themselves are not mentioned here.[18]

U. Cassuto takes a different route and parallels the term ביום to the forty days Moses was on Sinai. Hence, if the term refers to the forty literal days Moses spoke to YHWH on Sinai, then it is impossible to see ביום as a literal day. However, there are three problems with this:

---

18. An objection to the latter statement can be raised by looking to the rest of the chapter of the genealogy of the Levites; but even if this latter argument is removed, the previous two arguments still stand. Either way, it is clear that the term ביום refers to the day in which this genealogy was recorded, not the longer time period over which the events of the genealogy transpired.

1. There is nothing to indicate that Moses spoke to God for the entire forty days he was up on the mountain. Deuteronomy 9:9–11 and 17 seem to indicate that the fast lasted forty days, but the actual speaking to Moses was at the end of the forty days (cf. Exod 34:28).

2. If it is the record, and not the events, that are described by the word תולדת, then it would certainly not take forty days for Moses to record the genealogy. Again, the text seems to indicate that what Moses received was at the end of his fasting and prayer.

3. What Cassuto fails to understand here is that the forty days is a figurative number that represents a time of testing and trial (see chapter 7). Hence, there is no conflict between the literal use of ביום and the figurative time period of forty days.

Argument from Numbers 7

However, there have been passages cited that seem to suggest the idea that ביום must mean a longer unit of time. Cassuto argued that Numbers 7:1–84 supports the idea that ביום may indicate a longer expansion of time than that of a literal day. He argued that, since "the offering of sacrifices of the princes lasted twelve days," ביום here could not possibly refer to a single day.[19]

However, the consecration performed by Moses in v. 1 was completed on a particular day. This was the day the altar was anointed and all of the furniture set up. The offerings the leaders of the tribes bring are brought up on the day Moses completed his consecration of the altar (v. 2). Their offerings are separate offerings brought up in carts to the place the altar/tabernacle is located; and again, we are told that they brought these up in the carts on the day Moses completed his consecration (vv. 3–10).[20] In v. 11, the reader is told that YHWH instructed Moses to have each leader present the offerings, which he brought up in the cart on the day that Moses completed his consecration, before the altar one day at a

---

19. Ibid. 99–100.

20. Some English translations obscure what is being said by translating קרב as "offering up," which makes it sound as though the leaders are presenting their offerings right then and there. The text, however, tells us that the offerings are only brought near and placed before the altar on that day. At that point, each group of tribal leaders takes their turn over a period of twelve days to present their offerings to YHWH. Hence, קרב only speaks of the bringing of the items offered before the altar. The presentation of these items occurs during the twelve days that follow.

time for as many leaders as brought up offerings. It is at this point that the reader must realize that there are three events occurring here:

1. The completion of the dedication and anointing by Moses of the tabernacle, its furnishings, and the altar.
2. The transporting (i.e., bring near to the altar) the offerings in carts that will later be presented before the altar.
3. The actual presenting of the items that were previously brought up in the carts one by one in successive days.

In the first two cases, these events take place on the actual day that Moses finished his consecration of the tabernacle with its altar. In the last case, however, the reader is informed that the offerings brought up on that day by the leaders of the various tribes are offered up individually by each leader for the following twelve days. Hence, the events presented can be confusing to the cursory reader in that the same type of language is utilized throughout the text. Nonetheless, indications within the narrative display the distinction between the individual events.

Hence, the use of ביום in v. 10 refers to event # 2, not event # 3. The day Moses completes his consecration *via* anointing of the altar is the same day the leaders bring up the offerings in carts. This is the same event referred to in v. 84, providing an *inclusio* for the pericope which refers to the individual dedications of event # 3 in order to present the entire dedication event in one package; but the use of ביום in each of these cases does not refer to the twelve days, but instead to the single day on which Moses anointed the altar.

This is made even more explicit by the fact that the reader is told both in v. 10 and v. 84 that the day to which the author is referring is ביום המשח אתו "on the day it [the altar] was anointed." The leaders, of course, do not anoint the altar. That was accomplished in Moses' consecration of the altar. This tells the reader that the consecration, which included anointing the altar, and the offering up of the individual items by the tribal leaders over the consecutive days that follow, are separate events.

The consecutive days in vv. 11–83 also use the term ביום in an indisputably literal fashion, as it collocates each day with an ordinal number: "on the first day," "on the second day," "on the third day," etc. If one is still in doubt, v. 88 makes it plain that "this was the dedication for the altar *after* [אחרי] it was anointed." There can be no doubt, therefore, that the term ביום in 7:1 does not refer to the sequence of the twelve days which follow.

Arguments from Cultic Uses

Still, others claim that uses found in cultic contexts support the idea that בְּיוֹם is weakened to refer to a generalized period of time. For instance, Sæbø states that "in Lev. 14:57, with the meaning 'when' in a noun clause, *yôm* has lost all trace of the meaning 'day.'"[21]

However, there seems to be confusion between the semantic domain (i.e., the cultic context here) of the word בְּיוֹם weakening its meaning, so that it can refer to a longer period of time, and the gnomic use of יוֹם, which finds its parallel in most, if not all, languages. Simply because the word "day" is generalized as a recurring and repeatable time unit does not mean that the time unit itself refers collectively to all of the recurrences that it describes. In other words, one is able to say, "I will give you a present on every Christmas Day for the next twenty years," without suggesting that the word "day" in "Christmas Day" can refer to twenty days as a whole. Instead, this is a single, literal day that recurs in the future.

Simon DeVries comments upon this distinction with what he considers to be the gnomic, or cultic, use of יוֹם:

> As we analyze the use of the present *yôm*, we soon see that a basic distinction needs to be made between the day that is historically present in existential distinctiveness and the day that is present only in gnomic discourse or in cultic regulation. The latter refers to a "today" that is continually repeated and hence continually present.
>
> The gnomic present . . . is the present to which the wisdom sayings pertain, hence it is repeated and repeatable as long as the sayings are true. The cultic present is very similar: it is the ongoing present to which every sort of ritual and cult legislation pertains. These two kinds of present, are, together, ideologically opposite to the historical present. The essential difference is that the historical present is always unique—an experience unto itself—whereas the gnomic and cultic present is everything but unique. If the historical present is disjunctive, even irruptive, the gnomic/cultic present is repetitive, cyclical, and institutional.[22]

Therefore, the attempt to use a gnomic use of יוֹם as an example of a day that can refer to a longer period of time is misguided. A gnomic day describes a day that is unknown as to the specificity of when it

---

21. *TDOT* 6:15.
22. *Yesterday, Today, and Tomorrow*, 45.

will occur. In fact, a gnomic day can be repeated over and over again. Therefore, the gnomic יוֹם still refers only to a single day. Upon which day, out of the many in the future, the particular repeated day mentioned falls, is unknown. Hence, this literal day may fall on one or more days in the future, each individually describing the event that is to take place on "a day" such as this.

Hence, בְּיוֹם here does not refer to a long period of time. Instead, it references a single, literal day that may be repeated many times in the future, but it is repeated in a distributive sense, not in a collective sense, and therefore, cannot be taken collectively as a long period of time.[23]

Arguments from Contexts concerning Affliction/Trouble and the Alleviation/Deliverance from It

Further arguments are inferred from passages that seem to describe the day as an entire period of the affliction, judgment, or salvation within the individual's experience. The passages that are often used in support of the lengthened meaning of בְּיוֹם mainly fall into three categories: judgment contexts, affliction contexts, and salvation contexts. In each of these, a literal day is the most viable of the meanings suggested.

A. Judgment contexts: the literal day the sentence for a crime is carried out
B. Affliction contexts: the literal day affliction begins
C. Salvation contexts: the literal day affliction is alleviated

Gershon Brin has argued that the construct forms x-יוֹם and x-יְמֵי are idiomatic expressions that emphasize the character of x, and in this way are similar. However, he notes an important difference between the two.

> There is nevertheless a certain distinctiveness to the plural form, in that the term connoted by it is more on the order of a more abstract concept: e.g., יְמֵי בַחוּרוֹת, יְמֵי נְעוּרִים ("days of youth"), etc. Hence, whereas x-יוֹם (such as יוֹם מְצוּקָה) generally refers to a *moment*, that is, the definition received is focused upon a specific point, x-יְמֵי allows the descriptive adjectives to relate to an ongoing, continued *period of time*, and not only to one specific point.[24]

---

23. Cf. also the "future day" (DeVries, Ibid., 47–51). The term בְּיוֹם is employed to refer to a day that will or may occur in the *future*. Hence, it must be spoken of generically because it has not yet occurred, or is not yet known if it will occur.

24. Brin, *The Concept of Time in the Bible*, 55.

This is equally true for x-בְּיוֹם and x-בְּיָמִי, the difference being only the spherical function of the preposition. Proverbs 6:34 (לֹא יַחְמוֹל בְּיוֹם נָקָם) describes the day of vengeance as a literal day of judgment in which the husband does not show mercy and the sentence for adultery is carried out.[25] Hence, eschatological descriptions that describe the ending of the present order of things reference the day upon which the tide turns rather than the entire period of the eschaton (e.g. Isaiah 13:13: וּבְיוֹם חֲרוֹן אַפּוֹ). The Day of Judgment, wrath, vengeance, power, etc. are literal days when the sentence for crimes committed is carried out.[26]

The uses of the term in these texts, as Brin's study suggests, indicate a moment rather than a long period of time. Hence, each use evidences a reliance upon the concept of a literal day upon which an event begins, ends, or is carried out.[27] John R. Wilch noted the distinction between יוֹם and עֵת in these contexts when he described them as having different nuances, and further stating that *"yōm* retains its basic temporal connotation of '(the same) day' even when referring to the occasion of a particular event, as in Isa 10:3—'And what will you do on the day of punishment *(leyōm pekuddāh)?*"[28] There is simply no warrant, beyond a traditional perception, that the term בְּיוֹם should ever be translated in the understanding that it means a longer period of time than a day.

DECONSTRUCTING בְּיוֹם: AN ANALYSIS OF THE PREPOSITION בְּ

To understand the term בְּיוֹם, one must first understand the preposition בְּ. It cannot be simply assumed that בְּ is an indicator of time. In fact, it is not. Instead, בְּ is a primary indicator of sphere. The sphere in which the preposition is located is further defined by its object. Understanding the

---

25. Cf. Prov 11:4.

26. As DeVries (*Yesterday, Today, and Tomorrow*, 44) points out: "All these refer to the suppliants present day of suffering."

27. See Job 20:28; Psalm 18:1; 27:5; 41:2; 59:16; 77:3; 102:3 as verses that indicate that the term is to be understood as a literal day that befalls the individual in which he or she calls out to YHWH. It is on that same day the person calls that he expects to be delivered from it (see also Jer 16:19). Similarly, Jeremiah 51:2 conveys the day of calamity to be a single day in which Babylon is overthrown. The time of distress may last longer than a day, but the emphasis is on the literal day upon which the trouble for the individual begins. The days of Psalm 110:3 and 5 are likewise seen each as a literal day in which God will display His power by overcoming the enemies of the anointed king.

28. Wilch, *Time and Event*, 91.

preposition in terms of time stems not from the preposition itself, but a further interpretation of the context in which it is employed. In essence, it is an extrapolation determined by the reference of the boundaries of the sphere defined by the object of the preposition. In other words, time is to be found in the context and perhaps in the object of the preposition בְּ, according to the particular lexeme used, not within the preposition itself. A translation of the preposition can be based upon the larger syntax of the discourse in which it is employed, but itself carries no such temporal significance.

Hence, the definition found within GKC seems confused between the syntax of the preposition and the referential semantics which are created by the substantive's defined boundaries.

> Underlying the very various uses of this preposition is either the idea of being or moving within some definite region, or some sphere of space or time (with the infinitive, a simultaneous action, &c.), or else the idea of *fastening on* something, *close connection with* something (also in a metaphorical sense, following some kind of pattern, e.g. the advice or command of someone בְּעֵצַת פ׳ בִּדְבַר פ׳, or in a comparison, in Gn 126 בְּצַלְמֵנוּ כִּדְמוּתֵנוּ *in our image, after our likeness*; cf. 127, 51.3) or finally the idea of *relying* or *depending upon* . . . , or even of merely *striking* or *touching* something.[29]

What GKC seems to observe is the locative and instrumental functions of בְּ. Since our present study is concerned with its *contained* locative function (i.e., that which demands a translation of בְּ as "in"), we will leave the other uses of בְּ for another day.[30] A contained locative is that which describes something *within* the boundaries of the following-

---

29. GKC §119h.

30. Indeed, the uses are many, as Jouön §133c notes: "בְּ properly means *in* (and thus contrasts with אֶל). In the first place it expresses the fact of finding oneself *in*, or moving *in* or *into*, a place. But it has many other meanings: *on, against, with, by, for*. The origin of some of these meanings has been explained in various ways. We shall note only the main uses. בְּ is sometimes used for simple proximity, for contact; with a nuance of hostility it has the (frequent) meaning of *against* (= עַל). It sometimes expresses participation in something (Germ. *an*): Ex 12.43 אָכַל בְּ 'to eat *at* something" (contr. אָכַל מִן *to eat of* or *from* 34.15). In the temporal sense בְּ is far more common than לְ. בְּ expresses the idea of accompaniment ([*together*] *with*), the idea of instrument or means (*with, by*); the idea of equivalence (one things *for* another) whence the בְּ *pretii* [= of price]; the idea of instrument cause (cf. § 132e). For בְּ transitivity, cf. § 125 m–mb. With the infinitive בְּ is use in the temporal sense (§ 1661) and the causal sense (§ 170j). Verbs expressing the idea of *confiding in, ruling over, rejoicing in* take בְּ. With verbs of perception, especially *to see*, בְּ indicates either the idea of intensity or of pleasure, or duratively."

substantive. The phrase X + בּ + Y means that X is to be understood as contained within Y and not outside of it. Thus, the preposition limits the sphere, within which X must function, to the object of the preposition. GKC describes this use as the spherical use of the preposition.³¹ Thus, when Genesis 2:7 says that God breathed בְּאַפָּיו, it is understood that the boundaries set for the location are to be defined no further than that which is *in* his nostrils. The reader then understands that בּ describes only that which is inside the defined boundaries, not outside of them. In the same way, when בּ is coupled with the infinitive in Gen 2:7, the reader understands that it defines only the boundaries which do not go beyond the creation event of the heavens and earth.

The temporal boundaries, however, are not defined by the infinitive construct הִבָּרְאָם in 2:4,³² but instead must be determined by the larger context; but it is the time of the event that is precisely in dispute. If the seven days of Genesis 1 are symbolic of the temple purification, as suggested in Chapter 3, then to what time period does the event of "their having been created" refer? The infinitive is not employed for the purposes of defining the boundaries of time but rather the boundaries of the event. In other words, the record of the heavens and the earth does not begin in eternity, but refers to the period in which they are organized or created.

Time and event, however, are so closely related that it may seem tedious to suggest a distinction, but one seems necessary for the purpose of understanding the semantics of the infinitive. The event is the activity taking place upon the object being created, whereas temporal boundaries refer to the time it took to bring about that activity. Therefore, the confusion concerning to which time period the infinitive may refer might also be a product of the confusion between time and event.

Either way, however, the reader understands that the defined boundaries of בּ reside within the sphere of "their being created," and

---

31. Ibid., Arnold and Choi (*GBHS* 102–3), however, make no attempt to generalize its function, and instead seem content to note its referential uses as spatial and temporal.

32. "The infinitive being atemporal, the time and the aspect of the action can only be ascertained from the context" (Jouön §124s). It may sound contradictory, then, when Jouön states that "with the infinitive בּ is used in the temporal sense" (§133c), but it is clear that by "temporal" Jouön is referring to simultaneity between two events. Hence, it is concluded: "בּ indicates, properly speaking, the inclusion of an action *within* the period of another . . . בּ is used for the simple indication of time, without any special nuance, like Engl. '*on* his coming' or '*when* he came,' especially if the action is durative: '*while* he was coming" (§1661).

stretch no further beyond those boundaries. The time at which said action took place, however, remains undefined by either the preposition or the infinitive.³³

Instead, the adverbial use of בּ with the infinitive simply synchronizes the activity of the verb with the activity surrounding the event. In this case, בּ + the infinitive הִבָּרְאָם is synchronized with the word בְּיוֹם as its temporal qualifier, not the seven days of Genesis 1, as is often assumed, but which are too distant from its grammatical context. The temporal indicator in the text of Genesis 2 is the word בְּיוֹם immediately following the infinitive construct. Hence, the infinitive is contemporaneous with the term בְּיוֹם, not synonymous in meaning with it, as is often assumed.

IN THE DAY

These factors now become significant for our study of the word בְּיוֹם. The observations concerning the defined boundaries that pertain to the sphere in which בּ is contained, the fact that the infinitive does not carry a specified temporal measurement, and therefore, is not synonymous in meaning, and the figurative referent of the seven days in Genesis 1, which is often employed in harmonization with the term, all come together in collaboration to free the interpretation of בְּיוֹם from its false designation as a temporal adverb.

Furthermore, if it is the case that the בּ preposition does not within itself define temporality, but instead the containment of something within the sphere of its object, then the temporal boundaries of the term בְּיוֹם must be defined by the word יוֹם, not the use of the preposition.³⁴

---

33. Note that the infinitive itself is often employed in order to specify the experienced event that occurred on a particular יוֹם in the past, with the emphasis being placed on the qualified event rather than the time of the event. The plural, however, in contrast to the singular, emphasizes the time of the event (DeVries, *Yesterday, Today, and Tomorrow*, 43).

34. Williams (*Hebrew Syntax*, 44) cites an initially convincing example of the preposition retaining a temporal meaning in Amos 4:7, which he says expresses a "point of time." However, the בּ here seems more likely to be one of duration. In other words, it defines the temporal boundaries within the adverb עוֹד. Thus, "in there being still/yet..." is glossed in English as "when there was still/yet," but this attempt to make the English flow more smoothly should not be seen as assigning meaning to the preposition which retains its most common function as the contained locative. It is עוֹד that limits the time period to the three months until harvest, not the preposition, which only finds its location in what follows it.

If it is determined that the lexical boundaries defined by the singular noun יוֹם do not exceed what can be considered a literal day, then neither would there be any evidence to suggest that the term בְּיוֹם means anything beyond a literal day as well. Hence, the term would have to be understood within the temporal boundaries of the lexeme יוֹם, and translated either "in the day," or "when" only in the sense that "when" is to be understood within the boundaries of a literal day, not beyond those boundaries which might suggest a longer period of time.

WHEN IS "WHEN"?

A further observation of these facts can now be made by asking the question, if the temporal indicators are within the larger context, not the בְּ preposition, what in the context is indicating the time frame, or the "when," of the event?

The construction בְּ + infinitive functions as a temporal circumstantial, contemporaneous to the time of the event, but it does not tell the reader when that event occurred. Hence, neither the preposition nor the infinitive plays a role in determining the time of creation in Genesis 2.

In fact, there are only two possible answers to this question. The first, and the most common interpretation, is to take the seven days in Gen 1 as the "when" of the event. The word בְּיוֹם is then reinterpreted as a generic circumstantial, weakening the semantic boundaries of the term יוֹם so that it may refer to a generalized time period, similar in function to the infinitive construct, and is therefore a non-literal day referring to the seven literal days in 1:1–2:3.

However, this interpretation functions from the belief that בְּיוֹם itself can refer to a longer period of time than a literal day, and is furthered by the belief that there must be a harmonization of a literalistic interpretation of the days in Genesis 1. However, as stated before, the adverbial force of such a use does not come from the preposition בְּ, nor are the days of Genesis 1 to be taken as a literal measurement of time. It, therefore, must be shown that the collocation בְּיוֹם somehow takes upon itself this function by expanding the lexical boundaries of the word יוֹם beyond the regularly defined semantic boundaries that normally denote a literal day, even though the constituent parts of the word do not do this

---

Furthermore, the adverb עוֹד carries with it the idea of continuation, and the translation, "I withheld rain from you in continuation/duration of three months until harvest," makes better sense contextually. Either way, however, the preposition's semantic range should not be mistaken for what "sounds better" with an English gloss.

in and of themselves. If it can be shown that the word's lexical meaning does not expand beyond its basic meaning of a single day, then this option is no longer viable.

Furthermore, one ought to ask the question just how it can be that the preposition that functions within the sphere of its object, and therefore is limited by it, can expand the boundaries created by that object. In other words, the preposition is defined by its object, not the other way around. If this is the case then it is impossible for the preposition to expand the semantic boundaries of its object.

A BRIEF COMMENT ON THE WORD יום

There have been numerous studies of the word יום and its uses in the biblical text. The word appears 2,304 times in the Hebrew Bible, of which 1,452 appear in the singular. Of these, it is clear from a synchronic analysis of the word that יום in the singular, apart from a collocation with itself (hence making it plural),[35] refers to a literal day, whether in the sense of "daytime" or as a 24 hour period of time, and is not used to refer to a longer amount of time (in terms of temporal measurement) than that.[36] The failed attempt to attribute the analogy of Psalm 90:4 (a thousand days = a day) to the lexical meaning of the word itself is the last dying hope a now debunked method of lexicography. One cannot import the analogy into other texts that do not indicate the same analogy,

---

35. See the phrases יום יום or יום ביום, along with its variations (*TDOT* 6:14–15). Also cf. עד היום הזה, which includes the time period from a certain point עד "to" the current day of speaking. This, however, is expressed in the preposition, not the word יום itself, which only refers to the current day. The phrase דבר יום ביומו, used 16 times in the Hebrew Bible, sometimes used with a preceding preposition like ל or ב, literally translates as "the matter of the day in its day," which is then glossed as "daily," or "daily activity." The phrase יום ביום, used six times in the Hebrew Bible, sometimes with prepositions as well, simply means "day after day," or "day by day." It is this collocation that refers to a longer period of time than a single day. However, "daily," would also be an appropriate rendering for this construction as well. The reason why this refers to a longer period of time than a day, however, is that it is literally "day on day," referring to a group of days, one after the other.

36. For a summary of the argument, see Freitheim, "Days of Creation," 12–30. Although I disagree with Freitheim on whether or not the numbers are symbolic from a larger narrative referential standpoint, we both agree that the lexical meaning of the term does not expand beyond that of a basic "day." See also Judisch, "The Length of the Days," 265–71 and Fouts, "Selected Lexical Studies," 79–90. The lexicons are notoriously ambiguous and confuse the plural and singular uses. Hence, they are of little use in answering this question.

nor does the analogy in the verse itself indicate that the author is saying that a thousand years is equivalent to a day, but only that a thousand years in the *eyes of YHWH* are יוֹם "like a day." The text nowhere says that a thousand years is a day, and in fact, the analogy is lost unless the reader understands what a literal "day" means. Without the support of this verse, the uses of יוֹם in the singular all support the confinement of the term's lexical meaning to its literal referent of 24 hours or less.

A SYNCHRONIC ANALYSIS OF THE TERM יוֹם

It should be no surprise that the יוֹם with the definite article refers to a specific day. The same can be said for its more emphatic demonstrative form בַּיּוֹם הַהוּא.[37] What is also clear, however, is the indefinite יוֹם is often interchangeable with the definite form. Only rarely does it appear that a translation of "a day" is appropriate.

Of the 216 uses of יוֹם in the indefinite singular, whether with or without being collocated with a finite verbal form, there seems to be little evidence to suggest that the word is weakened to mean a longer period of time that would extend beyond the semantic boundaries that suggest a literal day. Having examined all 216 occurrences in the Hebrew Bible, not one justifies such a conclusion unless one takes this very occurrence in Gen 2:4 and interprets it against a literalistic view of the seven days in chapter 1. In fact, that is exactly what commentators have done.[38] Genesis 2:4b is either the only, or at least the primary, verse quoted to substantiate that יוֹם can be semantically weakened and refer to a longer period of time than a day.[39] However, if the seven

---

37. See the lengthy discussion by DeVries (*Yesterday, Today, and Tomorrow*, 57–136).

38. This fact might indicate that the original pointing on this particular phrase may have been definite. The conflict with Genesis 1, however, for ancient scribes who took it literally, would have led to an indefinite pointing as well as a reinterpretation of the term. Cf. the LXX, however, which sees no conflict between the accounts in its translation of the infinitive as ὅτε ἐγένετο and יוֹם as ᾗ ἡμέρᾳ. However, as noted before, the definite and indefinite forms are often interchangeable in function. Furthermore, the indefinite may reflect the nature of the primeval day (see below). It may be, therefore, that no emendation is necessary.

39. BDB, 400.7dg; *HALOT SE*, 401; *TDOT* 6:15; *TLOT*, 529; Westermann (*Genesis 1–11*, 183) cites GKC §114e in support of taking the בְּ in יוֹם as a determination of a time period (Ibid., 224); but GKC clearly states that this is the case with בְּ + infinitive, not בְּ + יוֹם + infinitive, as it is in Genesis 2:4b. It may be that this construction creates a circumstantial with the infinitive, but the semantic boundaries of the substantive יוֹם

days in Gen 1 are figurative, then the most prominent argument for this idea no longer stands.

בְּיוֹם + Perfective/Imperfective

It is then suggested by scholars that the weakening of the boundaries is a collaborative effort accomplished by the use of יוֹם + preposition + a verbal form, especially the infinitive.[40]

The term בְּיוֹם appears 590 times in the singular (a little over 200 times in the indefinite singular[41]), and of those, the collocation of בְּיוֹם + finite verb appears around 75 times in the Hebrew Bible.[42] Of these 75, it is collocated with an infinitive 64 times. It appears as בְּיוֹם + imperfective only three times with the specific lexis קרא, each referring to the specific day upon which YHWH was called to give aid (Ps 56:10; 102:3; Lam 3:57). It appears eight times as בְּיוֹם + perfective, each time referring to a literal day as well.

בְּיוֹם + Infinitive

It has for some time been assumed that בְּיוֹם plus the infinitive functions as the beginning of a circumstantial, temporal clause as does בְּ plus the infinitive. It is clear that בְּ plus the infinitive does in fact function as an indicator of a circumstantial clause,[43] but it remains to be seen as to whether בְּיוֹם carries that same grammatical function.

In Gen 5:1-2, בְּיוֹם refers to the day God made humans, something with which those who take the 7 days of Genesis as literal would also agree. The pattern further displays the literalness of the phrase in that it is parallel to 2:4 with variations found in additional appendages (e.g. סֵפֶר collocated with תּוֹלְדֹת), the identity of the object created (humans instead of the heavens and the earth) and elaborative information about the object conflated with 1:27–28.

---

remain even within this construction. It is יוֹם that expresses a unit of time, and the בְּ + infinitive that simply is contemporaneous to it.

40. *TDOT* (6:15) notes only "about 70" occurrences. Note that the example cited again for this is Genesis 2:4b.

41. This is confirmed by a computerized count, as well as a manual count of the listed appearances in Evan-Shoshan.

42. Ibid.

43. GKC §134.2g

אלה תולדות השמים והארץ בהבראם ביום עשות יהוה אלהים ארץ
ושמים

> These are the birth [records] of the heaven and the earth: When they were created, on the day of YHWH God's making earth and heaven . . . (2:4)

זה ספר תולדת אדם ביום ברא אלהים אדם בדמות אלהים עשה אתו
זכר ונקבה בראם ויברך אתם ויקרא את שמם אדם ביום הבראם

> This is the birth record of the human: On the day of God's creating the human, as the likeness of God He created him, He created them male and female. And He blessed them and called their name "human" on the day of their creation [lit. of their being created]. (5:1)

The parallel can be observed in the following chart:

2:4	5:1-2c	5:2d
demonstrative	demonstrative	---
תולדות	ספר תולדת	---
object created	object created	---
ב with infinitive of creative verb with suffix	---	infinitive of creative verb with suffix
ביום	ביום	ביום
infinitive of creative verb	infinitive of creative verb	---
God as subject	God as subject	---
reiteration of object created	reiteration of object created	---
---	---	conflation of material from 1:27-28

It is evident that the term in 5:1 refers to a specific day upon which אדם was created. The parallel in 5:1-2 indicates that the ב is employed according to its basic use as the locative sphere, which is contained within the lexical boundaries of יום, i.e., a literal day. It is clear from the latter passage, however, that God made and called the male and female ʾādām "on the day of their creation." It is doubtful that the text is attempting to communicate that God named them "human" over a long period of time. It is far more likely, therefore, that the day is a literal one, which is not meant to convey a measurement of time within itself, but instead designate the temporal boundaries of an event.

If the term ביום in 5:1 is meant to parallel 2:4b, as is abundantly clear, then the day of 2:4b is also a literal day. Hence, one must conclude that the day upon which man was made in 5:1 is the day that the entire chapter of Genesis 2 describes.

In fact, one must ask the pertinent question, "If the author sought to communicate the same circumstantial idea found in בהבראם, why did he not simply place the ב preposition on עשות?" Instead, Ezekiel 43:18 uses the construction ב + יום + העשותו to refer to a literal day upon which the altar is built and dedicated. There is simply no evidence that ביום + infinitive weakens the semantic boundaries of the term יום; and in fact, all of the evidence points in the opposite direction. It may be that the ב in ביום creates a temporal circumstantial out of the infinitive construct when it precedes it, as it seems to do here in 5:1, but this provides nothing toward the idea that the meaning of the substantive יום can, therefore, refer to a longer period of time than a literal day.

CONCLUSION OF LEXICAL ANALYSIS

The fact that the term ביום can be used to describe a day that can be distinguished from other days, denote a specific type of day, measure other days in distinction from it, and is interchangeable with the term יום in certain instances,[44] displays the fact that a literal day (whether referring to a single day or a type of day) is always in view. If one could not distinguish the day, to which it referred, from other days, then even the cultic uses that are gnomic would not indicate to the reader the sacred

---

44. Cf. 4QpsJub[a] 1:7, where יום הבראם rather than ביום הבראם occurs with the same meaning (i.e., "the day of creation"/"on the day of creation"). This should be enough to indicate that the term with the ב preposition is not needed. Here, יום stands on its own, and conveys the same idea with or without the preposition. Yet, יום is not stretched beyond its normal range of meaning, a fact known from the lexica. Hence, יום does not mean one thing and ביום another. Yet, if יום always refers to a literal day, then ביום would follow suit and also convey something occurring within the temporal sphere of a single day. Hence, neither the grammatically singular word on its own, nor with the preposition, nor with any of its verbal collocations, as we have seen, can be construed as having an expanded meaning.

time these events were to be observed. The attempt to apply the generic circumstantial "when" that denotes an unspecified time period is not a result of the evidence marshaled. Instead, the specific circumstantial "when" would be appropriate only if the translator/reader were aware that the term referred to a specific and literal day, i.e., that it referred to the specific day upon which the action/event described took place. If, therefore, the translation "when" is employed in the attempt to convey a reference to a larger period of time, such as a week, a year, or an epoch, it is at this point that the interpretive error has been made.

What this does is create a conflict for the literal view, for if the two accounts were to be taken literally, a contradiction, surely obvious to the author, would appear.[45]

LITERAL *AND* SYMBOLIC

One possible solution to the literal conundrum is to say that the term as a whole took on a different semantic meaning with its common usage that has no connection whatsoever to its constituent parts. This, of course, is very plausible, but must be proven through synchronic research, and in fact, the contrary manifests itself as the victor.

The second possibility is that the larger context refers to the literal day in which everything was made in 2:4b–25. In other words, that the author either means to convey that all of these things created were made on a single day, or that it is "upon a day when" these things were still unmade that God began creating. In both cases, יוֹם retains its literal meaning as "a day."[46] Of course the former is contradictory to the literal view of Genesis 1 and the latter is not; but we have already seen that such reservations are no longer needed, since the days of Genesis 1 do not

---

45. The common misguided attempt to take the day of Genesis 2 as the sixth day fails on numerous points. If the accounts are literal, the animals and humans are created in the wrong order, the heavens and earth are said to be created either in seven days, or at the beginning on the first day in Genesis 1 (assuming one does not accurately identify it to be an introductory statement in parallel to the following account), instead of the on the sixth, and most importantly, vegetation is created on the third day in Genesis 1, but on the supposed sixth day of Genesis 2, no plant life has yet come about. If one then argues, in an attempt to assail this objection, that there is a reordering of the event by the author in an effort to communicate something theological, then he has approached a more literary reading than a literal one, and hence, to a degree, has conceded the point being made by this book.

46. I would concur, then, with the translation of the LXX (ᾗ ἡμέρᾳ), Vulg (*in die*), NASB, NKJV, and NRSV ("in the day") contra the NIV "when" and Luther *zu der Zeit*.

need to be read as literal, but can instead be read as literary. However, the idea that בְּיוֹם describes the first day in a larger sequence of days upon which the creation event took place is untenable. The entire creation account in Genesis 2 is the main clause/body to the circumstantial in v. 4b.[47] Hence, since the infinitive construct informs the reader that בְּיוֹם is to be understood as occurring within the event described by it, and the infinitive runs simultaneous to the remainder of the creation account in chapter 2, then the term בְּיוֹם refers to the time period within which the creation of Genesis 2 took place. Hence, the author is attempting to communicate that creation here has taken place upon a single day.

Although considered by Patristic and Medieval interpreters, this option was not considered before by most modern scholars largely due to the fact that the seven days in Genesis 1 were seen as literal days, and therefore, were seen as contradictory to the idea that the second creation account argued for a single day in which creation took place. But, as we have seen, it would be a mistake to take the days in Genesis 1 as literal either for the purpose of harmonization or for the purpose of contradiction. In light of the previous discussion concerning Genesis 1, the seven days should no longer be taken as essentially literal. With this obstacle removed, it is now ideal to take the word בְּיוֹם in 2:4b as it is most commonly, if not always, taken to be a literal description of a day upon which an event occurred. This conclusion is consistent also with the two sets of numbers found in the account of the deluge, where one set is figurative and the other literal, and has some commonality, therefore, with Genesis 1 and 2.

THE PRIMEVAL DAY

There is, however, another type of "day" for which the term בְּיוֹם may be contextually employed here, and that is the primeval day. The primeval day is not a day that is known. In fact, the term is employed to denote a time period for which the writer does not have exact details.[48] This does

---

47. Andersen, *Sentence in Biblical Hebrew*, 86–87.

48. The primeval day is a subcategory of the unknown day that is often used literarily, and is similar to the modern storybook beginning as, "once upon a time." This unknown day is used in this fashion in numerous places (1 Sam 1:4; 14:1; 2 Kings 4:8, 11, 18; Job 1:6, 13; 2:1). Although this day is usually combined with the *wayyiqtol* form of the root היה, the point is that a day can refer to an unknown day where the author has little to no further knowledge pertaining to its specificity, and/or is simply using it to set the scene within the narrative.

not mean that he or she employs the term to refer to a long period of time, simply because the time, whether it is a longer or shorter period of time, is not known by the author.

Instead, the day represents an unknown period when the world was first made. In Egyptian texts, this is referred to as occurring *m zp tpj* "on the first occasion." In Sumerian texts, it is described as ud re.at.ta "in days of yore."[49] However, because the time is not known, it is also referred to as g$_6$ire.at.ta[50] "in nights of yore," and mu re.at.ta[51] "in years of yore."[52] In KAR 4, it is described simply as u$_4$ "a/the day" heaven and earth were separated.[53] In fact, the Sumerian remote demonstrative ri/re in some of the constructions mentioned above indicates that the author is speaking of a time that is not within his sphere of accessibility.[54] Since it is beyond his ability to access the time in which creation occurred, if there is such a thing as time before time in the first place, he uses the language of common time units to refer to it. It, therefore, can only be described as "that/those distant day/days," that/those distant night/nights," and "that/those distant year/years." Yet temporal language is being employed to represent, not measure, a time that is unknown to the author. He is not attempting to use this temporal language in an effort to say that creation took place literally during these time periods, but instead uses the language of these time periods as literary symbols representing the "time" of origins for the purposes of narration. The fact that this time period is really unknown may explain why other Mesopotamian texts, written in both Sumerian and Akkadian, refer to the time of the beginning without

---

49. This appears elsewhere in variation: ud ul.el.re../ta\, "in the long gone far off days," is constructed from a large attestation in other texts by Kramer in the dispute poem *Bird and Fish*. For a translation and commentary see Kramer, "Sumerische Litteraire," 99–108; and Krispijn, "Dierenfabels in het oude Mesopotamie," 131–48. Cf. also Vanstiphout, "Debate Poems," 271–318; and "Debate Poems: Part II," 347–48; as well as his "Bird and Fish," *NABU* (1991) no. 104. Another variation reads ud re.a (cf. u$_4$.ri.a in other texts), lit. "in the day").

50. g$_6$ re.a in *Gilgamesh, Enkidu, and the Netherworld* (i.e., *Gilgamesh and the Ḫuluppu Tree*). See Black et al., *Gilgamesh, Enkidu*," and Shaffer, *Sumerian Sources*, 1–6.

51. As in the other temporal designations, mu re.a in some texts.

52. *Enki and Ninmaḫ* (Jacobsen, *The Harps That*, 151–66).

53. Pettinato, *Das altorientalische Menschenbild*, 74–77. See Clifford's English translation (*Creation Accounts*, 49–51), which although is based on Samuel N. Kramer's French translation, stays true to the original text in most places.

54. Yoshikawa, "Spatial Deictic System," 185–92. Cf. also the brief discussion in Edzard, *Sumerian Grammar*, 50–51.

any specific temporal measurements at all.⁵⁵ This is largely due the fact that time is viewed as a created thing. Hence, creation cannot really take place in time, since time does not yet exist. The construction of time after or during creation in the bilingual prologue to the astrological treatise *Enūma Anu Enlil* illustrates this point:

e-nu ᵈa-nu ᵈen-líl u ᵈé-a ilānu^(meš) rabûti^(meš)
šamê^e u erṣeta^(ta) ib-nu-ú ú-ad-du-u gis-kim-ma
ú-kin-nu na-an-za-za [ú-š]ar-ši-du gi-is-gal-la
ilāni^(meš) mu-ši-tim ú-[x-x]-x ù-za-i-zu ḫar-ra-ni
kakkabāni^(meš) tam-ši-li-[šu-nu uṣ-ṣ]i-ru lu-ma-a-[ši]
mûša ūma mal?-ma?-[liš im-du-d]u ar-ḫa u šatta ib-nu-u
*ana sîn šamaš x x [x purussê šamê]^e u erṣetim^(tim).*⁵⁶

When Anu, Enlil, and Ea, the great gods,
>Had created heaven and earth, had made manifest the token,
>Had established the "stand," had fixed the "station,"
>Had appointed the gods of the night, had distributed the courses,
>Had [installed] stars as (astral) counterparts, had designed the "images,"
>Had [measured] the length of day and night, had created month and year,
>Had [ordered] the path for Sin and Šamaš (and) had made the decrees concerning heaven and earth.⁵⁷

Hence, day and night, as well as the astrological markers that measure them are a part of the created order. Thus, the first act of creation cannot really be spoken of as though it occurred within a measurement of time, since measurements of time had not yet been created. The terminology of temporal language, therefore, should not be taken literally, but literarily.

---

55. For instance, cf. *enūma eliš* "when on high" (Ee I.1), *inūma ilu awīlum* "when gods were man" (*Atra-ḫasīs* I.1), *e-nu ᵈa-nu ᵈen-líl u ᵈé-a ilānu^(meš) rabûti^(meš) šamê^e u erṣeta^(ta) ib-nu-ú* "when Anu, Enlil, and Ea, the great gods, had created heaven and earth" (the second Akkadian prologue to *Enūma Anu Enlil*).

56. This transliteration is taken from Horowitz, *Mesopotamian Cosmic*, 146–7. Also cf. SpTU 3 67 in Ibid., 141.

57. Translation offered by Landsberger and Wilson, "The Fifth Tablet,", 172; see Reiner and Pingree, *Babylonian Planetary Omens*; Rochberg-Halton, "TCL 6 13," 207–28.

Genesis 1 may record one of the ways this unknown time is addressed in the author's mind (i.e., בראשית, a general reference to the beginning, associated with concepts that would be translated as "on the first," or "on the head").[58] These expressions can be utilized precisely because the author is unconcerned about what cannot be known in the first place. What is important for the author to communicate to his audience, however, are the descriptive elements of chaos that precede creation followed by the reversal of those chaotic elements in creation, which are more to the point, since their audience is far more concerned with the ability of the deity to overpower chaos than they are about mathematical measurements concerning the exact time periods of creation.

This view of the primeval day would make sense in the biblical text, not so much from a mathematical standpoint, but from an ancient literary one, since the anthropogony in Genesis 2 is the one which would be considered, not the "literal," but the "real" account to the ancient reader.[59] Although the anthropogony in Gen 1:26–27 has a few paral-

---

58. There is some connection between Genesis 1 and Egyptian texts that use *m zp tpj* as a way of describing the unknown, primeval time. The 𓅓 *m* in Egyptian is equivalent to the ב in Hebrew. Likewise 𓊪// *tpj* means "first" and is etymologically related to the word 𓁶 *tp*, which means "head" (See the relationship between the hieroglyphs belonging to the two terms in Faulkner, *Dictionary of Middle Egyptian*, 276). The Hebrew word ראשית/ראשון "first"/"beginning" is related to the word ראש and also means "head" (see James K. Hoffmeier, "Some Thoughts on Genesis 1 & 2," 42) Perhaps, ראשית is used in Genesis 1, therefore, to describe the primeval time, a time unknown in which creation took place. cf. also the phrase *ina rēš* in certain theogonic texts (e.g., William H. Hallo, "The Theogony of Dunnu," 403). Aquila, interestingly enough, translates בראשית as κεφαλαίῳ (Wevers, *Greek Text of Genesis*, 75).

59. By distinguishing the term "literal" from "real," or "reality," I mean only to suggest that reality can be described in mythic language without one's view of reality itself becoming myth. The ancient Israelites would have viewed the events described within this account as the events that took place in reality, but they would not necessarily have seen the text as literal in its descriptive presentation of those events. This seems clear from the fact that no attempt was made to edit content that, if taken literally, is contradictory (e.g., the sequential contradictions between Genesis 1 and 2). The reality has now been clothed in the cultural symbolism that makes up the conceptual world of the ancient reader, and resonates with his or her audience when these more aesthetic aspects of language and understanding are utilized.

The account in chapter 2 would have been more plausibly the story that an ancient Israelite would have believed as the more "literal" of the two. By this, I do not mean to say that they would have seen the text as a literal presentation of the events, as though language objectively captures events anyway, but rather that the perhaps symbolic use of mythic imagery, used as the most common form of literary language in the ANE, points to literal persons and actions that took place. The ancient reader, for example,

lels within ancient Near Eastern texts, the most popular anthropogony found throughout various Mesopotamian creation accounts would be the far more likely to be taken as a depiction of reality. Add to this that the author seems preoccupied with his polemic against the argument made by the Mesopotamian epic *Atra-ḫasīs*, and the connection seems no less than a sure thing, since the Mesopotamian creation-flood story carries with it the likeness of this anthropogony in chapter 2, and not the anthropogony found in Genesis 1.

Furthermore, the creation-flood narrative pattern in Genesis follows a figurative scheme in the first report and a more "literal" one in the second.[60] For instance, the flood in the first account uses the symbolic numbers seven (the number of purification/sanctification) and forty (the number of trial).[61] The second uses a literal number (150),

---

would have believed that Adam and Eve were real persons, that they were made by God, that they shared a fellowship with God, and that God's commands, therefore, as reflected in the text, are literary presentations of real commands that were binding.

Whether they also believed that the mythic presentation of the garden, the trees, the way in which God made the woman, by dismissing the animals as legitimate helpers and pulling a piece of flesh out of Adam's side, is more difficult to ascertain. Certainly, in the more literalistic Second Temple interpreters one finds a belief in all of the elements mentioned that ignores the original literary intent; but as argued before, this hermeneutic is brought on by the perceived looming threat of pagan corruption and cultural infiltration into the religious mind of Judaism under Hellenistic rule (post Antiochus IV) rather than a grappling with the literary dimensions of the text.

60. By "literal" I still mean to say that this number is not necessarily a number that corresponds to the temporal unfolding of the event, but that it represents the time of the event, as opposed to the figurative number that expresses a literary concept found within the narrative.

61. Noah must endure the rains for forty days and forty nights (Gen 7:4, 12; 8:6); the Israelites are tested at the foot of Sinai for forty days and forty nights while Moses is on the mountain (Exod 24:18; 34:28); the period of waiting to hear back from the spies is forty days (Num 13:25); the Israelite nation must wander for forty years in the wilderness, an anticipatory period where the reader is left to wonder if the nation will endure (14:33–35; 32:13; Deut 2:7); see especially Deut 8:2: "You shall remember all the way which the Lord your God has led you in the wilderness these forty years, that He might humble you, testing you, to know what was in your heart, whether you would keep His commandments or not." Moses' life is dissected into forty year increments (something which is implied in Exod 7:7 and interpreted as such in Acts 7:30); the forty year rest for Israel in the Book of Judges is also a trial which they fail (Judg 3:11; 5:31; 8:28); Israel is taunted by Goliath for forty days (17:16); David's difficult reign is forty years (2 Sam 5:4), as was Solomon's (1 Kgs 11:42); Elijah's journey to Horeb is forty days and forty nights, during which he must be sustained on a single meal (19:8); and Nineveh's trial to see if they will repent is forty days (Jon 3:4); cf. also the temptation of Jesus in the wilderness, which lasts for forty days (Matt 4:2; Mk 1:13; Lk 4:2) in parallel to Deut 9:9.

having no connection to anything symbolic in the ancient Near East or the Hebrew Bible.

If this is indeed the case, then the first account in Genesis 1 gives us the symbolic number of seven days in its purification of the universal temple (later celebrated by Israel to remember God's sovereignty over everything through its Sabbath); and the second account gives us a literal number (i.e., "one day"[62]). The word בְּיוֹם then does not counter its other 215 uses, but rather its meaning is consistent with them; and our present study either restricts the timetable of creation to a single day, or removes such temporal restrictions from the event by not supplying a timetable in the first place.

One might, therefore, conclude that the literal number with which the author conveys God's "timetable" for creating everything is in a single day that represents an unknown period of time, as Augustine and other ancient interpreters seem to indicate. Hence, one historical view is vindicated above the others.

It seems more likely, therefore, that the literal day here functions as a literary representative of the time of creation, not the literal measurement of a time that itself cannot be measured. In other words, since the author does not know the chronology of the creation days, having taken place in a "time" of non-time and a history of a time when there was no history, it is likely that he simply supplied a literary use of בְּיוֹם in accordance with other ancient Near Easter creation accounts that simply describe the creation of the world taking place on a day. U. Cassuto identifies this as the poetic tradition concerning Paradise.[63]

As stated many times before, this does not mean that the word בְּיוֹם means a longer period of time. As I have just shown, the word refers to a literal day, and the appropriate linguistic guidelines for honest lexicography should not be overstepped in order to advance some sort of correspondence theory that attempts to make the text compatible with modern origins theories. Hence, although my conclusions may mimic those of BDB when it indicates that בְּיוֹם can mean "the time of" in a generic sense because it is "representing the act vividly as that of a

---

62. Cf. the numerical use of the indefinite singular of יוֹם/*ym* in Ugaritic literature (Sivan, *A Grammar of Ugaritic*, 93).

63. Cassuto, *Genesis I*, 99.

single day,"⁶⁴ the road to that destination leaves the integrity of our lexicographical methodologies intact.

However, I am now speaking about that which the "day" may represent in its literary context. As I have discussed before, just as one must ask both what the word "pig" literally means within its lexical boundaries and to what it refers within its semantic domain (i.e., within the context of its symbolic narrative) one must also ask what the phrase "in the day" means lexically and to what it refers within its literary context. Just as the pig, in the story of "The Three Little Pigs", must be understood as a literal pig in order for the reader to grasp the imagery of the narrative, one must also understand that the pig symbolically represents a human being, who must build his or her life out of things that last. The narrative has not changed the *meaning* of the word "pig." Instead, it has only indicated the word's *referent*.

Failure to understand this concept is in reality a failure to understand literature as a whole. Hence to misunderstand literature, the vehicle through which God communicates to His people, is to misunderstand the Scripture itself. Let me therefore restate the above in no uncertain terms.

The lexical meaning of the term בְּיוֹם itself is not expanded by grammatical or syntactical modification. However, literary uses of a term may have two significations:

1. The lexical meaning that conjures up within a reader's mind a picture or sense of the object described; and
2. The object outside the text to which the term refers.

In the case of "The Three Little Pigs," the object described lexically as a "pig" immediately conjures up images the readers mind of a morbidly obese farm animal, along with its numerous characteristics, as soon as the word in the story is read or heard. However, the object outside of the text to which the pig in the story refers is a type of human person who makes wise or foolish decisions. The lexical term "pig" does not mean "person who makes a life decision," but in the larger context of the story and literary purpose, the term does refer to that person. In the same way, the term יוֹם in the singular, regardless of its grammatical and syntactical associations, literally means "day"; but in its literary context may refer to an object or event that exceeds its lexical range of mean-

---

64. BDB 400; followed by Driver, *Genesis*, 37.

ing as within the narrative—in this case, the term בְּיוֹם, which literally means "in a day," refers to an unknown period of primordial "time."

In this way, the text must be seen as a whole, rather than exclusively in terms of broken grammatical and lexical units of information. Lexical information is needed to support the picture the narrative creates, but without an understanding of the external referents, i.e., that to which the imagery refers, the story of "The Three Little Pigs" is simply about the hazardous plight of farm animals in their quest to build better housing.

It also needs to be understood that this is not an allegorical approach to literature, as allegory is not contained by its literary and historical context. Instead, as I have argued before, the approach I am suggesting employs a symbolic interpretation of literature that should be compared to that of interpreting an impressionistic or abstract painting. Likewise, the symbolic narrative of Genesis 2 has not changed the literal meaning of the term בְּיוֹם, but it does indicate its referent. Since the day is not known, yet the primordial creation must begin at some point in time, a day in the literature is used to represent an unknown time when creation occurred in reality. It is doubtful, therefore, in light of ancient Near Eastern parallels and the context of the passage, that the author believes creation took place on a literal day. After all, the account in Genesis 2 begins with an already made world that simply does not yet have plants, humans, and animals to inhabit it. There is nothing of the abyss, the heavens and their host, etc.[65] Of course, there is simply no need to mention these things, since the account itself is a symbolic portrayal of creation, a romantic rather than realist depiction of the historical event. Hence, the account differs significantly from Genesis 1, having no need to harmonize what is caste in the symbolism of the ancient Near Eastern world.

---

65. Of course, the same can be said for Genesis 1, since the dark earth already exists, although covered by water.

5

A New Look at the Punishment of the Primeval Couple

IN HIS GROUNDBREAKING ARTICLE, "Sanctuary Symbolism in the Garden of Eden Story,"[1] Gordon J. Wenham suggested that the garden was being presented by the author of Genesis as a localized temple, and that the phrase "in the day you eat of it, you will surely die," is therefore, to be understood "symbolically in terms of later cultic legislation."[2] In other words, as the temple represents the presence of God within the community, this had implications for the person expelled from the community, since he or she "was to enter the realm of death."[3] The imagery, then, is one of the couple moving from the sphere of the community over which the temple resides (i.e., a community of order and life sustained by the presence of God and His divine symbol of sovereignty) into the sphere of chaos, characterized as the netherworld or the land of death.

In conjunction with Wenham's suggestion, the previous analysis concerning the term ביום indicates that the term refers to a literal day. If the term ביום must refer to a literal day, then how does one who disagrees with Wenham's analysis explain the use of the term in 2:17? It will be my purpose in this chapter to show that Wenham's suggestion is the only viable one, both in the context of the ancient Near Eastern

---

1. Originally published in *The Proceedings of the Ninth World Congress of Jewish Studies, Division A: The Period of the Bible* (Jerusalem: World Union of Jewish Studies, 1986), 19–25, and reprinted in Richard S. Hess and David T. Tsumura (ed.), *I Studied Inscriptions from before the Flood: Ancient Near Eastern, Literary, and Linguistic Approaches to Genesis 1–11* (SBST 4; Winona Lake, IN: Eisenbrauns, 1994), 399–404.

2. Ibid., 404. This suggestion was made in skeletal form by early interpreters as well (Kugel, *Traditions of the Bible*, 110), but Wenham's argument has given academic meat to their claims.

3. Ibid.

conception of death, and within the literary use of temple symbolism and its implications for chaos and creation.

It is important first to understand that the command appears three times within the pericope, each time evidencing significant alterations from the previous appearance.

ומעץ הדעת טוב ורע לא תאכל ממנו כי ביום אכלך ממנו מות תמות
(Gen 2:17)

"From the tree of the experience of order and chaos,[4] you will not eat, for on the day you eat from it, you will certainly die."

ומפרי העץ אשר בתוך הגן אמר אלהים לא תאכלו ממנו ולא תגעו בו פן תמתון
(Gen 3:3)

"From the fruit of the tree which is in the middle of the garden," God said, "You are not to eat from it, nor are you to harm it,[5] lest you die."

---

4. "Good and evil" should be seen in terms to the creation and preservation of humanity itself. What is ordered for the benefit of human life is "good" and what flows toward chaos is "evil." Likewise, contra von Rad (*Genesis*, 78), the phrase does not refer to omniscience, but rather, according to the usual employment of ידע in the Book of Genesis, refers to the experience of both order and chaos, rather than simply the order with which they have been only briefly acquainted. Vogels, although with some deficiency in description, comes close to suggesting this in his article "'Like One of Us,'" 145–50. The concept of טוב ורע as "order and chaos" will be pursued further in this chapter.

5. The word *nāgaʿ* is, with the exception of the Hiphil participle in 28:12, employed in Genesis to describe harm being done to something. One "touches" something in order to do damage it in some way. YHWH *yĕnaggaʿ* touches/harms Pharaoh and his household with great *nĕgāʿîm* "touchings"/"harmful things" (12:17); Abimelech warns his people that *hannōgēaʿ* "the one who touches/harms" Abraham or Sarai will be put to death (26:11); Abimelech also goes to Isaac and declares that *nĕgaʿănûkā* "we have not touched/harmed you," but instead declares to him that they did only what was beneficial to him (26:29); finally, the angel wrestles with Jacob and *wayyiggaʿ* "touches/harms" Jacob's groin (32:26, cf. also v. 33; See also comment on 20:6 concerning the "touching" of Sarai). It should be made clear that this is the common *reference* of the word in Genesis, not the *meaning* of the word, which is simply "to touch."

If the word *nāgaʿ* refers to touching in order to do harm in the Book of Genesis, then here the prohibition of J may have been originally, "You are not to eat from it, nor are you to harm it. Otherwise, you will die." The idea would be that they were not to eat from those trees, but neither were they to destroy them. God has placed them into the garden for a reason (although the reason is never told to us explicitly, it forms a special meaning within the theology of Genesis). Augustine seems to have this interpretation

Note that, in the repetition of the command, the temporal indicator בּיוֹם is not mentioned. It is not until the serpent mentions what will occur "on the day" that בּיוֹם is mentioned again.

כי ידע אלהים כי ביום אכלכם ממנו ונפקחו עיניכם והייתם כאלהים
ידעי טוב ורע

(Gen 3:5)

"For God knows, that on the day you eat from it, your eyes will be opened, and you will become like God, experiencing[6] order and chaos."

The final statement of the command is also different than the one in 2:17, since the woman only states the phrase, "lest you die" (an atemporal and less emphatic assertion), rather than stating "in the day you eat of it, you will absolutely die."[7] It is this statement that is distorted, rather than just the previous command. The crux of the interpretative situation mainly concerns how God is able to say that the two humans are going to die the day they eat of the fruit and yet, when in fact they eat of it, they do not die that day.

HISTORY OF INTERPRETATION

As discussed before, some Second Temple,[8] later rabbinic, and Christian interpretations incorporate the idea of Psalm 90:4, "for a thousand years

---

of the command (*Gen. litt.* 8.15.33). Therefore, the woman would not necessarily be distorting the command. However, in the final state of the text, it seems R may be setting the command in 2:16–17 against the woman's alternate version of it in 3:2–3.

6. The word ידע in the context of the Genesis narrative carries the idea of having experience with something or someone, and often conveys the idea that one has mastery over the thing known. Hence, the serpent is telling the woman that the human couple will not only experience order with chaos, but will also have control of it—a clear falsehood known to all its ancient readers, although eluding many of its modern interpreters.

7. Cassuto's argument (*Genesis I*, 145) that the words in 3:3 are too far removed from those in 2:17 is not convincing.

8. E.g., *Jub.* 4:29–30: "And at the end of the nineteenth jubilee in the seventh week, in the sixth year, Adam died. And all of his children buried him in the land of his creation. And he was the first who was buried in the earth. And he lacked seventy years from one thousand years, for a thousand years are like one day in the testimony of heaven and therefore it was written concerning the tree of knowledge, 'In the day you eat from it you will die.' Therefore he did not complete the years of this day because he died in it." This theory, designated the "day-year" theory, was also followed by certain

is like yesterday when it passes by and like a watch in the night." This Psalm is traditionally attributed to Moses, and therefore, was connected to Genesis (also traditionally thought to have been written by Moses). Hence, the statement made by God, that they would die "in the day" they ate of the tree, is true, since Adam (who, according to Genesis 5:5, lived to be 930 years old) and Eve (who is said by Second Temple interpreters to have died around the same time) died before a thousand years was up.

Justin Martyr claimed:

> Now we have understood that the expression used among these words, "According to the days of the tree [of life] shall be the days of my people; the works of their toil shall abound," obscurely predicts a thousand years. For as Adam was told that in the day he ate of the tree he would die, we know that he did not complete a thousand years. We have perceived, moreover, that the expression, "The day of the Lord is as a thousand years," is connected with this subject.[9]

Irenaeus also stated:

> And there are some again, who relegate the death of Adam to the thousandth year; for since "a day of the Lord is as a thousand years," he did not overstep the thousand years, but died within them, thus bearing out the sentence of his sin. Whether, therefore, with respect to disobedience, which is death; whether [we consider] that, on account of that, they were delivered over to death, and made debtors to it; whether with respect to [the fact that on] one and the same day on which they ate they also died (for it is one day of the creation); whether [we regard this point] that with respect to this cycle of days, they died on the day in which they did also eat, that is, the day of the preparation, which is termed "the pure supper," that is, the sixth day of the feast, which the Lord also exhibited when He suffered on that day; or whether [we reflect] that he (Adam) did not overstep the thousand years, but died within their limit.[10]

Patristic writers in times of Roman persecution. Danielou comments concerning Justin Martyr: "Since the Asiatics, following the lead of apocalyptic, regarded the messianic reign as a return to Paradise, it was natural that in it the length of life should be the same as Adam's ought to have been (cf. *Jubilees* XXIII, 27)" (*Development of Christian Doctrine*, 392).

9. *Dialogue*, 81; *ANF* 1:239–40.
10. *Haer.* 5.23.2; *ANF* 1:551–2.

A New Look at the Punishment of the Primeval Couple   105

Chrysostom took ביום to refer to a literal day, but then believed God's act to be one of mercy, where He delayed the punishment to a time in the future.[11] He is followed by Speiser, who states that "the point of the whole narrative is apparently man's ultimate punishment rather than instantaneous death."[12]

Nahum Sarna, stating his assessment that humans were always mortal, sees the "death" as referring to expulsion from the garden, but only because this would cut off the couple's access to the tree of life (i.e., immortality).[13]

Other scholars attempt a more existential answer and state that the couple died spiritually in that they were cut off from God's presence. This argument is not explicit, however, and although partially true, is more midrash than exegetical. This is not to say that it is completely wrong to develop this into a more advanced lapsarian theology, only that a more exegetical step, concerned primarily for the immediate text, must precede it.

Another way of interpreting the phrase, however, is gleaned from the word that is commonly translated "in the day" found in 2:17. It has been argued in Chapters 1 and 2 that the Hebrew words יום should be understood as a literal period of a day without extending its lexical range beyond that period. However, many commentators believe that ביום refers to a much longer period of time than that of a single day. It was thought that the preposition, which can be used temporally, can cause a word to become adverbial, specifically a temporal adverb, when connected to a noun conveying a measurement of time like a day. Hence, the translation "when" is often given to it. It is argued that in Gen 2:4b, the statement "When YHWH God created the earth and heaven," obviously refers to the longer period of time described in Chapters 1 and 2, not just a single day.[14] Because of this, the term ביום does not necessarily restrict the period to that literal day in which Adam and Eve would have

---

11. PG 53:138. See also Smick, "Mythological Elements in Job," 213.

12. *Genesis*, 17. This is a seemingly inconsistent statement made by Speiser, as he concludes upon the same verse that ביום refers to the "moment" the man eats of the tree (Ibid.). One can only surmise that he means to harmonize these two statements by viewing the process as having begun at that moment, but only finalized at Adam's much later physical demise.

13. *Genesis*, 21. This interpretation is shared by Vogels, "'Like One of Us,'" 150–55.

14. Arnold, *Genesis*, 56.

to die. However, if the collocation means "when," or "at the time," then it is "at the time" they eat the fruit that they will die, then the punishment remains within the temporal parameter of the action taken.[15] In other words, if X will occur at the time of Y, then Y cannot occur at a time much later than Y. Therefore, if death will occur at the time the fruit is eaten, then death cannot occur at a later time. Death must occur at that same time if ביום is to be taken as a circumstantial temporal indicator corresponding to their eating the fruit.

However, ביום in fact does not mean a longer period of time than a day as we have seen; and it is my contention that they did die that day, and by this I do not mean spiritually (although that would be implied). I would contend that they died physically that day.

The problem in interpreting this text is the same as the one we have encountered throughout—namely, that moderns are reading an ancient text and reading modern concepts into ancient words. When a modern individual looks at the word "die" he or she thinks of annihilation or non-existence from life. This is largely due to the naturalistic materialism that pervades our worldview.

However, the ancient mind thinks of death as separation from the created land (which is the land of the living) to the uncreated land (which is the land of the dead/the netherworld). Death is expulsion from the created world to the netherworld, from what is organized to what is disorganized, from a life-sustaining environment to a chaotic and hostile one. For instance, one need only compare the identification of the abyss with the netherworld due to the fact that it is an uncreated place. The wilderness is used in the same way, as discussed before, as the realm of the wild beasts (as opposed to the domesticated animals within the civilized/created world). Hence, the primordial/uncreated state of the world is covered by the abyss and uncultivated land is understood as the "realm of the dead." This concept is also connected to the imagery of the serpent in Chapter 3. Hence, a brief look at the temple imagery as creation and the serpent imagery as chaos will illumine the netherworld imagery in the ancient Near Eastern concept of death.

---

15. See Skinner, *Genesis*, 54.

THE TEMPLE OF GENESIS 2

As I have already discussed, the presence of the temple is an instrument of creation through which the deity orders society and holds chaos at bay. As Genesis 1 is creation described in terms of a temple, so Genesis 2 also uses this imagery in a different way. Scholars, of course, have oft noted the shared imagery between Eden and the Jerusalem temple,[16] together with Wenham. E. M. Bloch-Smith has argued that the temple represents God's victory over the sea and the acceptance of His people into His presence, and provides a shared theme of the divine victory over chaos in Genesis 2.[17] Here in Genesis 2, chaos is a desert wasteland rather than the cosmic sea, as in Genesis 1, and God accepts humanity, as His creation, into His presence. The garden imagery, both in Genesis 1 and in the Jerusalem temple, certainly communicate what temples often do, i.e., that the deity has brought fertility out of barreness, abundant life out of death, a fruitful creation out of an uninhabitable chaos.

Sanctuary Symbolism

There are numerous elements that indicate that the garden is meant by the author to symbolize a temple. The first and foremost of these is the garden itself. It hardly needs to be argued that temples in the ancient Near East, specifically in Mesopotamian texts, are usually described as gardens. This is due to the fact that gardens are representative of life and fruitfulness (i.e., fertility that counters death/chaos). Hence, text after text refers to the temple as a garden sanctuary with fruit bearing trees and plants.

However, by itself, a garden does not indicate that a temple is in view. This is where the rest of the imagery in Genesis 2 is helpful. The rivers that flow out of the garden in vv. 10–15 are reminiscent of the divine streams that flow from the deity's heavenly temple. These are waters of life and purification. In Ugaritic literature, ʾIlu abides on the paradisal mountain at the center of the world that contains two sources

---

16. Smith ("Like Deities, Like Temples," 6–10) notes a wide range of scholars who have come to this conclusion (e.g., Widengren, *The King and the Tree of Life*; Clifford, *The Cosmic Mountain*; Wallace, *The Eden Narrative*; Batto, "Paradise Reexamined," 33–66; Morris and D. Sawyer (eds.), *A Walk in the Garden*; Stager, "Jerusalem and the Garden of Eden," 183–94; Stordalen, *Echoes of Eden*; Callendar, *Adam in Myth and History*).

17. Bloch-Smith, "Who Is the King of Glory," 24.

from which four rivers flow out.[18] Nick Wyatt observes that the place from whence these rivers spring indicates temple imagery.

> Temple symbolism also placed the resident god at the centre of the universe. This is the omphalos, the place of true reality, the still centre of the turning world. El, the absolute deity, is immovable, and all other deities revolve around him.[19]

Ezekiel 47:1-12 also employs the imagery of river and garden in reference to the temple. The fresh water that produces life represents the prosperity that the presence of the deity brings to the area in which it resides.[20] In this same way, the temple of paradise in Genesis 2 is the source of four rivers, indicating the abode of YHWH and His image, which also exists at the center of the world.[21]

The pure gold and precious jewels that are mentioned in vv. 11-12 often adorn the inside of temples, and have often been compared to the jewels in the tabernacle.[22] The tree of life has often been paralleled to the menorah in the tabernacle, which itself mimics the burning bush on the proto-temple of Mount Sinai.[23] Whether this connection is appropriate is disputable, but there is little doubt that the tree itself represents the type of life and order that often characterizes the presence of the temple.

The cherub that guards the sanctuary and the tree of life is a dead giveaway, in that cherubs surround the throne of God and both guard and represent His presence in the temple. As Wenham notes, cherubs were often placed at the entrance of temples in the ancient Near East.[24] The cherub is situated at the entrance of the garden sanctuary, which seems to indicate that the garden is hedged off, and is, therefore, an enclosure that can only be accessed from a single point of entry at the east side.[25]

---

18. Wyatt, *Religious Texts*, 52 n. 63.

19. Ibid., n. 64.

20. Hence, there is a common ancient Near Eastern motif of gods dwelling near fresh water.

21. Although in our present text there is one source, not two.

22. Chilton, *Paradise Restored*, 32-36; Wenham, "Sanctuary Symbolism," 402.

23. Meyers, *The Tabernacle Menorah*. Meyers is followed by Wenham, "Sanctuary Symbolism," 401.

24. Wenham, "Sanctuary Symbolism," 401.

25. Ibid.

The cult image is made of clay, given some of the deity's essence, and performs royal/priestly functions as God's representative in order to maintain the sanctuary and facilitate life. The cult image in the ancient Near East, and the making of אדם in Genesis 2 parallel one another at numerous points. Man is a clay image that is crafted and then enlivened by the deity as a representative of his or her sovereignty over, and presence in, a localized area.[26]

The work given to the man is in the language of temple service. Wenham observes:

> The description of Adam's job in Eden, also suggests it is a sanctuary. He was told 'to till and keep it' leʿobdâ ûlĕšomrâ. The midrash drew attention to passages where these terms were used separately. It did not note though that the only other passages in the Pentateuch where these verbs are used together are to be found in Num 3:7–8, 8:26, 18:5–6, of the Levites duties in guarding the ministering in the sanctuary.[27]

Finally, the idea that the garden is described in terms of a temple is also seen by its parallel to Genesis 1:

Genesis 1

A Introductory statement: Creation of Heaven and Earth (v. 1)

B Parenthetical statement concerning the chaotic state of the world, i.e., disordered and not occupied by אדם (v. 2)

C Creation of human habitation in terms of a temple (vv. 3–25)

D Creation of אדם (male and female) as God's royal cult image (vv. 26–27)

E Distinguished as male and female (זכר and נקבה), and told to be fruitful and multiply and to rule over creatures (v. 27c–28)

F Food is given to the cult image to eat (v. 29)[28]

---

26. Schüle, "Made in the Image," 11–14.

27. Ibid.; also see Schmutzer, *Be Fruitful and Multiply*, 194–5.

28. Cf. KTU² 1.4.vi, where an inaugural banquet is held in order to celebrate the completion of Baʿal's temple.

Genesis 2

A´ Introductory statement: Creation of Earth and Heaven (v. 4)

B´ Parenthetical statement concerning the chaotic state of the world, i.e., disordered and not occupied by אדם (v. 5)

C´ Creation of אדם (male) as God's royal cult image (v. 7)

D´ Creation of human habitation in terms of a temple (vv. 8–14)

F´ Food is given to the cult image to eat; kingship is implied (vv. 15–20)

C´ Creation of אשה (i.e., a female אדם) as God's royal cult image (vv. 21–23)

E´ Distinguished as male and female (איש and אשה), and told to join together to become one flesh (vv. 24–25)

It would take another book to deal with each of these here in detail, and there are other elements, such as God initializing the reversal of chaos by natural elements (e.g., wind to water and water to dry land in 1:2c and 2:6) that could be mentioned, but the suggested parallels above should suffice for now. Of course, it must be mentioned that the creation of Genesis 1 ends in an established and peaceful order with Sabbath observance as the pinnacle indicator of God's victory over chaos, whereas the creation of Genesis 2 ends in the victory of chaos in chapter 3. Of course, in the author's mind this is but a temporary victory and God has vindication in its ultimate end (50:20).

Outside the Temple

If humans are God's cult image within the sanctuary, or are simply protected by the sanctuary, then going outside the sanctuary is entering the realm of chaos that had previously held back those forces. The garden sanctuary is cultivated, but the humans are now entering the uncultivated שדה that described the disorder and chaos of the land in v. 5, the symbol for chaos in the second creation account. It is important to remember that chaos is synonymous with death, as order is synonymous with life. To die is to enter into the land of chaos, the land of "uncreation." Outside of the perimeters of the garden, the land and wild animals were subdued and ruled over by the man. Hence, they are brought to him and named by him (2:19–20), a signification of divine authority over another, as it decrees a fate to its subject. This rule changes, however, once the wild bull of order mixed with chaos are sought by the human beings and God grants their wishes by cursing the ground (3:17–19). The human couple, of course, will not be able to fill the role of deity in subjugating chaos as the serpent promised, and they will ultimately succumb to its destructive forces without the aid of deity.

THE SERPENT OF GENESIS 3 IN ITS ANCIENT NEAR EASTERN CONTEXT

It is important to note here that when one does a comparative study between the Hebrew Bible and other ancient Near Eastern texts that the evidence should not only be sufficient to display the existence of such concepts in the ancient Near Eastern world, but that these ideas would have been known by the Israelite authors/recipients as well. Many abuses materialize when one attempts to conform the text of Scripture to obscure ideas and practices that would hardly have been known by most of the ancient Israelites.

Similarly, when the imagery of the narrative as a whole is missed, this tends to turn the purpose of the story on its head. An interesting example of this is the common notion among scholars that the serpent in the story is the hero, who tells Eve the truth, since she does not die.[29] God is, therefore, the villain, who tells the lie that Adam and Eve will die on the day they eat of the fruit; and the woman is also a liar in saying that the serpent deceived her (3:13).[30] Understanding the imagery means everything if one is to interpret the passage as it was meant to be understood by its ancient reader. I will attempt to show, therefore, the intersection between the serpent, as it is depicted in Genesis 3, and three common motifs found in the ancient Near Eastern world: the common use of animal imagery for supernatural beings, the serpent as enemy of the gods, and the fact that talking animals signify a supernatural presence.

The Use of Animal Imagery to Symbolize the Supernatural

Although the use of animals to represent something supernatural is widespread in the ancient Near East, the larger portion of the evidence is derived from Egyptian religion. Most are familiar with the large im-

29. Charlesworth, *The Good and Evil Serpent*, 307–11.
30. Ibid., 307.

ages of gods, which have the bodies of humans and the heads of animals or are entirely animals. However, what many do not realize is that this is not because the Egyptians worshipped animals.[31] Nor is it that the Egyptians thought that their gods looked like the animals used to depict them. As James Allen comments:

> To an Egyptian, the image of a lion-headed woman, for example, conveyed two things at once: first, that it was not the image of a human female, and was therefore a goddess; and second, that the goddess in question was Sekhmet. Such images were not an attempt to portray what the gods might look like if they could be seen; instead, they are nothing more than large-scale *ideograms*.[32]

This phenomenon occurs when a god is noted for a particular attribute and is in turn depicted as an animal with a similar characteristic. Therefore, Horus, associated with the sun god, who soars in the sky, is depicted as a falcon. Sobek, who is the god of fresh water and the Nile is depicted as a crocodile (the animal which rules the water). At Ugarit, both ʾIlu, who is the creator god in Ugaritic myth, and Baʿal, the storm god (i.e., the god who brings rain) are associated with fertility, and thus are depicted as bulls, largely because the bull (due to its strength and the length of its phallus) is an animal which often represents fertility in the ancient Near East.[33] Likewise, when speaking of a goddess, a cow (because of the milk it provides) is also an animal which often represents a goddess's fertility.

Animals are, therefore, often regarded as symbols in epic literature of larger concepts. This fact alone does not indicate that the serpent is meant to be symbolic in Genesis 3, since the other animals in the garden seem to be literal; but the idea that animals in literature are capable of adopting symbolic nuances that represent their distinctive characteristics does contribute to a collective case toward seeing the serpent as symbolic here.

31. Although this may be something that happens later under the Greek infiltration of (and syncretism with) Egyptian culture.

32. Allen, *Middle Egyptian*, 44.

33. Likewise, Baʿal, as the storm-god, is depicted in the same manner because of his association with rain and fertility in the land. Similiarly, the golden calf in the Exodus narrative is likewise meant to convey the idea of YHWH's strength and fertility (eg., "I delivered you from Egypt with a mighty hand," "I will bring you into a land flowing with milk and honey," etc.).

A New Look at the Punishment of the Primeval Couple 113

Talking Animals Signify a Supernatural Presence

In the Egyptian tale, *The Shipwrecked Sailor*,[34] a man has an encounter on a mystical island with a talking snake. The snake has a beard and is covered with gold. These characteristics, to an ancient Egyptian reader, are significant because the beard represents either a god or a king (usually they are not mutually exclusive in Egyptian culture), and the skin of the gods, in Egyptian thought, is made of gold.[35] It is also clear that the being is supernatural since he tells the sailor that once he returns home he cannot come back to the island, due to the fact that only water will be in the place the island is now, indicating to the sailor that the island is not physically there. This is supported by the fact that the island is called the "Island of the *k3*," the *k3* being the immaterial life-force/spirit of all living beings. The talking snake here signifies to the sailor that he is in the presence of someone who is supernatural, not simply a snake with extraordinary vocal chords.

A biblical example is that of the notorious Balaam and the supernatural ability of speech given to his donkey. Even though the donkey here is not seen as divine, his speaking indicates the presence of a supernatural being (i.e., the adversarial angel standing in front of him). The donkey's mouth is said to be opened by God, and He seems to do so in order to communicate to the spiritually-inept seer that a supernatural force is present and standing in the way as an adversary (Heb. *śāṭān*). This is to signify to Balaam the presence of a supernatural force.[36]

These examples show that when an ancient person encountered a talking animal in a text, he or she did not believe it was because animals could talk, but that it was a literary omen that signified the presence of a supernatural being. Therefore, despite the attempt of certain Second Temple interpreters to state otherwise,[37] it is doubtful that the ancient

---

34. See Lichtheim, "The Shipwrecked Sailor," 83–85.

35. E.g. in the *Destruction of Mankind*, Re's skin is said to consist of gold (*AEL* 2:198). See also Hornung, *Conceptions of God*, 134; Leitz, *Magical and Medical Papyri*, 36, IV.8–9; and Robins, "Cult Statues," 6.

36. Although the irony in the passage is the fact that Balaam, the Seer, doesn't see the angel himself, nor does he "see" the omen of a talking animal to understand that there is a supernatural presence, but rather his donkey which does see all of this has to inform him explicitly.

37. See *Jub.* 3:28, "On that day [the day of the Fall] the mouth of all the beasts and cattle and birds and whatever walked or moved was stopped from speaking be-

Israelites really believed that animals could talk anymore than modern individuals do.

The Serpent as Enemy of the Gods

In Egypt, Seth, who is the evil god is depicted by numerous unclean and destructive animals, but he is mainly depicted as a serpent (the apophis). He is the arch-nemesis of Re, the Sun-god, since he seeks to swallow Re up in darkness.

The Hittite myth of Illuyanka conveys also the great battle between the storm god and the serpent. In this text, the storm god's cohort conspires with a mortal man to kill the serpent and his offspring.[38]

In the Ugaritic myth of the Baal Cycle, Baʿal smites Lôtan (= Leviathan), who is called "the fleeing serpent," "the twisting serpent," and "the close-coiling one with seven heads."[39]

This corresponds to the seven-headed dragon/serpent in Mesopotamia, the most notable of which is Tiamat, who is later depicted in Mesopotamian art as a serpent/dragon.[40] The correspondence between Ee and the Bible, then, may be between the enemy identified as the serpent in both accounts. If this is the case, the *Chaoskampf* of the Bible would begin in Gen 3, not Gen 1; and the serpent, therefore, would be seen as the supernatural enemy of God in the garden. The difference between this serpent and that of the one in other ancient Near Eastern accounts is that this one counters God indirectly through the people that He has made. There is no hint that the serpent ever attacks God Himself, and he even takes rebuke and punishment from God without a quibble (which is less of an argument than the man and woman give to God).

---

cause all of them used to speak with one another with one speech and one language" (Wintermute, "Jubilees," 60).

38. Hoffner ("The Hittite Illuyanka Myth," 122–3) makes an excellent point in cautioning the modern reader not to contextualize the serpent in this story, and I would extend it to the mythic serpent imagery in the entire ancient Near East, within our modern concepts of snakes and dragons.

39. Translation by Pardee, "The Baʿlu Myth," 265.

40. The evidence for the dominant Mesopotamian view of the serpent being utilized as a symbol for the demonic is overwhelming within the incantation texts alone. See, for instance, Geller, *Evil Demons: Canonical Utukkū Lemnūtu Incantations*.

Craftiest among the Beasts of the Field

In the Gilgamesh Epic, Gilgamesh finds a plant which has the power to give him everlasting life, but is stolen from him by a serpent. He then states that UR.MAH šá qaq-qa-ri du-un-qa e-te-pu-uš,⁴¹ literally "the lion of the ground enjoys its fortune." The word for lion here (UR. MAH = nešû) is often a designation for supernatural beings.⁴² The word *qaqqaru* "ground" is a term which is often used in mythological texts like Gilgamesh to refer to the netherworld.⁴³ The statement would be understood as something like, "the demon of the netherworld enjoys its fortune" (the two elements of wild beast and land used metaphorically). This metaphor is established further by the fact that Gilgamesh is in the netherworld at the time.⁴⁴

This brings us to a further point in the Genesis text that is often missed by more literalistic interpretive methods. The meaning of the phrase חית השדה is often taken for granted by scholars in Gen 3:1 to exist merely as a geographical description for the purpose of background information (although it is recognized by most scholars to be more than merely topical in other Scriptures, such as its use in Leviticus and Numbers, where the land outside the camp represents the netherworld/the land of chaos and death, and the animals that reside there are painted as agents of chaos).⁴⁵ Often in the Hebrew Bible, the beasts of the field are antagonistic to the community of God (e.g., Exod 23:29; Lev 26:22; Isa 56:9; Jer 12:9). They represent creatures outside of the holy sphere (e.g., garden, camp, or nation) organized and ruled by God. They instead are creatures in the uncreated/unorganized lands, which represent the land ruled by the demonic.

---

41 Line 306 in Parpola, *Epic of Gilgamesh*, 113. See the meaning of *qaqqaru* mentioned here in section A1d in *CAD* Q, 116.

42 *CDA* 251. Cf. also the suggestion concerning the phrase *nešû šá qaqqari* as a chameleon, the animal which disguises itself by shifting in appearance.

43 *CAD* Q, 124, section A9; *CDA* 284.

44. Cf. the imagery of the Hebrew Bible, where the lion will lay down with the lamb, where the animals are used as synecdoche for "the wild will lay down with the domesticated," which in turn signifies that the land of the living will have no more conflict with the land of the dead/death.

45. Stadelmann, for instance, fails to note the contrast of the field (a term that describes the uncreated/chaotic condition in 2:5) with the garden and interprets the phrase as referring to a "hunting ground" (*The Hebrew Conception*, 138). However, he does note the use of שדה in terms of a countryside that is contrasted to a city, i.e., structurally inhabited as opposed to lacking structure and human habitation (Ibid.).

Note that the שדה is placed in contrast to the garden in three different instances:

1. The state of the שדה was said to be a lifeless place (2:5), that parallels the primordial chaos of 1:2, with the garden, being a cultivated sanctuary, as distinct from it.
2. Every חית השדה has to be brought to Adam presumably from outside the garden (2:19). It is not a creature that normally dwells within it. This point becomes significant mainly because this serpent is not a creature of the garden. It is a creature from outside the garden—a creature of the field.
3. The vegetation from which man will now eat, once he is banished from Eden and the trees are no longer accessible to him, are plants of the שדה (3:18).

The comparison can be made of both the wilderness and the abyss, since both are used in the ancient Near East to refer to the uncreated area of the earth. In Ee, the wild beasts and demons come from Tiamat (the uncreated abyss). The text is as follows:

> *um-ma ḫu-bur pa-ti-qat ka-la-[mu]*
> *uš-ra-di kak-ku la maḫ-ri it-ta-lad* MUŠ.MAḪ.[MEŠ]
> *[zaq-t]u-ma šin-ni la pa-du-[u] at-ta-[ʾi-i]*
> *[im-t]u ki-ma da-mu zu-mur-[šú-nu] uš-ma-al-[li]*
> GAL.UŠUM.[MEŠ] *na-ad-ru-ti pul-ḫa-ti ú-šal-[biš-ma]*
> *me-lam-ma uš-taš-šá-a i-li-iš um-taš-[šil]*
> *a-mi-ir-šu-nu šar-ba-bi-iš li-iḫ-ḫar-[mi-im]*
> *zu-mur-šú-nu liš-taḫ-ḫi-ṭam-ma la i-né-ʾu-ú i-[rat-su-un]*
> *uš-zi-iz ba-aš-mu* MUŠ.ḪUŠ *u* ᵈ*la-ḫa-mu*
> UD.GAL.MEŠ UR.IDIM.MEŠ *ù* GIR.TAB.LÚ.U₁₈.[LU]
> UD-*mi da-ab-ru-ti* KU₆.LÚ.U₁₈.LU *ù ku-sa-r[iq-qu]*
> *na-ši kak-ku la pa-du-ú la a-di-ru ta-ḫ[a-zi]*⁴⁶

> Mother Hubur, who can form everything,
> Added countless invincible weapons, gave birth to monster serpents,
> Pointed of fang, with merciless incisors(?),
> she filled their bodies with venom for blood.
> Fierce dragons she clad with glories,
> Causing them to bear auras like gods,

---

46. Lines 133–44 according to the standardized text found in Talon, *Babylonian Creation Myth*, 38.

> (saying) "Whoever sees them shall collapse from weakness!
> Wherever their bodies make onslaught, they shall not turn back!"
> She deployed serpents [bašmu], dragons, and hairy heromen,
> Lion monsters, lion men, scorpion men,
> mighty demons, fish men, bull men,
> bearing unsparing arms, fearing no battle.[47]

The same concept is displayed in the Ugaritic epic of Baʽal. Leviathan comes from Yammu (the uncreated sea). The two foes in the cycle are Yammu (the uncreated sea) and Môtu "death," "the netherworld" (the uncreated desert land/ the uncultivated fields), where it is said that "the sun, luminary of the gods, glows hot,"[48] that it "craves the pool (as do) the wild bulls" and "(craves) springs as (do) the herds of deer."[49] Môtu "death" is simply the netherworld then, who is described both with the imagery of the outlands/desert/wilderness as well as the abyss.[50]

The uncultivated land, where the wild beasts rule, is used as a symbol of Môtu "death," the netherworld. The well watered portions of the earth, the pasture land or cultivated fields, are said to exist up to the border of "death's realm."[51] Any place which is uncultivated, whether the sea or the desert, is used as imagery for the netherworld, or "death's realm." Thus, Môtu states that his throat is the throat of a lion in the wasteland and the gullet of the "snorter" in the sea.[52]

The same concept is found within Egyptian literature with the uncultivated land/desert/wilderness ruled by Seth.[53] It is within this land, not in the cultivated lands, where the apophis (the serpent) dwells. When the sun-god Reʽ goes down into the wilderness/netherworld, he is then attacked by the serpent. The difference here in Genesis is that the serpent has come out of the netherworld and into the created lands. Genesis 2:19–20 may offer the occasion as to why the serpent was there

---

47. COS 1.111:392.
48. KTU² 1.4.viii.21–22; COS 1.86:264.
49. KTU² 1.5.i.15–17; COS 1.86:264.
50. Cf. "descend into the throat of Môtu, son of ʼIlu, into the watery depths of the beloved warrior of ʼIlu" (COS 1.86:265), although it must be granted that this is a reconstruction of the text (see fn. 215).
51. KTU² 1.5.vi.7; COS 1.86:267.
52. KTU² 1.5.i.15–16; COS 1.86:264.
53. Another example can be seen in a First Intermediate Period text found in *The Book of the Dead* (COS 1.18:27–30) that describes the netherworld as going to the hostile desert.

(although J seems to be speaking of literal animals there). Supposedly all of the world's creatures are made by God and named by Adam in 2:19–20, but it is clear that not all lived in the garden. In fact, God must bring each animal from the place He made it into the garden for Adam to name.[54] Therefore, the serpent is a creature from among the "uncreated" outlands, not an indigenous creature to the garden. He is instead a creature from the uncultivated field, i.e., the "realm of death."

This interpretation is also illumed by the fact that YHWH tells the serpent that ועפר תאכל כל ימי חייך "dust you will eat all the days of your life." Eating dust is a common metaphor applied to those who live in the netherworld.[55] In fact, the reference belongs specifically to the house of Ereshkigal, who rules the underworld.

Finally, there is a contrast between the domesticated animals and the wild animals in 3:14. Where the בהמה represent domestic animals, the חית השדה represent the wild animals, the "animals of the field." These designations do not imply anything about the nature of the animals themselves, of course, but instead mark off boundaries between civilized and uncivilized land. These then become symbols of creation and chaos, and as such, often represent the land of the living and the land of the dead (i.e., the netherworld).

THE *CHAOSKAMPF* OF GENESIS

What is even more important than the evidence marshaled from the ancient Near Eastern background of the temple, the serpent, and the realm of death is the context of the Book of Genesis itself. The literary context is clearly woven together by a concern for chaos in the world and how it fits into God's work within such a world. The book will continually present the world as a place that is hostile toward human life, a place

---

54. It is likely that, since they are made from the dust (2:19), they are made in the same place that the man was originally. Note that their designation as כל חית השדה "every animal of the field" (i.e., wild animal) already exists, and is used in a merism with כל עוף שמים to indicate that all of the animals are included.

55. E.g., "To the netherworld, land of n[o return], . . . to the gloomy house, the seat of the ne[therworld] . . . where dust is their sustenance and clay their food" (BM III.19: 499). Likewise, cf. KTU² 1.5.i.18–19: *hm . imt . imt . npš . blt . hmr* "Look, in truth does my throat devour clay" (Wyatt, *Religious Texts*, 118), which refers to Môtu, the king of the dead/netherworld/desert. Also cf. the connection between the death of humans, described as returning to dust in Genesis 3:19, and the fact that the agent of the now cursed lands is sentenced to eat dust.

of ḥāmās, a word that describes that very hostility in relation to human preservation.[56] *Chaoskampf*, which describes a war between the primary deity and personified chaotic forces, is absent from Genesis 1, but begins in Chapter 3 and following.[57] Threats to God's creation, the life of His image that represents His victory over death and chaos, jump out at the reader at every turn. The serpent, as a symbol of wisdom, makes no sense in this context if not combined with the serpent as a symbol of chaos as well.

CONCLUSION

The expulsion from the garden (i.e. the created, organized land, which is ruled by God), then, removes the human couple from the cultivated land that is conducive to life and places them in the hostile wilderness (i.e., the uncreated, disorganized land, which is ruled by the demonic) in which human life will be threatened. This idea is made explicit in P (specifically in the Book of Leviticus, where one is cast outside the camp into the wilderness if unclean, as well as the idea of the scapegoat, which is sent out to the wilderness-demon Azazel[58]).

The idea that the wilderness here carries the connotation of the netherworld, i.e., the land of death, is illuminated by the fact that the reader is introduced to it, at the beginning of the pericope in 2:5, in terms of its parallel to the chaos of Genesis 1:2, and its associations with the serpent in 3:1.

Further evidence of this fact can be seen in the contrast between the שדה and the garden sanctuary/temple. The temple, where the cult image (i.e., אדם) resides, is a place of order where chaos is held at bay. Outside the temple, however, is the realm of chaos. To be removed from the temple in order to be ultimately buried outside of it, evidences that the cult image, which once was enlivened by the deity's essence, has been defiled and is no longer under the complete protection of the deity's

---

56. Cf. Frymer-Kensky's analysis of חמס (6:11, 13), usually translated as "violence," and how it refers often to sexual immorality (i.e., sexual acts that run counter to the procreative command in 1:28–31) and murder ("The Atrahasis Epic," 154).

57. Paas, *Creation and Judgement*, 78–81.

58. Lev 16:8–10. The uncultivated field in ancient Mesopotamia had to undergo an exorcism of sorts in order to free the land of the demons who ruled it. For example, cf. the field in Tablet 1:59–60 of the Utukkū Lemnūtu series, where evil creatures (i.e., evil spirits) dwell (Geller, *Evil Demons*, 94–95, 192).

sanctuary. It has entered the realm of chaos. It has died. This, of course, is comparative imagery being utilized by the author to make a point about God and mankind. Hence, there are not exact parallels in every instance. Instead, the author wishes to convey the idea that humans were once dominant in their relationship with creation as God's image, and now, because of their disobedience, have gone out into a land where they will be dominated by it, even to the point of removing them from the land of the living completely. Hence, the reader must understand that the ancient author (as well as the ancient readers) had concepts of the world that existed in spheres of life and death. Inside the temple was the greatest amount of order and protection. As one went further from the courtyard, outside the community that surrounded it, into the wilderness, and finally into the netherworld, i.e., the depths of the earth, death and chaos increasingly took dominion over him or her. Hence, the expulsion of the couple into the realm of death outside the garden is better than that of Cain. The expulsion of Cain from a lesser sphere than the garden to an even worse sphere leads him to become afraid that he is now vulnerable to an agent of chaos who will completely overtake him and kill him, thereby immediately bringing him to the final sphere of chaos, i.e., the netherworld (4:11–14).

Therefore, the day the human couple eat of the tree is the very day they are removed from the created, organized land of God (and therefore good/beneficial) and sent out to struggle in the uncreated, disorganized land of the demonic (and therefore evil/unbeneficial).[59] This evil land will be set against them, since man was made to thrive only in the place that was created for him, and it will therefore *eventually* return him to the dust from which he was made. His physical death, however, is but an extension of his expulsion from the garden. It is the last sphere of death into which he must enter, and the ultimate consequence of entering a realm of chaos in the first place. Although the serpent promised the human couple that they would be like God in knowing both order and chaos, they are incapable of God's sovereignty to control it. Hence, once the land of chaos is entered, physical death is inevitable. In any case, the situation to an ancient Near Eastern reader is much bleaker than it is to

---

59. Athanasius interprets the text in a similar fashion when he says "they were incurring that corruption in death that was theirs by nature, no longer to live in paradise but cast out of it from that time forth to die and abide in death and corruption" (*Inc.* 3.4; *NPNF*[2] 4:37–38).

a modern reader, who too often simply sees the couple moving from a penthouse to a studio.

Man is no longer in the good creation, but now has entered into the evil lands. The wind is no longer at his back, but is now set against him, specifically his ability to obey the procreation command. Rather than being beneficial for sustaining his (and his offspring's) life, the new situation will eventually tear him down to the dust from which he was made. He, as the image of God, will now fight to survive in the realm of evil; and only with God's sovereign help will he be able to combat total annihilation from the earth. The rest of the book, of course, will display God as the one who causes the "good" to manifest itself through humanity's struggle within the chaotic world.

Hence, the punishment in Genesis 2:17 has to do with a reversal of creation. It is the act of sending those being punished back to the uncreated state. In the flood, it is a reversal of Genesis 1, but in Chapter 3, it is a reversal of Genesis 2. The humans, who were placed in the garden in the midst of uncultivated, hostile land, will now be placed outside of the garden sanctuary to be subject to the forces of chaos and eventually to decay.

Hence, the term ביום does in fact refer to a literal day upon which the couple are expelled from the garden, and therefore, enter the realm of death. This understanding is apparent only if one views the idea of death in terms of the ancient Near Eastern conceptual world, and refrains from reading modern assumptions about death into the text.

6

The Genealogies of the Two Seeds

WHEN ONE READS THE genealogies of Genesis 5–11, one is often struck by the extended number of years that are assigned to the life-spans of the patriarchs. This is especially the case in terms of the antediluvian patriarchs, some of whom live just short of an entire millennium. Compounding the problem are the variations within the major textual witnesses of the chronology. In the SP, Methuselah lives fourteen years past the flood. Yet, the text indicates to the reader that only Noah and his family survived what P depicts to be a universal flood. In the MT, this is rectified by shortening the length of years assigned to two of the antediluvians (Methuselah and Lamech), who fall just short of the year of the flood. Suspiciously, Methuselah dies the very year the flood waters come upon the earth, and Lamech dies only five years before. In the LXX, however, Jared, Methuselah, and Lamech all die in the year of the flood, a coincidence too grand to overlook. One might consider Methuselah's death as a coincidence, but if he or she understands the MT as the less reliable witness of the three major text types in which the numbers are attested, then the problem of taking the numbers as literal descriptions of each of the antediluvian life-spans become much more problematic.

Jeremy Hughes observes that the MT's higher figures, in terms of adding one hundred years or more to the year of begetting, would be inconsistent with the later story of Abraham, in Genesis 17:17, who is in disbelief that he might have a child at the age of one hundred.[1] He states that this "is hardly consistent with the higher set of figures, according to which his recent ancestors had fathered children well in excess of this."[2] Hence, this is a good indication that there has been a harmonization that

---

1. Hughes, *Secrets of the Times*, 10.
2. Ibid., 11.

has taken place in the MT and LXX transmissions in order to explain Abraham's reaction.[3] There seems to be no justification for the idea that the SP increased the numbers by 100 arbitrarily. The following partial chart, displaying the differences between the versions, is taken from Hughes:[4]

		MT	LXX	SP
(Gn 5.3)	Adam	130 + 800 = 930	130 + 800 = 930	230 + 700 = 930
(Gn 5.6)	Seth	105 + 807 = 912	105 + 807 = 912	205 + 707 = 912
(Gn 5.9)	Enosh	90 + 815 = 905	90 + 815 = 905	190 + 715 = 905
(Gn 5.12)	Kenan	70 + 840 = 910	70 + 840 = 910	170 + 740 = 910
(Gn 5.15)	Mahalalel	65 + 830 = 895	65 + 830 = 895	165 + 730 = 895
(Gn 5.18)	Jared	162 + 800 = 962	62 + 785 = 847	162 + 800 = 962
(Gn 5.21)	Enoch	65 + 300 = 365	65 + 300 = 365	165 + 200 = 365
(Gn 5.25)	Methuselah	187 + 782 = 969	67 + 653 = 720	167 + 802 = 969
(Gn 5.28)	Lamech	182 + 595 = 777	53 + 600 = 653	188 + 565 = 753
(Gn 5.32)	Noah	500	500	500
(Gn 7.6; 9.28)	age at flood	600 + 350 = 950	600 + 350 = 950	600 + 350 = 950[5]

Hughes gathers from the evidence that the modification of the numbers indicates that "Jared, Methuselah, and Lamech did in fact outlive the flood in the original Priestly chronology."[6] The support of this theory is captured in the SP's chronology concerning Methuselah. Regardless how one takes this evidence, however, there can be no doubt that the other numbers found in the textual witnesses are modified to end the life-spans just short of the flood in an effort to make the original text consistent.

The problem of this chronology is joined with those within the postdiluvian chronologies that essentially would cause all of those patriarchs to have lived simultaneously with one another, including the fact that most of them would survive well into the life of Abraham.[7] When

---

3. The LXX may be trying to harmonize an early interpretation that believes the patriarchs are slowly losing their longevity. Hence, with the exception of the length of life-span attributed to Kenan, the LXX's chronology declines as opposed to the numbers in the MT and SP that fluctuate.

4. Hughes, *Secrets of the Times*, 7.

5. Cf. the chart in Gardner, *The Genesis Calendar*, xi–xii.

6. Ibid., 13.

7. Hendel, *The Text of Genesis 1–11*, 78.

observed closely, numerous issues surface that evidence the numbers to be contradictory or inconsistent with the larger narrative. There was, therefore, an attempt by scribes to resolve these problems by modifying the numbers, so that contradictions might be alleviated.[8]

However, there was no need to do so if the numbers are understood to communicate larger concepts rather than literal chronologies depicting the actual temporal measurements of antediluvian and postdiluvian longevity. If one sees the chronology as part of the narrative language, and functions literarily rather than literally, then there is no need to play with the numbers.

Westermann concludes that the large numbers signify P's contention that their true life-spans, existing in a time now unknown to us, are therefore something that "cannot be measured by the standards of present-day history," so that "their astronomical numbers point to the extension of ancient time into an unimaginably distant past."[9] In this way, the numbers simply represent time periods unknown to the author in the same way that בְּיוֹם mentioned in the previous discussion represents the unknown primeval day. This is most likely the case, but there is more going on with these numbers than simple representation.

One of the problems affecting the interpretations of the genealogies of Genesis 4–11, both ancient and modern, is that they tend to presuppose that it is the author's purpose to communicate a historical succession of literal ethnic lineages. Because of this, modern scholars have shied away from any view that connected the genealogies to the seeds in 3:15, since

---

8. "As first systematically worked out by Klein, the initial problems were (1) a contradiction between the lifespans of three antediluvians (Jared, Methuselah, and Lamech) and the onset of the flood and (2) the coexistence of all of the postdiluvian generations (including Noah and Shem) during the lifetime of Abraham. The first problem was solved in the textual traditions ancestral to M, S, and G by three different strategies of revision for the chronology of Gen 5:3–32. The second problem was solved in the textual traditions ancestral to S and G by two overlapping strategies of revision for Gen 11:10–32; M shows no signs of revision in this chapter.

I have also argued that two other chronological problems derive from this initial textual situation: (3) an apparent contradictions between Lamech's lifespan and the implicit sense of the narrative sequence of 11:31–12:4 and (4) a contradiction between Shem's age at the birth of Arpachshad and the date of the flood. The third problem was solved in proto-S by reducing Lamech's lifespan so that he dies in the year of Abraham's journey (the problem is unresolved in M and G). The fourth problem was resolved by a redactor or scribe by an explicating plus specifying that Arpachshad was born two years after the flood" (Ibid.).

9. Westermann, *Genesis 1–11*, 353–4.

this would be seen as supporting an idea that some people are inherently good and some are inherently bad.[10] However, it is clear from the context that the genealogies are linked to the story of Cain and Abel, who are themselves linked to the two seeds mentioned in 3:15, as a literary way of communicating the author's theology symbolically. In other words, the two lines represent two types of people, i.e., those who follow God, living their lives in submission to the creation mandate as His images, and those who seek to become אלהים themselves. This is an abstract representation, not a literal description of ethnic behavior and identification. This, again, does not mean that the author does not believe that there is a literal succession of people that stem from Adam and Eve, but only that the details of this succession are molded to communicate the theological intentions of the narrative in regard to chaos and creation, and those who seek to be agents of one or the other. There is no question that the author believed that Adam had descendents and that Cain and Abel/Seth were his children; but his purposes are to transform those genealogical lines by painting them in a certain light to represent types of people (i.e., those who seek to become God's image and those who seek to become like God) rather than associating good and bad behavior to their biological ancestry. This literary purpose, therefore, is directly linked to the prophecy of the two seeds given to the serpent in 3:15. The text, therefore, reads as follows:

ואיבה אשית בינך ובין האשה ובין זרעך ובין זרעה הוא ישופך ראש ואתה תשופנו עקב

> "And I will place hostility between you and the woman, that is, between your offspring [זרע] and her offspring [זרע]. He will strike your head, but you will strike his heel."

Quite a few questions arise as one reads this text. What is the enmity between the two seeds? What is the distinction the author makes between them? The answer comes in the next few chapters of the book. In Genesis 4, we meet Cain and Abel, whom the author uses as a depiction of the two seeds. The firstborn offspring, Cain, is depicted as one

---

10. Westermann (Ibid., 343–44) calls this interpretation a "pre-judged and constricted concept of religion" precisely because he confuses the literary use of the genealogies with the literal link to ethnic identities. Wilson's view that the genealogies function as a form of political identification may also lead to these fears ("The Old Testament Genealogies," 200–23).

who does not have an upright spirit within him. Abel, on the other hand, has a right spirit within him and is pleasing to God. Cain, however, is bitter toward God and hates his brother, Abel. He becomes the first murderer by killing his brother. Seth, then, replaces Abel as the one who will continue the line of the woman's seed.[11]

Genesis 4 describes Cain's line. Although the text does not explicitly indicate that Cain is the first of the serpent's seed, the literary context is clear that he is meant to fill that role. In contrast, Seth is said to be given to Eve as זרע אחר "another seed" to replace Abel (4:25). That Seth is meant to be the woman's seed is, therefore, made explicit.

The first element of contrast, then, is that the serpent's offspring do not have an appropriate attitude toward God. They are seen as the unrighteous. The offspring of the woman, in contrast, have a right attitude toward God and are seen as the righteous. Hence, after Seth and his son are born, the statement, "Then he began to call upon the name of YHWH" (v. 26), is directly connected to Seth and his son Enosh.

That the serpent's line is characterized this way is made clear by Cain's disposition toward God and his subsequent fratricide. Seth, however, as Abel's replacement, is assumed to be righteous, as Abel was. He is said to be made in the likeness (בדמות and כצלמו) of Adam who was made in the likeness (בדמות) of God.[12] It is at the point that Seth and his son Enosh are born that the text tells us that men began to call upon the name of YHWH.

We are told that the Enoch in the line of Seth walked with God. The Lamech in the line of Seth also gives life to Noah, and this line culminates in the statement that Noah, in contrast to the whole world, finds favor with God.

Secondly, the most prominent element of their righteous or unrighteous status is found in their actions of either preserving or reversing creation by either saving or taking life. Where the line of Cain begins it also ends. Cain's line culminates in Lamech, who proclaims himself to be a greater murderer than Cain. Seth's line, however, culminates in Noah, who ends up preserving humanity through the flood, and becomes the

---

11. Eve literally states that she calls his name שת "because God appointed [שת] for me another seed [זרע] under Abel, for Cain killed him." The terms שית and זרע are undeniably connected to the statement in 3:15, where God אשית "appoints" hostility between זרעך and זרעה (i.e., the seeds/offspring of the serpent and the woman).

12. This harkens back to 1:26–27, where God makes the male and female in His likeness and according to His image (צלמנו כדמותנו and צלמו).

rightful heir to the command to "Be fruitful and multiply, fill up the earth and swarm upon it."

Finally, Cain's line is characterized by technological advancement. He builds a city, his offspring rule it, and they become the inventors of musical instruments, and bronze and iron tools, as well as being involved in animal husbandry. In other words, they are the founders of urban civilization (i.e., the collection of people into groups). The instruments are most likely related to festivals, the tools may be related to the building, farming and military divisions that characterize urban culture; and the dwelling in tents of those practicing animal husbandry may be related to those on the outer city limits, who sell and trade in livestock.[13]

In contrast to the urbanites, the offspring of Seth are characterized by four things: walking with God (Enoch), long life (Methuselah), seeking rest from the hardship of mankind, i.e., desiring to reverse the curse (Lamech), and finding favor with God (Noah). In other words, the line of Seth seeks the perpetuation of human life and its preservation in God, while the line of Cain seeks power through achievement, invention and organization. Whereas the creativity of the individual is spent on the advancement of culture in the line of Cain, the creativity of the individual in the line of Seth is spent on preserving human life. Hence, one practices creation as the image of God in being fruitful and multiplying and one practices creation in attempting to be like God in the subjugation of chaos through the power of human organization.

Such an observation is subtle, of course, and not immediately apparent at first glance, but will become much clearer as the primeval history develops and has its culmination in the building and destruction of a city with a tower that is built in a human collaboration that seeks to obtain the divine power to control the environment of order and chaos through construction.[14]

The distinction between the seeds may also be seen in the variation of names between the two groups. Excluding the two representative sons, since the story of Cain and Abel (with Seth provided as Abel's replacement seed) portrays the two characteristics of the sons as consistent with

---

13. It is possible that this is also an indication that there are those who have the urban mindset, i.e., pursuing craft over creation, and do not fulfill the creation mandate in rural areas as well.

14. Although the text does not explicitly state that the line of disrepute is responsible for the building of the tower, it can be safely inferred from 10:10 that it is.

their respective lines.¹⁵ The placement of Adam at the beginning of the Sethite list exists in order to convey to the reader that the Sethite line, as opposed to the line of Cain, fulfills the purpose of Adam as God's image. The mention of the three sons of Noah at the end of the Sethite line is set in the narrative as that which characterizes Noah, not the sons themselves.¹⁶ Hence, eight names remain in each line that represent the distinction of the two seeds mentioned in 3:15.¹⁷ Many of the names show more than just a coincidental similarity. There are two Enochs, two Lamechs, a Jared and Irad, a Mahuyel and a Mahallel, a Metushael and a Metushaleh, three variations of Cain, and three variations (one of which shares dual similarities with Cain) of Jubal, leaving only Enosh ("human"), the beginning of Seth's line, and Noah (along with his sons), the end of Seth's genealogy here, as purely distinctive names within the record.

חנוך	אנוש
עירד	קין
מחויאל	מחללאל
מתושאל	ירד
למך	חנוך
יבל	מתושלח
יובל	למך
תובל קין	נח (שם חם יפת)

15. Cain serves the cursed ground (4:2), and gains disfavor from God when he offers up the product of the ground to Him (vv. 3–5; see Herion, "Why God Rejected," 52–65). He is a creature of the field like the serpent, and murders Abel there (v. 8). Abel's offering, however, is acknowledged by God (cf. the connection of the term ישע יהוה in the Aaronic blessing in Numbers 6:26 to the concept of blessing and favor), offering Him a product that is not a part of the curse (v. 4).

16. The genealogies of the sons come after the flood narrative in 10:1–9.

17. If the emphasis of the genealogy in chapters 4 and 5 is with the eight names of each group, then the now abandoned view that the list shares some correspondence to the SKL in its antediluvian list may have some support, since each list would then focus upon eight individuals before the flood.

The name of Cain's son, Enoch, could be derived from the West Semitic root חנך, which either means "to initiate"[18] or "to dedicate."[19] It is also possible that it is related to the Sumerian sign UNUG, which refers to the city of Uruk.[20]

Either way, Cain's Enoch is characterized by the city. In contrast, however, Seth's first son is named אנוש, which simply means "human." The significance of this is found in the fact that this name is nowhere else attested. Instead, the author desires the reader to catch the contrast between those who are concerned with city life and those who are concerned with individual human life, the collective versus the individual.

The reader can see this contrast again between the second son in Cain's line, עירד, which is most likely a Hebrew wordplay conjoining the words עיר "city" with the first known city of Eridu.

The third in Cain's line, מחויאל, may mean "one who strikes down God," a possible reference to Cain who struck down Abel.[21] However, it may also mean "one who blots out God," or "God blots him out."[22] In contrast, the Sethite counterpart מהללאל "praise of God" reflects the emphasis on the godly character of the woman's seed.

The fourth in Cain's line, מתושאל, means "man/warrior of the grave/realm of death," which is fitting for this group. It is also possible that מת is the older form of מות without the *mater*, the *waw* is the *yod* preformative for the third person masculine singular, and שאל is the

---

18. Hess, *Personal Names*, 39.
19. *DNWSI* 1:388.
20. Hess, *Personal Names*, 39.
21. This reading takes מחו/י as an example of phonemic confusion between *wāw* and *yôd* in the process of transmission, or possibly, its presence is an instance of archaic preservation and the *yôd* is simply a modernization (Hendel, *The Text of Genesis 1–11*, 48). Since the Syriac variant may display the common mistake of phonemic confusion made in transmission, it is not too much to suggest that this very thing may have happened with the second ו/י, which might suggest an original name of מחואל, where the ה of the suffix has syncopated.
22. מחה is used in 6:7, 7:4, and 7:23. The suggestion that מחו/י is a form of מיח/מחוה, which would suggest the meaning "God preserves my life," as some scholars have argued (Skinner, *Genesis*, 117; Hendel, *The Text of Genesis 1–11*, 48; Hess, *Personal Names*, 41–43), is not likely from both a linguistic and contextual standpoint. One would expect מיחתיאל for this, not the current form as it stands, and if the contrast between Cain and Seth's line is as I have suggested, a more sinister name would be expected.

verb that means "to ask." This conjecture would then read the name as "he asks for death."²³

Methuselah, in contrast to this, would mean "he sends death away," and is more probable than the far reaching suggestion that מתו means "man" and that שלח is some sort of ancient DN unknown outside of the onomastica.²⁴ Instead, it is simpler to see from both the Hebrew root and the context that the name has something to do with the figure's long life. The *waw* before שלח is the well attested phonemic shift made from the *yod* when consonants are prefixed to it. The word מת (*mū/mōt*) appears here without its *mater* as it does occasionally occur in earlier Hebrew spellings.²⁵

The three sons are mentioned, not in an effort to give the reader any information about their characteristics, as that will be done later. Instead, they exist in this genealogy simply to show Noah's faithfulness to the procreative command, and as such, to secure the only information we have of him thus far: that he is a preserver of human life through its perpetuation *via* procreation.

The remaining sons in the genealogy are characterized, not by their names, since their names are either identical, or almost identical, to one another, but by what is said of them. Cain's Enoch is characterized by the city he builds for him; but Seth's Enoch is characterized by his moving with God and his reward of immortality, i.e., being taken up and never dying. The reader must assume that Seth's Kenan is in contrast not to Cain, but to Tubal-Cain, who is the "sharpener" of all bronze and iron devices. Kenan gives birth to numerous offspring, but Tubal-Cain gives birth to sharp plowing equipment (perhaps meant to be speculative of the farmer Cain killing his younger brother in the field by striking him with something).

Cain's Lamech, of course, is notoriously known for his boast of killing a young boy; but Seth's Lamech gives birth to Noah. Hence, as the legacy of Cain is murder, the legacy of Cain's Lamech is also murder, specifically the murder of a boy. Conversely, as the legacy of Seth (to preserve the line of the woman's seed that would have existed through

---

23. Although names often exhibit variations in word order, it would seem odd that the active verb followed its object. This latter suggestion, therefore, may seem less probable.

24. Contra Westermann, *Genesis*, 357.

25. *DNWSI* 2:707; cf. 2 Kgs 15:5; Isa 53:9.

Abel) is the preservation of human life, so the legacy of Seth's Lamech is giving birth to a boy (i.e., Noah) who will preserve human life.

What is even more interesting, however, is the amount of children mentioned in both genealogies. In Cain's genealogy, only Lamech is said to give birth to more than one child; and when given the opportunity, he takes another child out of the world. In Seth's line, however, the phrase, ויולד בנים ובנות "and he gave birth to [more] sons and daughters" is assigned to every individual within the Sethite genealogy. The contrast the author wishes to convey becomes clear as the literary elements of the text reveal themselves. Cain's line is concerned for empire and inheritance of power; but Seth's line is concerned for human life and preservation. Cain's line, therefore, concerns itself with building and crafting in order to achieve power over chaos; but Seth's line is concerned with overcoming chaos as God's images (5:1), who perpetuate human life and gain victory over the chaos that threatens human life by being fruitful and multiplying.

Furthermore, even though there is little likelihood that the genealogies have any direct connection to the Sumerian King List,[26] their general purposes contain the same basic rationale.[27] If long life and succession is given to a group of people, it shows that the divine favor is with that particular group. Hence, as kings are given long life and kingship itself granted succession, the favor of the gods is evidenced to be upon that individual and that institution. In the same way, the genealogies in Genesis are portrayed in terms of longevity and succession, only in this case, longevity and succession is given to the line of Seth. The line of Cain is absent of any discussion of how long this group lived, and they certainly are not portrayed as living past the flood. Hence, the line of Cain is not said to be granted long life or succession.

The reader must keep in mind the initial symbolism in Genesis. Humans were made to be God's cult image (בצלם and כדמות, i.e., "as God's image" and "like God's likeness") by seeking to subdue chaos in the world through procreation (1:26–31), but then failed in this role by

---

26. Hasel, "The Genealogies," 361–74. For a solid translation of the list, see Oppenheim, "Historical Texts," 265–6.

27. Although it must be noted that the two genres are distinct from one another (Westermann, *Genesis 1–11*, 472), the pattern employed by the two accounts (list of individuals and successions characterized by abnormal longevity, an interruption of the list with a mention of the flood, and a pattern of larger numbers assigned to individuals in the antediluvian period with smaller numbers assigned to those in the postdiluvian period) cannot be overlooked.

seeking to become כאלהים "like God" (3:5). Similarly, the two seeds (i.e., lines of offspring), one line of the woman and one line of the serpent, each are described in terms of seeking one role or the other. The line of Cain is described as pursuing knowledge/skill/mastery and having a general disposition toward chaos.[28] The line of Seth, however, is not characterized by skills they have obtained for themselves, but instead by the lives they have created, their walking/moving with God and with creation, and by the idea that they are made as the image and likeness of the original man, who is the image and likeness of God. Ultimately, the genealogies, although interrupted by the flood narrative, have their aim in dividing the two groups again between those who pursue divine knowledge through building a city with a tower, and those who seek to follow God and perpetuate human life (i.e., Abraham's/Israel's line).[29]

The reader is capable of grasping the message well. The line of the serpent perpetuates the serpent's mandate to become like gods, killing humans (i.e., reversing creation as inhabited), building cities into which people will flock (i.e., hindering the filling up of the entire land/earth that is to be cultivated as habitation), and seeking divine knowledge to become divine themselves (even the control over human life is the prerogative of the divine), whereas the woman's offspring perpetuate God's mandate to rule over the earth through creation and procreation (i.e., cultivating land/habitation, increasing inhabitants, and preserving life). Where they both may seem similar, they are actually worlds apart in the mind of the author. The former seek to establish their own rule through the destruction of land and people. The latter, however, seek to establish the rule of God over chaos through the procreation and preservation of the human life that represents Him. The former is characterized by those who seek to be "like God" (3:5) in determining their own plan for the world. The latter are characterized as in the "likeness of God's and Adam's image" (1:26–28; 5:1–3) in following the plan laid out by the Creator. Although, the full connection of the genealogies to the creation of man as God's cult image is missed, Claus Westermann does note the connection between the Sethite line and the creation mandate.

---

28. The intention of the author to link the two narratives is, in Westermann's mind, "unmistakable" (*Genesis 1–11*, 285–6), but he fails to specifically link the genealogies to the two seeds in 3:15.

29. A descendent of Ham (i.e., Nimrod), the cursed son, is described as the one who builds the tower (Gen 10:6–10)—thus, perpetuating the idea that those seeking to be "like God" are those who are of the serpent's seed.

P is saying here that the plan of God in creating human beings is spelling itself out. The blessing and its power have been bestowed on the creature. The imperative, "be fruitful and multiply and fill the earth," is being carried out in Gen 5. The power of the blessing shows itself effective in the relentless rhythm and steady succession of generations that stretch out across time. The real meaning of the creation of a man and a woman in Gen 1:26–31 can only become clear when generation follows generation according to the rhythm of begetting and birth, life-span and death, as presented in Gen 5.[30]

Hence, Enoch, a key character in the line of Seth, is said to have יתהלך "walked/moved with God," which, contextually speaking, most likely describes his subjection to God as His cult image that indicates his movement with creation and submission to God's creative plan in reversing chaos. To move with God is to be in reception of His creative and preservationist work in the world rather than to be in resistance to it.

This same contrast is seen again after the flood, as the descendents of Shem are displayed as having long life-spans and characterized only as having children (10:21–31; 11:10–26), but the line of Ham, who has one of his children cursed by Noah, builds the city with a tower (10:6–20; 11:1–9).[31]

CONCLUSION: THE LITERARY FUNCTION OF THE ANTEDILUVIAN NUMBERS

The genealogies themselves, therefore, function as literary devices that seek to display a contrast between the two seeds of 3:15. The similarity of the names, with variations that reflect the characteristics of each respective line, bears this out. It seems clear, then, that the primary function of the abnormally long life-spans in the genealogy of Genesis 5 is also

---

30. Westermann, *Genesis 1–11*, 348.

31. It seems clear that the long numbers in the SKL are meant to display something other than a literal historical record measuring the precise amount of years that these kings reigned. An example of this are the first twenty-three, postdiluvian kings who are said to have reigned collectively for 24,510 years. However, in a list of the rulers of Lagaš, it is said that, in the days after the flood, the young men, after being raised for a hundred years, lived for another hundred years (e.g., ud-ba lu$_2$-tur dan$_3$-dan$_3$-na-ka mu 100 i$_3$-ak nam-buluĝ$_3$-ĝa$_2$-ni-ta mu 100 bi$_2$-in-ak "in those days, the pure young man endured for 100 years, and following his upbringing, he endured another 100 years [BM 23103, 14–16], no doubt a rhetorical expression as well. This is far from the thousands of years detailed in the SKL.

not meant to convey literal time periods, but instead provides the reader with a couple similarly conceived ideas that function as literary descriptions of the group to which they are ascribed.

The first idea is that the long numbers, as they do in the Sumerian King List, display divine favor with this particular group of people.

The second idea it conveys is that this group is to be identified as the seed that perpetuates human life. What is predominantly characteristic of these types of people for the author is the very children they have bore in submission to the creation mandate of the divine image in 1:26–31.

Finally, the numbers, together with the continued succession of this line, convey that this group is the reason why God's favor remains upon humanity in general. It is because of this group that humans survive both because they seek to preserve human life and because they secure the deity's favor and help in their plight against chaos. This fact is made explicit in the flood narrative, where Noah saves humanity because he finds חן "favor" with God (6:7–8). It exists as well in the theme's resurgence, both in the Abrahamic blessing, conveying the idea that all nations will be blessed because of him, and in the Jacob/Joseph Cycle, which portrays the deliverance of numerous people groups as a result of God's favor with Joseph. They are in contrast to the wicked in the world—those who become agents of chaos in their practice of חמס, i.e., that which threatens the order of human life and preservation.

As the numbers in the Sumerian King List are not meant to convey literal years in which these kings reigned, the numbers associated with the two genealogies in Genesis 5 are also not meant to convey literal numbers, but rather they exist as symbolic figures that seek to convey the three elements above in continuity with the larger message of the narrative, i.e., that God's creative acts against chaos continue through those who seek to live as His representative images in the world *via* their obedience to the procreative command in 1:28–31.

What is gained from this understanding is a theology much richer than that of reading "narrative time" literally in a very symbolically driven context, and something that provides a more meaningful, theological contribution to the overall message of the book than that of simply acknowledging literal time periods is capable of achieving.

7

The Days of the Deluge

APART FROM CREATION, THE ancient individual considered the flood one of the most significant events in human history. Because of the prominent position it held in ancient history, it was used in a variety of ways. It is used to argue for population control (e.g., *Atra-ḫasīs*), explain why humans do not have immortality (e.g., GE), and as a segue from the primeval world to the still distant but civilized world of the author (e.g., the king lists). Whatever the individual authors of ancient times did with the flood story, one must conclude with R. W. L. Moberly that "within the ancient world, of which Israel was a part, a story of a flood was in some way a *given*."[1]

PATIENCE AND TRIAL IN 120 YEARS

When an individual reads that God has set a lifespan of 120 years for humankind in Genesis 6:3, whether speaking of the age before the flood or the human life-span in general, he or she has often assumed it to be a literal number. The idea that the number refers to the age before the flood has been categorically rejected by modern scholars. It is still possible to see the number this way, but it is less likely in view of the preceding and following genealogies that display the human life-span as getting shorter. What is clear, however, is that if one is to take the 120 years as referring to human life-spans in general, then the genealogy of Shem in 11:10–33 is in conflict with this statement if both are to be taken literally. Even if one grants that Shem was "grandfathered in," his sons and grandsons are blessed with life-spans that range between 230 and 438 years.[2] Of course, as we have seen, the life-spans themselves

---

1. Moberly, *Theology of Genesis*, 108.
2. The LXX and other early interpreters saw a contradiction in the literal interpreta-

symbolize the life-giving occupation with which the godly adorn their lives. Hence, only Shem's line is spoken of in terms of length of life in contrast to Ham's line, which builds the city with a tower.

There is another way of seeing the time periods apart from literal depictions of real events. It is possible that the number of years in Genesis 6:3 are meant to convey something about God's patience and desire to preserve mankind. The text states:

ויאמר יהוה לא ידון רוחי באדם לעלם בשגם הוא בשר והיו ימיו מאה ועשרים שנה

> And YHWH said, "My spirit will not abide with man forever due to the fact that he is also flesh, so his days will be 120 years."

The word רוח, appearing throughout chapters 1–11, signifies God's creative acts toward human life and preservation. The question becomes whether the 120 years is a reference to God sustaining human life in general with His רוח, or simply refers to the remaining time left before the judgment of the flood when God removes favor from mankind that was once expressed in His preservation of human life *via* His רוח.

O. Gruppe defended the ancient proposal that the 120 years signified a time of grace that God bequeathed to mankind before the flood. He saw a connection between a Phoenician myth, where three generations of humanity (interpreted by Gruppe as consisting of 30 years each) had provoked the gods to anger, and thus, initiated the flood.[3]

---

tion and sought to interpret it differently. Kugel discusses the ancient desire to harmonize the lengthened life-spans of the postdiluvian patriarchs with the time frame given in Genesis 6:3: "These words spoken by God were not taken by most interpreters at face value, that is, as if God were now decreeing that humans could not live more than a hundred and twenty years each. How could such an interpretation be correct, when so many later biblical figures lived considerably longer? (Noah himself lived to the age 950, while his son Shem lived to 600, his grandson Arpachshad to 438, his great-grandson Shelah to 433, his great-great-grandson Eber to 464, and so forth.)

And so, these words were instead interpreted as a warning: if human beings don't improve, I will destroy them *a hundred and twenty years from now*. Alternatively, what God might have meant was, I will destroy the wicked people of this generation at an early age (for those days, at least), namely when they are one hundred and twenty years old. In either case, God's words did not announce a fundamental change in human longevity but warned of an impending punishment of the *flood generation alone*" (*Traditions of the Bible*, 183).

3. *Philologus*, 100ff. as quoted in Childs, *Myth and Reality*, 53–54. This view was held by Augustine, Jerome, Luther, F. Delitzsch, and E. A. Speiser (Westermann, *Genesis 1–11*, 376). Rashi also seems to have viewed this period as a provisional timeframe where God

Childs rejected this view based on form critical issues and an argument from silence.[4] He later conceded, however, by stating that "in its present position as an introduction to the flood, one cannot help see some connexion with a period of grace before the coming catastrophe."[5] Westermann rightly observes, however, that there is a conceptual parallel between the limiting of the human life-span and the divine exclusion of human beings from the tree of life.[6] As humans are not allowed access to immortality, their life-spans are also prevented from even coming close to it through shared longevity with the divine that may have resulted in the belief that humans were not distinct from the gods/angels, and thus the text speaks of the cohabitation of humans with divine/semi-divine beings in 6:1–4.[7] Whether Westermann is correct in his identification of the בני אלהים as divine beings, it must be acknowledged that the statement concerning 120 years comes on the heels of this obscure union.

However, although conceding this point, one might also compare the 120 years with three sets of forty in other texts. One example of this might be the three days journey Jonah takes into the city of Nineveh in order to communicate that a forty day trial would commence after which, if the Ninevites did not repent, the city would be destroyed. It has been pointed out, by numerous commentators, that the city is not large enough that it would take three days to travel through it. Furthermore, when Jonah finishes his message, he sits up on the hill above the city in order to watch and see what happens to it. Are we really to believe that he sits there for forty days in the scorching hot sun until he realizes that God is not going to destroy it? The numbers are surely understood as symbolic, and may in fact, have some continuity with our present passage in that three and forty are coupled together in both texts.

Another closer example is that of the exodus from Egypt to the promised land set within the individual segments belonging to Moses' lifespan of 120 years, each segment divided into periods of individual trials (1 x

---

desires humans to repent (see his commentary in Silberman, *Bereshith*, 28).

4. Ibid., 54. See also Skinner, *Genesis*, 144–5.

5. Ibid., 58. Child's main concern, leading him to reject Gruppe's analysis, is that he saw the divine statement as something that should be universally applied rather than existing in the text merely as commentary for that specific antediluvian generation.

6. *Genesis 1–11*, 376.

7. Ibid.; Westermann also notes that the emphasis is not so much on the identification of the "sons of gods," but on what they do (Ibid., 367). For his fuller discussion of the subject, see his comments in Ibid., 365–73.

40 = temptation of Egyptian nobility, 2 x 40 = trial of humility in the wilderness, and 3 x 40 = the trial of dealing with hard-hearted people, both Egyptians and Israelites alike in the exodus and wilderness wanderings). Moses' life itself serves as a template for viewing these periods as trials in which God is seeking the obedience of His subjects. In essence, his life represents YHWH's testing of His people along with the divine desire to save humans through their adherence to the message proclaimed.

There may be a foundation for this understanding in the use of the literal number as well. In 1 Kings 9:14 and 10:10 (= 2 Chron 9:9), 120 talents of gold are given to Solomon by Hiram and the Queen of Sheba as a sign of friendship, an offering of goodwill. Likewise, the Levitical priests, blowing trumpets, number 120, and clearly desire to invite God's presence (2 Chron 5:12). Hence, the number may communicate an invitation of friendship. If this is true, then it is possible that the number, in terms of God granting a lifespan of 120 years to humans, is a gesture that reflects the divine desire for humans to be delivered through the trial of life. If individual life-spans are in view in Genesis 6:4, then this would mean that an individual human life itself is portrayed as a time of test and a trial that God genuinely desires that individual to pass. Although there certainly is a literal reference here to the shortening of individual life-spans, the symbolic number represents something deeper and far more connected to the narrative, since God will have to destroy humans, who have become agents of chaos, but still desires to preserve them through Noah and his family.

When all is said and done, the number may be simply a literal reference, but it does provide an interesting suggestion toward the literary use of the number if the above turns out to have some connection to it. The symbol of the divine intent to save is summed up in the rainbow at the end of the flood, creating an *inclusio* when coupled with the understanding of the 120 years we noted above. The goal of the flood, then, is not simply to bring about horrific destruction upon the earth, but "its goal is the divine decision never again to wipe out life on the earth."[8] R. Moberly describes it quite beautifully:

> The rainbow is one of the most unusual, beautiful, and moving of all recurrent natural phenomena. Its symbolic resonances are many, and one can imagine it variously . . . It usually appears after a time of heavy rain when the sun comes out and shine again but

---

8. Moberly, *Theology of Genesis*, 110.

while dark clouds are still in the sky; and often the dark clouds are a backdrop for the many colors of the rainbow. Thus, when the rainbow is viewed in the light of the preceding Flood narrative, its appearance at the very moment when one can see both darkness and light in the sky comes to symbolize God's commitment to light over darkness, to beauty over chaos, to life over death.[9]

Hence, the 120 year period, rather than being a literal measurement of time, may be a subtle way of communicating God's desire to save. The text is not communicating the literal length of an individual human life, as though the author of Genesis and the Psalmist conflict.[10] Instead, each person's life will be a time of trial in which opportunity to repent from each individual's participation in חמס, "acts against human life and preservation," will be granted.[11]

THE ARK AND THE NUMBER SEVEN

It is obvious to even the cursory reader that the flood account intersects with the creation account in more than just a few points. The waters that threatened the existence of humankind at the beginning of P's account now return to threaten the existence of humans again. The ark itself becomes in many ways another creation account. One of the most prominent features of both the creation and flood account is that the divine act of creation/destruction takes place in seven days.

Chaos and the Number 7

The biblical account of the deluge gains its symbolic time periods of seven from its purposeful interaction with Mesopotamian tradition. In the Sumerian flood story, the *Eridu Genesis*, the parallels are evident.

> DAG-me-a a-ma-ru ugu kab /dug$_4$\-[ga . . .] ba-/ur$_3$\ [. . .]
> numun nam-lu$_2$-ulu$_3$ ḫa-lam-e-/de$_3$\ [nam-bi ba-tar]
> ud 7-am$_3$ ĝi$_6$ 7-am$_3$

---

9. Ibid., 110–11.

10. Both writers have the same experience. They, no doubt, knew that the majority of people only lived to their seventies and eighties. Ps 90:10: "As for the days of our life, they contain seventy years, or if due to vigor, eighty years, yet all there is to show for it is labor and sorrow; for soon it is gone and we fly away."

11. It is also possible that the referent is left ambiguous so that a connection can be made, both to the time left before the flood, giving humans a period of time to repent, and to individual human life-spans in general.

> a-ma-ru kalam-ma ba-ur₃-ra-ta
> ᵍⁱˢma₂ gur₄-gur₄ a gal-la im-ḫul tuku₄-tuku₄-a-ta
> ᵈutu i-im-ma-ra-e₃ an ki-a ud ĝa₂-ĝa₂
> zi-ud-su₃-ra₂ ᵍⁱˢma₂ gur₄-gur₄ ab-BUR₂ mu-un-da-buru₃
> šul ᵈutu ĝiš-nu₁₁-ni-da ᵍⁱˢma₂ gur₄-gur₄-še₃ ba-an-kur₉-re-en
> zi-ud-su₃-ra₂ lugal-am₃
> igi ᵈutu-še₃ giri₁₇ ki su-ub ba-gub
> lugal-e gud im-ma-ab-gaz-e udu im-ma-ab-šar₂-re[12]

> A flood [will sweep] over the cult-centers;
> To destroy the seed of mankind . . .
> After, for seven days (and) seven nights,
> The flood had swept over the land,
> And the huge boat had been tossed about by the windstorms on the great waters,
> Utu came forth, who sheds light on heaven (and) earth.
> Ziusudra opened a window of the huge boat,
> The hero Utu brought his rays into the giant boat.
> Ziusudra, the king,
> Prostrated himself before Utu,
> The king kills an ox, slaughters a sheep.[13]

In the 11th Tablet of the Epic of Gilgamesh, the duration of the flood is described as follows:

> 6 ur-ri ù 7 mu-šá-a-ti
> il-lak šá-a-ru a-bu-bu me-hu-ú[14] i-sap-pan KUR
> se-bu-ú UD-mu ina ka-šá-a-di it-ta-rak me-hu-ú a-bu-bu qab-la
> ša im-tah-ṣu ki-ma ha-a-a-al-ti
> i-nu-uh A.AB.BA uš-ha-ri-ir-ma im-hul-lu a-bu-bu ik-la
> ap-pal-sa-am-ma UD-ma šá-kin qu-lu
> ù kul-lat te-né-še-e-ti i-tu-ra a-na ṭi-iṭ-ṭi
> ki-ma ú-ri mit-hu-rat ú-šal-lu
> ap-ti nap-pa-šá-ma UD.DA im-ta-qut UGU BÀD ap-pi-ia . . .
> a-na KUR.ni.ṣir i-te-mid GIŠ.MÁ
> KUR-ú KUR.ni-ṣir GIŠ.MÁ iṣ-bat-ma a-na na-a-ši ul id-din
> 1-en UD-ma 2-a UD-ma KUR.ni.ṣir KIM.MIN
> šal-šá UD-ma re-ba-a UD-ma KUR.ni.ṣir KIM.MIN
> 5-šá 6-šá KUR.ni.ṣir KIM.MIN
> 7-a UD-ma i-na ka-šá-a-di

12. Black et al., "The Flood Story," lines C22–D11.

13. *ANET*, 44.

14. Parpola's transliterated *h* = *ḫ* here.

ú-še-ṣi-ma TU.MUŠEN ú-maš-šir
il-lik TU.MUŠEN i-tu-ram-ma
man-za-zu ul i-pa-áš-šum-ma is-sah-ra
ú-še-ṣi-ma SIM.MUŠEN ú-maš-šir
il-ik SIM.MUŠEN i-tu-ram-ma
man-za-zu ul i-pa-áš-šum-ma is-sah-ra
ú-še-ṣi-ma a-ri-ba ú-maš-šir
il-lik a-ri-bi-ma qa-ru-ra šá A.MEŠ i-mur-ma
ik-kal i-šá-ah-hi i-tar-ri ul is-sah-ra
ú-še-ṣi-ma a-na 4 TU$_{15}$. MEŠ at-ta-qí ni-qa-a
áš-kun sur-qi-nu ina UGU ziq-qur-rat KUR-i
7 u 7 DUG.A.DA.GUR$_5$ UG.A.DA.GUR uk-tin[15]

Six days and seven nights
Came the wind and flood, the storm flattening the land.
When the seventh day arrived, the storm was pounding,
The flood was a war—struggling with itself like a woman writhing (in labor).
The sea calmed, fell still, the whirlwind (and) flood stopped up.
I looked around all day long—quiet had set in
And all the human beings had turned to clay!
The terrain was as flat as a roof.
I opened a vent and fresh air (daylight?) fell upon the side of my nose.
I fell to my knees and sat weeping,
Tears streaming down the side of my nose.
I looked around for coastlines in the expanse of the sea,
And at twelve leagues there emerged a region (of land).
On Mt. Nimush the boat lodged firm,
Mt. Nimush held the boat, allowing no sway.
One day and a second Mt. Nimush held the boat, allowing no sway.
A third day, a fourth, Mt. Nimush held the boat, allowing no sway.
A fifth day, a sixth, Mt. Nimush held the boat, allowing no sway.
When the seventh day arrived I sent forth a dove and released it.
The dove went off, but came back to me;
no perch was visible so it circled back to me.
I sent forth a swallow and released it.
The swallow went off, but came back to me;
no perch was visible so it circled back to me.
I sent forth a raven and released it.
The raven went off, and saw the waters slither back.
It eats, it scratches, it bobs, but does not circle back to me.

15. Lines 128–36 and 141–58 in Parpola, *The Epic of Gilgamesh*, 110–11.

> Then I sent out everything in all directions and sacrificed (a sheep).
> I offered incense in front of the mountain-ziggurat.
> Seven and seven cult vessels I put in place.[16]

Although the bulk of the lines are missing in the flood account in the Babylonian text of *Atra-ḫasīs*, it is clear that the story is identical to the other flood accounts especially the one found here in GE.[17] This, together with other key elements, tells us that the story was well preserved in its details, and that the author of Genesis is likely interacting with the text of *Atra-ḫasīs* specifically.[18]

The parallel between the two accounts, from the birds that are sent out, in order to discover whether dry land has yet appeared, to the offering of sacrifices after the flood (8:20–21),[19] are striking. What is significant for the present study, however, is the use of the number seven within the story. The flood is sustained for seven days, and birds are then sent out after another seven days to discover dry land. Seven days is given also for the length of time that Noah waits until he sends a bird out to discover dry land.[20] In the Genesis account, the logic of the earlier flood narrative has been worked out. Hence, Noah waits for seven days and sends out a bird. He then waits for another seven days before he sends out the next one.

One might conclude that perhaps the ancient tradition that predates the Genesis account simply records the actual time period of the event. However, as we have seen, the number seven carries great significance in ancient Near Eastern literature, and it is more likely that, just as in the Genesis account, the Mesopotamian uses of the number seven within its flood accounts are also meant to convey concepts of purifica-

---

16. Translation offered by Kovacs, *Gilgamesh*, 101–2.

17. This is evident by the fact that the opening and closing of the flood narrative are virtually identical.

18. There is no doubt that the text was well known by West Semitic peoples even before the Babylonian Exile, as evidenced in its attestation in an Ugaritic document (see Lambert and Millard, *Atra-ḫasīs*, 131–3).

19. Cf. also the line in the Gilgamesh Epic: DINGER.MEŠ *i-ṣi-nu i-ri-šá* DINGER.MEŠ *i-ṣi-nu i-ri-šà* DÚG.GA "the gods smelled the savor, the gods smelled the sweet savor" (lines 160–1; see also *ANET*, 95).

20. Although the MT and the Gilgamesh Epic send out the birds in different order, Cassuto notes (*Genesis II*, 18) that in the LXX version, as in the Gilgamesh Epic, the raven is sent out and does not return: καὶ ἀπέστειλεν τὸν κόρακα τοῦ ἰδεῖν εἰ κεκόπακεν τὸ ὕδωρ καὶ ἐξελθὼν οὐχ ὑπέστρεψεν ἕως τοῦ ξηρανθῆναι τὸ ὕδωρ ἀπὸ τῆς γῆς.

tion and recreation through chaos. In fact, all of God's destructive acts in the Bible are seen as acts of purification rather than meaningless acts of devastation. In the *Eridu Genesis* and GE, the flood lasts for seven days. This is also true of the account in *Atra-ḫasīs*. What is only shared by the *Atra-ḫasīs* and the biblical account, however, is the seven night/day countdown to the flood.[21]

This sort of deconstruction in terms of seven is well attested in mythic literature. In *The Descent of Inanna to the Netherworld*, the gatekeeper to the Netherworld removes a piece of clothing from Inanna, one for every level that they get closer to the netherworld, until she is stripped of all of her adornment and clothing.[22] The relevant elements evident within the pericope read as follows:

> abula 1-kam-ma ku₄-[ku₄-da-ni-ta]
> tug₂-šu-gur-ra men edin-na saĝ-ĝa₂-na lu₂ ba-da-an-ze₂-er ...
> abula 2-kam-ma ku₄-ku₄-da-[ni-ta]
> na₄za-gin₃ di₄-di₄-la₂ gu₂-na lu₂ ba-da-an-ze₂-er ...
> abula 3-kam-ma ku₄-ku₄-da-ni-ta
> na₄-nunuz tab-ba gaba-na lu₂ ba-da-an-ze₂-er ...
> abula 4-kam-ma ku₄-ku₄-da-ni-ta
> tu-di-da lu₂ ĝa₂-nu ĝa₂-nu gaba-na lu₂ ba-da-an-ze₂-er ...
> abula 5-kam-ma ku₄-ku₄-da-ni-ta
> ḫar kug-sig₁₇ šu-na lu₂ ba-da-an-ze₂-er ...
> abula 6-kam-ma ku₄-ku₄-da-ni-ta
> gi-diš-nindan eš₂-gana₂ za-gin₃ šu-[na] lu₂ ba-da-an-ze₂-er ...
> abula 7-kam-ma ku₄-ku₄-da-ni-ta
> [tug₄pala₃] tug₂ nam-nin-a bar-ra-na lu₂ ba-da-an-ze₂-er

After she had entered in,
someone had slipped off her kaffieh and aghal, the desert
    headdress, of her head ...
After she had entered through the second great gate,
someone had slipped off her the pure yardstick
    and measuring line ...

---

21. *Atra-ḫasīs*: *ba-a-a' a-bu-bi 7 mu-ši-šu iq-bi-šu* "He announced to him the coming of the flood for the seventh night" (Lambert and Millard, *Atra-ḫasīs*, 90–91). כי לימים עוד שבעה אנכי ממטיר על הארץ "for in seven days I will bring rain upon the earth" (Gen 7:4).

22. Being stripped of one's clothes is often a symbol of humility gained from the presence of chaos. Hence, tearing one's clothes was a common response to calamity in one's life. Likewise, in *The Descent of Ishtar to the Netherworld*, once Ishtar is stripped of her clothing, chaos ensues.

> After she had entered through the third great gate,
> someone had slipped off her the small lapis lazuli beads
>   of her neck...
> After she had entered through the fourth great gate,
> someone had slipped off her the yoked oval stone beads
>   of her chest...
> After she had entered through the fifth great gate,
> someone had slipped off her the gold rings of her hands...
> After she had entered through the sixth great gate,
> someone had slipped off her the breast-shields   (named)
>   "O man, come hither, come hither"...
> After she entered through the seventh great gate,
> someone had slipped off her the robe of office, the robe
>   of queenship of her back.[23]

Moving toward the netherworld (i.e., the land of chaos and death), the number seven takes a prominent role. It looks toward the reversal of the prosperity and fertility of human life.[24] In other words, it works against the human and toward chaos. In the same way, the countdown to the reversal of creation is presented in the same seven days that it took to order that creation: "Once it became seven days, the water of the flood came upon the earth" (7:10; see also v. 4).

---

23. Translation offered by Jacobsen, *The Harps That*, 213–15. Cf. also *The Descent of Ishtar to the Netherworld* in Foster (*Before the Muses*, 500–1):
> He brought her in the first gate,
>   he loosed and removed the great tiara of her head...
> He brought her in the second gate,
>   he loosed and removed the earrings of her ears...
> He brought her in the third gate,
>   he loosed and removed the beads of her neck...
> He brought her in the fourth gate,
>   he loosed and removed the garment pins of her breast...
> He brought her in the fifth gate,
>   he loosed and removed the girdle of birth stones of her waist...
> He brought her in the sixth gate,
>   he loosed and removed her bracelets and anklets...
> He brought her in the seventh gate,
>   he loosed and removed the loincloth of her body.

24. In the Akkadian version, the text states, "As soon as Ishtar went down to the netherworld, the bull will not mount the cow, the ass will not impregnate the jenny, the young man will not impregnate the girl in the thoroughfare, the young man has slept in his [bedroom?], the young girl has slept by herself" (Ibid., 502). Thus, chaos strips the land of its fertility/prosperity in the same way that the Gatekeeper stripped Ishtar of her clothes that represent her powers to sustain fertility/prosperity.

At this point, one might see a contradiction between this statement and the comments concerning the seven day structure of the temple and its connection to order and creation; but such a contradiction is merely superficial. It is through the very chaos of the flood that God seeks to preserve human life.[25] It is, in fact, an act of salvation toward humanity. Through it, God has decided to destroy chaotic agents in the world, i.e., those who threatened the perpetuation and preservation of human life, in an effort to save humankind. In essence, God's acts of chaos toward chaotic agents, in the Book of Genesis, are acts of creation toward His people. They seek to remove those elements that threaten human life in order that God's people might be preserved through the destruction of those elements. The seven day structure, then, describes the act of purity through chaos in that destruction must take place in order for renewal to come about.

This is not a biblical novelty. As it is clearly seen above, this concept of creation through destruction is a common one in the ancient Near East. It is the foundation of the concept of justice in the law codes, the concept of war in the annals, and the concept of divine love that subdues chaotic forces in order to preserve the deity's people. Hence, the number seven is suited for divine acts of chaos, as they are also divine acts of purification, creation, and order.

This is confirmed by the fact that the flood begins with a seven day countdown until the chaotic waters, i.e., waters of purification, come upon the earth (Gen 7:4, 10), and ends with Noah waiting for seven days to send out the final dove which discovers that creation (i.e., the reversal of the chaotic waters) has commenced once again (8:10). In doing so, the Genesis account is attempting to convey creation through destruction, order through chaos, and life through death. Neither the ancient Near Eastern accounts of the flood, nor the flood in Genesis, are likely meant to record a literal time frame during which the flood occurred. Instead, the septadic time frame is of a literary nature, conveying these concepts of chaos and creation in the ancient Near East.[26]

---

25. Even in the Akkadian version of the myth above, the goddess Ishtar returns from the netherworld victoriously. Hence, some have entitled the myth along those lines. See Lapinkivi's designation of the myth as *The Neo-Assyrian Myth of Ishtar's Descent and Resurrection*.

26. The time frame of the flood is another example of a primeval time unknown to the author. Hence, the Unidentified fragment noted by Lambert and Millard states that the flood occurred "in the day, [in that remote] day, in that night, [in that remote] night, in that year, [in that remote] year, when the flood . . . in the primeval day, that day . . . in

THE ARK AS A TEMPLE

Scholars have, for some time, seen the ordering significance of the ark within the chaotic waters.

Susan Niditch astutely notes:

> That which is special about this tale of chaos and creation is that the chaos has within it one small island of cosmogonic order, the ark. Within the ark are maintained human beings and beasts, pairs of creatures in their species... Food, the produce of the fertile land, is also aboard (6:21). Only Noah and his family retain calendrical time-consciousness, counting each day the water falls upon the earth, noting the passage of day and night.
>
> The ark not only represents the maintained ordering of the natural realm with its calendar, fertility, and species. It also maintains a state which Genesis 2–3 portrays as a step beyond the ordering and defining of nature, the state of social structure and culture. The ark itself is a culture-intensive structure built with man-made tools and complex prepared materials.[27]

Thus, the connection of the flood with the creation account, as well as its preservation of order has been thoroughly noted by scholars to be a case where "cosmos floats on chaos."[28] However, what has not been significantly pursued by scholars, perhaps because of its speculative nature, in evaluating the symbol of the ark, whether in terms of its description within the Mesopotamian or biblical accounts, is that the ark is meant to shelter the individual from the waters of chaos much like the temple does in ancient Near Eastern society. As discussed before, it is through the temple that the deity provides protection from chaos to his or her community. A universal symbol for chaos in the ancient Near East is water, especially large bodies of water, which may have been adopted through the course of having to deal with disastrous flooding that often occurred in Mesopotamian history. In both accounts the boat is made of many rooms, as are temples in the ancient world. In the biblical text, the boat is sectioned off into three levels that mimic the three main sections of the sanctuary (i.e., the courtyard, the holy place, and the holiest place).[29] Likewise, as the cosmic temple in Genesis 1 is structured in

---

the remote year, the year... after the flood had been brought about" (*Atra-Ḫasīs*, 16).

27. Niditch, *Chaos to Cosmos*, 22–23.
28. Ibid., 23.
29. It is possible that this instead may be linked to three levels in the temple, i.e.,

sevens, especially in reference to the seven days, the flood account is also structured in sevens, especially seven days in reference to the entrance and departure from the ark (7:2–4; 10; 8:10, 12).

As discussed before, creation in Genesis 1 is described in terms of a cosmic temple. The flood account parallels the account in Genesis 1 in much of its language and imagery, especially concerning the animals that are male and female and לְמִינֵהוּ (1:11–12, 21, 24–25; 6:20; 7:14).[30] Similarly, 6:21 may be purposefully drawing from 2:9 and 16, both of which speak of food that is given to the humans that God places into a sphere of protection, a sanctuary in the midst of chaos.[31] Although somewhat speculative in isolation from the larger evidence, the verbal and noun form of כפר "bitumen," as are their cognates in GE, are used to refer to the bitumen that is used to smear on the boat as a sealing agent and its application.[32] There is a homonymic/homographic connection with the verbal forms of כפר/*kapāru*, here referring to the application of bitumen to the boat, which also refers to the blood that is smeared on the cultic items and walls of the sanctuary in order to expiate it. What is more interesting, however, is that its cognate *kupru* (כפר), also used to refer to the bitumen with which the boat/ark is sealed, is the sealing agent used to waterproof temples and palaces in Mesopotamia.[33] Finally, as in the rest of the accounts, an altar is erected and sacrifices are offered outside the boat.[34]

---

the ground level and two upper chambers (cf. 2 Chron 3:9), or the ziggurat that often had three levels (John M. Lundquist, "What Is a Temple?" 211). Cf. also the statement by Davey ("Temples of the Levant," 112) that "despite considerable conjecture, most scholars reconstruct the temple with a series of three storeys of side rooms built around the *hêkāl* and the *debîr* (1 Ki. 6:5) although C. Watzinger extends them to the front of the temple. There is also a general consensus that the temple was constructed on a platform and approached by a flight of stairs."

30. The word mainly appears elsewhere in cultic contexts, and primarily refers to animals in those contexts (Lev 11:14–16, 19, 22, 29; Deut 14:13–15, 18). Beside these occurrences, the word only appears one other time in the Hebrew Bible (Ezek 47:10).

31. As the שָׂדֶה in Genesis 2–3 functions as a parallel to the chaos of תְּהוֹם in Genesis 1, so the sanctuary of the ark that guards humans from the chaotic waters is parallel to the garden sanctuary that protects the original couple from the chaos of שָׂדֶה. Hence, both spheres function symbolically as sanctuaries in the midst of chaos.

32. Gen 6:14 (cf. the homonym in Exod 29:37); cf. GE *kupru* in X.159, 263; XI.54, 65, as well as *kapāru* "to wipe clean" in X.165.

33. Leick, *Ancient Near Eastern Architecture*, 35.

34. Although the length and width of the ark are different than the temple for obvious reasons, the height is the same, i.e., thirty cubits (1 Kings 6:2; 2 Chron 3:3; although

Westermann quotes Benno Jacob as making the observation that "the ark and the tabernacle are the only buildings that the Torah describes."[35] He then continues to expound upon Jacob's observation.

> P looks to the Tabernacle, the place where Yahweh meets his people, as the goal of the history which begins with the covenant with Abraham and extends to the erection of the sanctuary in Jerusalem. The place where God allows his glory to appear is the place whence the life of the people is preserved. The ark corresponds to this in the primeval event where the concern is for the preservation of humanity and what is saved is natural creation. Such is the significance of the construction of the ark because by means of it God preserved humanity from destruction. The parallel between the ark and the tabernacle has a profound meaning. The people of Israel which alone has in its midst the place where God reveals his glory is part of the human race which exists now because it has been preserved by the same God.[36]

In fact, the measurements of the ark itself were once interpreted to be those of "a truncated pyramid, measuring 300 cubits by fifty at the base and only one cubit by one at the apex."[37] A pyramid, however, is not necessarily what is in view, and early interpreters did not see the connection between the shape of the ark and a temple or ziggurat.[38] If the ark is meant to be God's own ziggurat, then this would provide an interesting contrast between chapters 6–10 and 11:1–9, as well as providing the connection to the two seeds of the preceding and following genealogies in terms of those who seek to preserve human life (hence being כדמות אלהים "like God's likness/cult image"), as Noah does, and those who seek power (hence being כאלהים "like God"), as do the builders of the towered, cult city Babylon. If this is the case, then Noah fulfills his role as God's cult image, and thus, is placed within a temple for the purpose of his own preservation

---

see the LXX measurement of 25 cubits).

35. C. Westermann, *Genesis 1–11*, 421.

36. Ibid.

37. Cohn, *Noah's Flood*, 38. One can understand the idea that early interpreters had of the ark described as a pyramid, since the phrase εἰς πῆχυν (= אל אמה) "to a cubit" seemed to describe the idea that the ark was formed in a pyramidal shape from the bottom to the top.

38. Although cf. also Lundquist ("What Is a Temple?" 215), who states the common understanding that pyramids are also types of temples. However, it is more probable that the ark imagery mimics a temple of the Babylonian variety, specifically that of a ziggurat.

on a microcosmic level, and the persistence of order and human life in the midst of chaos on a macrocosmic one.

Still, other temples beside religious structures like the ziggurat, would also meet the description, since numerous temples were wide at the bottom, had more than one layer/level, and had a narrow pinnacle. It was not until the twelfth century that the ark was thought of in a different form more befitting a boat in the water,[39] or as I should say, more befitting a literalistic interpretation of the description of a boat in water. Understanding the ark as a temple, however, allows the reader to see the connections the biblical story has with the rest of the primeval history, which is largely concerned with God's ability to bring order (i.e., preserving human life) out of chaos (i.e., those destructive elements that exist in the world to destroy human life) by preserving His image and cleansing His temple of chaotic agents. In this case, the wicked people are the chaos from which God is delivering Noah, but the flood, as divine judgment that seeks to preserve His people, also becomes a threat to human life. It is the ark, then, that provides the protection from chaos, i.e., the protection that a temple normally supplies to the individual or community. For this reason, from its earliest appearances in Sumerian and Babylonian literature, the craft is described in cosmic terms as a sanctuary in the midst of the primeval sea, i.e., the waters of chaos. There is, therefore, a connection between the primeval hillock that emerges from the waters of chaos as sacred ground, which individual temples are meant to represent, and the ark, which is a protected sphere of order and creation, that emerges from the waters.

Finally, another parallel is gained between the cosmic temple in Genesis 1 and the flood narrative from the duty of, and language surrounding, the cult image in 1:26–31, which is re-established with Noah in 9:1–7.[40] As God's cult images, humans are to work toward perpetuating and establishing human life and the order that supports that goal. Hence, they are to work against chaos and for order, the primary occupation of the cult image. Here, however, the cult image has been removed

---

39. "But the ark remained pyramidal in shape until the twelfth century, when it came to be thought of as a rectangular house with a sloping roof" (Cohn, *Noah's Flood*, 38).

40. Indeed, one might make the argument that the ark is not a temple because God is never said to dwell inside of it; but this misses the fact that the deity dwells in a temple through his or her cult image. Hence, the fact that the image motif is continued in the flood narrative, at the very least, must give some credence to the idea that the ark functions as a temple.

from the ark and placed upon the earth. The ark, therefore, functioned only as a temporary sanctuary that held the contents of creation/order, and the image of God through which He preserves them, in the world of chaotic waters. Once chaos in the world subsided, its contents could be released into the larger cosmic temple that God had re-established through the subjection of those waters.

Hence, the number seven may be linked to the ark for the same reason that it is linked to the creation account in Genesis 1 (i.e., because it functions as a temple that provides order and protection for humans from chaotic forces). The seven day period surrounds the ark. It is the countdown to the flood once Noah is told to enter the ark; and it is the countdown that surrounds Noah's intention to leave the ark by looking for signs of chaos's defeat, i.e., dry land.[41]

However, each element can be interpreted as consistent with the story, absent of temple imagery. Still, it makes for an interesting suggestion, since it would provide an *inclusio* with chapter 1 for the primeval history. In any case, whether temple imagery is present or not, the number seven has been employed for theological purposes that convey God's re-creation of the world through chaos, and how those activities relate to His intentions toward humanity.[42]

THE NUMBER FORTY AS THE TIME OF TESTING

Noah must endure the rains for forty days and forty nights (Gen 7:4, 12; 8:6). As discussed before, this number, rather than being a literal time period, has a wide attestation in Scripture as a symbolic period of time representing trial and testing.

The Israelites are tested at the foot of Sinai for forty days and forty nights while Moses is on the mountain (Exod 24:18; 34:28), during which time, they fail the test by becoming fearful and creating a golden calf to represent God. Likewise, the time period used to describe the Israelites'

41. Wenham ("The Coherence of the Flood," 445) also notes the parallel between the pattern of the week mentioned in each account. The work of creation begins on a Sunday and ends on a Friday, the Sabbath observed the following day. Likewise, the flood narrative depicts the flood as being announced on a Sunday at its inception (7:4, 10), and Noah sends out the birds Sundays once it begins to abate (Gen 8:7, 10, 12).

42. The well known parallel between the ark and Moses' river basket also yields an interesting note. If these vessels were meant to mimic the *function* of a temple (i.e., to hold chaos at bay), then an *inclusio* is also created by the author of Exodus, who would have then begun his narrative with a sanctuary, keeping death and the waters back, and ended it with a temple/tabernacle.

wait to hear back from the spies consists of forty days (Num 13:25). The Israelite nation must wander for forty years in the wilderness, an anticipatory period where the reader is left to wonder if the nation will endure (14:33–35; 32:13; Deut 2:7). Deuteronomy 8:2 describes this time period in terms of testing: "You shall remember all the way which the Lord your God has led you in the wilderness these forty years, that He might humble you, testing you, to know what was in your heart, whether you would keep His commandments or not."

As also discussed before, both God's patience toward the world and Moses' life exists in terms of forty year increments (something which is implied in Exodus 7:7; Deuteronomy 31:2; and 34:7, and interpreted as such in Acts 7:30).

The forty year rest for Israel in the Book of Judges is also a trial which they fail (Judg 3:11; 5:31; 8:28). Israel is taunted by Goliath for forty days (17:16). David's difficult reign is forty years (2 Sam 5:4), as was Solomon's (1 Kgs 11:42). Elijah's journey to Horeb is forty days and forty nights, during which he must be sustained on a single meal (19:8). Finally, Nineveh's time of testing that they are given to repent is said to be forty days (Jon 3:4).[43]

The fact that each of these appearances of the number describes a time of testing and difficulty is more than mere coincidence. There is a clear biblical employment of the number that is meant to convey, not a literal period of time, but a time of trial. Whatever the literal time periods were, they were considered by the biblical authors to be less important to recapture in the text than the symbolic expression that sought to convey a much more meaningful idea (i.e., that God is patient and gives a time of opportunity for people to humble themselves and obey Him instead of immediately destroying them for their lack of obedience). In other words, God seeks to call back the wayward and strengthen the faithful through trial. This is what the textual data above bears out.

Here, we may safely conclude that the forty days of difficulty and trial for Noah and his family are meant to be strengthening, although the events that transpire after the flood concerning Ham may indicate that

---

43. Cf. the age of Isaac (Gen 25:20) and Esau (26:34), which are both mentioned in the context of difficulty, specifically in regard to elements threatening preservation (i.e., Rebekah being barren and Esau's foreign wives threatening the covenant community); also cf. the temptation of Jesus in the wilderness, which lasts for forty days (Matt 4:2; Mk 1:13; Lk 4:2) in parallel to Deuteronomy 9:9.

the event also serves as a testing period that draws out unfaithfulness. However, such may be too much to suggest for this specific text. Either way, it is clear that the number, rather than existing as a measurement of time, exists in the text to portray the flood as a time of testing for mankind, a time God graciously desires the test to be passed.[44]

THE OTHER TIME PERIODS OF THE FLOOD AND WHAT THEY MAY COMMUNICATE TO THE ANCIENT READER

Whether the numbers here are literal or symbolic in their meaning is a secondary consideration, since it is clear that the author is using these numbers in order to complete the narrative, not give literal chronologies that correspond to the event in reality. This is made clear from the literary structure. Gordon Wenham notes that the ark narrative is presented in a palistrophe:

```
A  Noah (6:10a)
B   Shem, Ham and Japheth (10b)
C    Ark to be built (14–16)
D     Flood announced (17)
E      Covenant with Noah (18–22)
F       Food in the ark (21)
G        Command to enter the ark (7:1–3)
H         7 days waiting for flood (4–5)
I          7 days waiting for flood (7–10)
J           Entry to ark (11–15)
K            Yahweh shuts Noah in (16)
L             40 days flood (17a)
M              Waters increase (17b–18)
N               Mountains covered (19–20)
O                150 days waters prevail ([21]–24)
```

44. Hence, the comparative observation with *Atra-ḫasīs* that "there are two major gods in opposition, one of whom (Enlil) decides to destroy all humans, and another god (Enki) decides to save the flood hero and his family" and that "in Israelite tradition a single god has taken on both divine roles—destroyer and savior—thus creating an inner tension in his character and a deep ambiguity in the story" (Hendel, "Genesis," 939) is only partially true in that the act of destroying is the act of saving. God has given humans who have made themselves into chaotic agents in the world a gracious chance to repent (e.g., the indication of the 120 years mentioned before). He now saves Noah and his family from those chaotic agents, as He tests them as well through the tribulation of the flood. The time units, therefore, give some indication that God's character is without inner tension in that every chaotic act performed upon the wicked is one that seeks to preserve those who would find favor with Him.

P	**GOD REMEBERS NOAH (8:1)**
O′	150 days waters abate (3)
N′	Mountain tops visible (4–5)
M′	Waters abate (5)
L′	40 days (end of) (6a)
K′	Noah opens window of ark (6b)
J′	Raven and dove leave ark (7–9)
I′	7 days waiting for waters to subside (10–11)
H′	7 days waiting for waters to subside (12–13)
G′	Command to leave ark (15–17 [22])
F′	Food outside ark (9:1–4)
E′	Covenant with all flesh (8–10)
D′	No flood in future (11–17)
C′	Ark (18a)
B′	Shem, Ham and Japheth (18b)
A′	Noah (19)

He then observes that the time spans used to describe various events within the palistrophe correspond to one another in an organized fashion.

> The 7 days of waiting for the flood is mentioned twice, and matches the 14 days of waiting for the water to subside. The 150 days of water prevailing correspond to the 150 days of water abating. In other words, the rise of the flood seems to take exactly the same time as its decline, namely 204 days, and these time spans are fitted very neatly into the palistrophe.[45]

His next comments are the most important for this study: "But closer examination suggests that some of these time spans are mentioned purely in order to achieve symmetry in the palistrophe."[46] The palistrophe itself is intended to create a literary picture of the rise and fall of the waters of the flood.

I have already discussed the nature of the numbers seven and forty, which are most certainly symbolic numbers; but the 150 days mentioned both as the duration of the flood, as well as the point after which the waters decrease, indicates, as Wenham argued, that this number is presented twice in order to meet the conditions of the palistrophe. There is a good indication, therefore, that the number, being associated with other symbolic numbers in the passage, as well as employed to meet

---

45. Wenham, "The Coherence of the Flood," 439.
46. Ibid.

the literary structure of the passage, although not specifically symbolic, does represent something other than a literal, precisely measured, time period.

Furthermore, another indication of the number's symbolic use exists within the passage. The text states that the flood began on the seventeenth day of the second month, but then tells us that the ark comes to rest five months later on the seventeenth day of the seventh month. Hence, 150 days exist between the commencement of the flood and its abatement. The problem is that 190 days (i.e., 150 + 40) are mentioned in the passage. Although Wenham gives a good argument that the ancients may have read the forty days into the 150 days, the text seems to suggest that יגברו המים אל ערץ "the waters were mighty upon the earth" (7:24) for the duration of 150 days, but the flood was only gaining momentum during the forty days (vv. 12, 17), only after which, it is said that the waters prevailed (vv. 18–20). Admittedly, however, it is possible to take the numbers as simultaneous if one were to take the number forty as literal.[47] As we have seen, however, the number is figurative, and even if one were to conclude that the author intended to harmonize the two, it would only be for purposes pertaining to the literary presentation of the event, as it contributes to the larger theological picture the author is painting, not a literal chronology.

Hence, Wenham observes that "in these ways even the chronology of the flood story becomes a vehicle for expressing theological ideas."[48] In other words, the use of time is subordinate to the author's theological message. It does not attempt to convey a literal time period, but instead represents an event with a chronology that suits the author's literary purposes.

This is a common practice in retelling stories. Even in the case of narrative speech, the authors of the ancient world do not always detail the exact conversations that were spoken in reality but instead only represent what was said in reality with conversations that are molded to the purposes of the narrative itself.[49] This explains why there is so much

---

47. This harmonization exists in 4QcommGen A (4Q252) 1:6–10. The author of the Qumran commentary, however, makes the flood a full 364-day year (1–2), changing the original timeline of the flood narrative.

48. Ibid., 445.

49. "Indeed, literary critics of the Bible have noted that dialogue often provides the central framework for the plot structure of a story. But the representation of speech extends beyond dialogue to perform a variety of narrative functions. It may introduce

variation when the same conversation is recorded in multiple accounts. The individual narratives mold the conversation or events to fit the theological message of the larger narrative in which they now reside.[50] Hence, the flood narrative uses temporal measurements as literary devices that support the flow of the story, pointing to concepts of creation, destruction, trial, and the divine intention to save.

The coherence of the message is supported by the time periods used to describe it. As the beginning of the flood narrative portrays God as grieving over people who have largely become agents of chaos in the world, allowing us to "witness the motives and feelings of God,"[51] the temporal language used conveys God's intentions toward humanity, i.e., He does not wish chaotic agents to thrive, but instead desires to save humanity that is threatened by those chaotic agents. If one understands "chaos" to mean that which threatens human preservation, something described by the word *ḥāmās* (perhaps a description of the line of Cain that now has become representative of much of antediluvian humanity) and the prescription for humans to deal with murderers on their own through implementation of the *lex talionis* after the flood (9:5–6), then the portrayal of God in the act of the flood must be understood as God's good intentions to actually save mankind rather than to destroy it. The

---

characters, recount their inner thought processes, elucidate their inner character, index social relationships, and provide background information for the narrative. Finally, the linguistic resources for representing speech and dialogue may be used when no speech or dialogue is being reported; in such cases, the forms of represented speech function solely as a narrative trope" (Miller, *The Representation of Speech*, 2). Also see Bar-Efrat, *Narrative Art in the Bible*, 41–45, 64–77; Sternberg, *The Poetics of Biblical Narrative*, 168; and Alter (*The Art of Biblical Narrative*, 69–70), who refers to some of this as "narration through dialogue" that manifests what is significant about the character, and I would add, as it contributes to the larger message of the narrative.

50. The question should be further pursued as to whether numbers that do not convey any theological or symbolic meaning are meant to communicate the author's belief in the real event, as existed with a measurable period of time—in other words, whether the author signifies what he views as a real, temporally-measurable event with time periods that have no symbolic referents associated with them, and still, are not employed to strictly measure time (i.e., they are still representative of time periods of an event the author believes to have occurred, but he is unaware of the exact measurements, so he employs somewhat arbitrary numbers that represent the unknown measurements). This is a possible suggestion in terms of the 150 days presented in the flood narrative, since the day has no symbolic link, and yet, is clearly used for literary purposes within the narrative. Such a study is beyond the scope of this present work, however, but would be an interesting notion to pursue.

51. Gelander, *The Good Creator*, 69.

seven day time frame that communicates God's creative activity, the 120 years, and the forty day time period, indicates God's desire for humanity to repent, be restored as God's image, and return to pro-creative, rather than pro-chaotic, activity in the world, something verified by God's instructions to Noah after the flood (9:1–7). The flood, therefore, must be seen ultimately as an act of creation rather than one of destruction.

Conclusion

IN CONCLUSION, I WOULD like to address what I consider the most important point of this study, and that is the repercussions that have resulted when interpreting the temporal language in the primeval history as polemic against a contemporary cultural concern. I would like to take *Jubilees* as a prime example. J. van Rutten sums up the author's guiding concerns in his rewritten version.

> Other passages that are closely related to the biblical text, those that include, for example, the verbatim quotation of one or more words, depart from the biblical text quite extensively. I have shown that the structure of passages has been altered, that certain phrases have been omitted, while others have been added. As far as the creation story (Gen 1:1–2:4a; *Jub* 2:1–33) is concerned, the overall framework of the seven days remains intact, and eight acts of creation are placed within a six-day framework. However, the structure of each day of creation has been fundamentally altered. Moreover, the context of the Creation Story has been changed because the Sabbath frames the account (*Jub* 2:1, 17–33), and *Jubilees* 1 has preceded the account of creation.[1]

He further notes:

> One of the main characteristics of the rewriting in *Jubilees* is the chronological framework, which is an absolute one (anchored in creation), and heptadic (years, yearweeks, jubilees). We have seen that all events acquire a date . . . the author has the tendency to present the biblical story as a sequence of events which ought to be presented strictly chronologically. In many places, this leads to a rearrangement of biblical material.[2]

What van Rutten observes here is Jubilee's reordering and subjugation of the text of Genesis to a literal chronological framework that argues against what is perceived as an infiltration of pagan ideas into

---

1. van Rutten, *Primeval History*, 372.
2. Ibid., 373.

Jewish culture. What has been produced is a well-fortified revision of Genesis that accomplishes the author's purpose in communicating to Second Temple Judaism that Judaism ought to continue practicing those things it has always been practicing due to their ordination by God through creation of the world and of Israel. What has ultimately resulted from this, however, is a loss of the original message of the book. Instead of preserving the biblical message, in his attempt to preserve literal time frames and chronologies, the author has, perhaps unwittingly, destroyed the divine message that the text originally sought to convey to the religious community. The same, however, can be said for those allegorical interpretations that are so far from the original intent of the text within its literary and cultural context that the message is no longer identifiable. The tragedy, therefore, of seeking to preserve the text, either by harmonizing, *via* reinterpretations and midrash, literal understandings of the text, or over allegorizing in an effort to preserve the integrity of larger religious commitments to which one might hold, is that the message itself is forever lost in the process. It is only in letting the text speak within its ancient and literary context that the message, through all of its rich and vivid imagery, is capable of retaining its original message—a message that the religious community has and will forever need to understand God, themselves, and the nature of the world in which they live from a divine perspective.

This study has centered on the contextually ancient Near Eastern and literary use of the language of time, and has concluded that the temporal language in Genesis 1–11 itself, rather than simply being the author's primitive beliefs about the time periods in which the events described took place, are a part of the larger argument the author wishes to communicate to his audience. An interpretation that seeks to establish a literal understanding of these time periods is, therefore, misguided.

What is gained from the understanding that Scripture is a piece of art that communicates theology is that the reader realizes the complex nature of interpreting the text. In fact, what one may now see is that biblical interpretation is more a matter of skill and reflection than technical form in evaluating a "plain reading" of any given text. As one cannot acquire the correct reference of the statement, "That sunrise is beautiful," by merely analyzing the meaning of the individual words in a literalistic fashion, so one cannot simply grasp the full meaning of the biblical text by analyzing it as a literalistic and technical piece of literature. Instead, the paper is the canvas, the ink the paint, and the words used are the picture painted in order to communicate concepts that both transcend culture and yet are conveyed within the parameters of its conceptual world.

Temporal language, as we have seen, belongs to this same form of artistry. The use of a time period in a particular text certainly conveys something real in the author's mind, but the actual measurement of that time period often conveys something that supports the theological message of the narrative. Attempting to establish the time period of primeval events by their symbolic representations within the narrative, therefore, is much like trying to establish the time period of Middle Earth in the Lord of the Rings. Tolkien's time period externally represents, not a fictional period long ago in the earth's history, but the early twentieth century.[3] Yet, the symbolic ages, internal time referents within the story, used set the stage of the narrative and attempt to convey ideas that support the world he created rather than existing literally to measure time. In a similar manner, the author of Genesis uses these time periods that, in his mind, represent real events, but the actual measurements of those time periods employed convey ideas that support the theology he desires to communicate. Confusion between the internal and external referents of time, therefore, is often at play in misinterpreting the intentions of the narrative and its use of the event it subjugates to its purposes.

Furthermore, if a director of a movie were to alter the chronology of historical events in order to support his thematic presentation of events, or a painter chose to alter details in order to express what he or she wished to say through his or her work, this form of artistic expression would be widely understood and admired. It is simply a matter of understanding the narrative artistry of the book of Genesis, its theological purposes, and its literary savvy that will yield for the interpreter the true intent of the temporal language the author has sought to weave in and out of the retelling of the event. Once this is understood, the beauty of the text shines forth, and the threat of unbelieving polemics fade as irrelevant, as they miss the mark when seeking to undermine inspiration by undermining a literalistic interpretation of a passage that is not meant to convey such a rigid literalism after all. With the threat past, the faith community will find greater joy in what the author has presented

---

3. Although Tolkien viewed it as timeless, representing any time period.

than in what he has not, and indeed, never intended to present to us in the first place.

What the author of Genesis 1–11 presents to us is a God who is sovereign over chaos, who seeks to create humankind and preserve it from destruction, and who desires for those humans He created to participate in the work of the creation and preservation of further human life. The implications for this theology are far and wide, and at the end of the day, yield a righteousness for God's people that the mere adherence to a particular calculation of time could never produce.

Bibliography

Abou-Assaf, Ali, et al. *La statue de Tell Fekherye et son inscription bilingue assyro-araméenne*. Etudes Assyriologiques. Vol. 7. Paris: Editions Recherche sur les civilisations, 1982.
Andersen, Francis I. *The Sentence in Biblical Hebrew*. The Hague: Mouton Publishers, 1980.
Alexander, Denis. *Rebuilding the Matrix: Science and faith in the 21st Century*. Grand Rapids: Zondervan, 2003.
Allen, James P. *Genesis in Egypt: The Philosophy of Ancient Egyptian Creation Accounts*. New Haven: Yale Egyptological Seminar Department of Near Eastern Languages and Civilizations Graduate School Yale University, 1988.
———. *Middle Egyptian: An Introduction to the Language and Culture of Hieroglyphs*. Cambridge: Cambridge University Press, 2000.
———. "The Memphite Theology." In *The Context of Scripture, Volume 1: Canonical Compositions from the Biblical World*, edited by William H. Hallo and K. Lawson Younger Jr., 21–23. Leiden: Brill, 1997.
Alter, Robert. *The Art of Biblical Narrative*. New York: Basic Books, 1981.
Aquinas, Thomas. *Summa Theologica*. Vol. 1, Part 1. Translated by Fathers of the English Dominican Province. New York: Cosimo, 2007.
Arnold, Bill T. *Genesis*. New Cambridge Bible Commentary. Cambridge: Cambridge University Press, 2009.
Arnold, Bill T., and John H. Choi. *A Guide to Biblical Hebrew Syntax*. Cambridge: Cambridge University Press, 2003.
Athas, George. *The Tel Dan Inscription: A Reappraisal and a New Interpretation*. JSOTsup 360. Copenhagen International Seminar 12. Sheffield: Sheffield Academic Press, 2002.
Atwell, James E. "An Egyptian Source for Genesis 1." *JTS* 51 (2000) 441–77.
Baines, John. "Palaces and Temples of Ancient Egypt." In *Civilizations of the Ancient Near East*, edited by Jack M. Sasson, 303–18. Peabody, MA: Hendrickson, 2000.
Bar-Efrat, Shimon. *Narrative Art in the Bible*. Translated by Dorothea Shefer-Vanson. Bible and Literature 17/JSOTsup 70. Sheffield: Almond, 1989.
Barr, James. *Biblical Words for Time*. London: SCM, 1962.
———. *The Garden of Eden and the Hope of Immortality: The Read-Tuckwell Lectures for 1990*. Minneapolis: Fortress, 1993.
———. "The Literal, the Allegorical, and Modern Biblical Scholarship." *JSOT* 44 (1989) 3–17.
———. *The Semantics of Biblical Language*. Glasgow: Oxford University Press, 1961.
Batto, Bernard F. "Paradise Reexamined." In *The Biblical Canon in Comparative Perspective: Scripture in Context*, edited by K. L. Younger Jr., et al., 33–59. Ancient Near Eastern Texts and Studies 11. Lewiston, NY: Edwin Mellen, 1991.

———. *Slaying the Dragon: Mythmaking in the Biblical Tradition.* Louisville, KY: Westminster John Knox, 1992.

Bavinck, Herman. *Our Reasonable Faith.* Grand Rapids: Eerdmans, 1956.

Beck, John A. "Geography as Irony: The Narrative-Geographical Shaping of Elijah's Duel with the Prophets of Baal (1 Kings 18)." *SJOT* (2003) 291–301.

Bendavid, Abba. *Parallels in the Bible.* Jerusalem: Carta, 1972.

Ben Isaiah, Rabbi Abraham, and Rabbi Benjamin Sharfman. *The Pentateuch and Rashi's Commentary: A Linear Translation into English, Genesis.* Philadelphia: S.S.& R., 1949.

Bird, Phyllis A. "'Male and Female He Created Them': Genesis 1:27b in the Context of the Priestly Account of Creation." In *I Studied Inscriptions from before the Flood: Ancient Near Eastern, Literary, and Linguistic Approaches to Genesis 1–11*, edited by Richard S. Hess and David T. Tsumura, 329–61. Sources for Biblical and Theological Study 4. Winona Lake, IN: Eisenbrauns, 1994.

Black, Jeremy, et al., eds. *A Concise Dictionary of Akkadian.* SANTAG 5. Wiesbaden: Harrassowitz Verlag, 1999.

———. "The building of Ninĝirsu's temple (Gudea, cylinders A and B)." No pages. Online: http://etcsl.orinst.ox.ac.uk/.

———. "Gilgameš, Enkidu and the Netherworld." No pages. Online: http://etcsl.orinst.ox.ac.uk/.

Borger, Rykle. "The Incantation Series *Bīt Mēseri* and Enoch's Ascension to Heaven." In *I Studied Inscriptions from before the Flood: Ancient Near Eastern, Literary, and Linguistic Approaches to Genesis 1–11*, edited by Richard S. Hess and David T. Tsumura, 224–33. Sources for Biblical and Theological Study 4. Winona Lake, IN: Eisenbrauns, 1994.

Botterweck, G. Johannes, et al., eds. *Theological Dictionary of the Old Testament.* 15 vols. Translated by John T. Willis, et al. Grand Rapids: Eerdmans, 1977–2006.

Brett, Mark G. *Genesis: Procreation and the Politics of Identity.* Old Testament Readings. London: Routledge, 2000.

Brin, Gershon. *The Concept of Time in the Bible and the Dead Sea Scrolls.* Studies on the Texts of the Desert of Judah 39. Leiden: Brill, 2001.

———. "The Formula X-יֹום and X-יֹום: Some Characteristics of Historiographical Writing in Israel." *ZAW* 93 (1981) 183–96.

Brooke, George J. "Genesis, Commentary On." In *Encyclopedia of the Dead Sea Scrolls*, edited by Lawrence H. Schiffman and James C. Vanderkam, 300–2. New York: Oxford University Press, 2000.

Brown, Francis, et al., eds. *A Hebrew and English Lexicon of the Old Testament with an Appendix containing Biblical Aramaic.* London: Oxford University Press, 1972.

Brown, William. *Structure, Role, and Ideology in the Hebrew and Greek Texts of Genesis 1:1–2:3.* SBL Dissertation Series 132. Atlanta: Scholars Press, 1993.

Callender, Dexter E. *Adam in Myth and History: Ancient Israelite Perspectives on the Primeval Human.* Harvard Semitic Studies 48. Winona Lake, IN: Eisenbrauns, 2000.

Calvin, John. *Calvin: Commentaries.* Translated by Joseph Haroutunian; The Library of Christian Classics XXXIII. Philadelphia: Westminster Press, 1958.

———. *Commentaries on the First Book of Moses called Genesis.* Translated by John King. Grand Rapids: Baker, 1979.

———. *Opera Exegetica et Homeletica*. Vol. 1. Brunsvigae apud C.A. Schwetschke et filium. M. Bruhn, 1882.
Cassuto, Umberto. *A Commentary on the Book of Genesis, Part I: From Adam to Noah*. Jerusalem: Magnes, 1998.
———. *A Commentary on the Book of Genesis, Part II: From Noah to Abraham*. Jerusalem: Magnes, 1998.
Charlesworth, James. *The Good and Evil Serpent: How a Universal Symbol Became Christianized*. New Haven: Yale University Press, 2010.
———, ed. *The Old Testament Pseudepigrapha: Volume 1: Apocalyptic Literature and Testaments*. Garden City: Doubleday, 1983.
———, ed. *The Old Testament Pseudepigrapha: Volume 2: Expansions of the "Old Testament" and Legends, Wisdom and Philosophical Literature, Prayers, Psalms and Odes, Fragments of Lost Judeo-Hellenistic Works*. Garden City: Doubleday, 1985.
Childs, Bervard S. "Critical Reflections on James Barr's Understanding of the Literal and the Allegorical," *Journal for the Study of the Old Testament* 46 (1990) 3–9.
———. *Myth and Reality in the Old Testament*. Studies in Biblical Theology 27. London: SCM, 1968.
Chilton, David. *Paradise Restored*. Tyler: Reconstruction, 1985.
Clark, W. M. "The Flood and the Structure of the Pre-Patriarchal History," *ZAW* 83 (1971) 184–210.
Clifford, Richard J. *The Cosmic Mountain in Canaan and the Old Testament*. Cambridge, MA: Harvard University Press, 1972.
———. *Creation Accounts in the Ancient near East and in the Bible*. CBQ Monograph Series 26. Washington DC: Catholic Biblical Association, 1994.
Clines, David J. A., ed. *Dictionary of Classical Hebrew*. 6 vols. Sheffield: Sheffield Academic Press, 1993–2007.
———. "The Image of God in Man." *TynBul* 19 (1968) 80–85.
Coats, George W. *Genesis, with an Introduction to Narrative Literature*. The Forms of Old Testament Literature 1. Grand Rapids: Eerdmans, 1983.
Cohn, Norman. *Noah's Flood: The Genesis Story in Western Thought*. New Haven: Yale University Press, 1996.
Cole, R. Alan, *Exodus*. Tyndale Old Testament Commentary 2. London: Intervarsity Press, 1973.
Coote, Robert B., and David Robert Ord. *In the Beginning: Creation and the Priestly History*. Minneapolis: Fortress, 1991.
Curtis, Edward M. "Man as the Image of God in Genesis in the Light of Ancient Near Eastern Parallels." PhD diss., University of Pennsylvania, 1984.
Danielou, Jean. *The Development of Christian Doctrine Before the Council of Nicaea, Volume 1: The Theology of Jewish Christianity*. London: Darton, Longman & Todd, 1964.
de Moor, Johannes C., and Klaas Spronk, *A Cuneiform Anthology of Religious Texts from Ugarit*. Semitic Studies Series 6. Leiden: Brill, 1987.
Dever, William G., "Palaces and Temples in Canaan and Ancient Israel." In *Civilizations of the Ancient Near East*, edited by Jack M. Sasson, 605–14. Peabody, MA: Hendrickson, 2000.
DeVries, Simon J., *Yesterday, Today, and Tomorrow: Time and History in the Old Testament*. Grand Rapids: Eerdmans, 1975.

Dietrich, Manfried, et al., eds. *The Cuneiform Alphabetic Texts from Ugarit, Ras Ibn Hani and Other Places*. 2d enlarged ed. Abhandlungen zur Literatur Alt-Syrien-Palästinas und Mesopotamiens 8. Münster: Ugarit-Verlag, 1995.

Dorman, Peter F., and Betsy M. Bryan, eds. *Sacred Space and Sacred Function in Ancient Thebes*. Studies in Ancient Oriental Civilization 61. Chicago: The University of Chicago, 2007.

Driver, S. R. *The Book of Genesis: Introduction and Notes*. London: Methuen, 1920.

Ebling, E. *Keilschrifttexte aus Assur religiösen Inhalts*. 2 vols. Leipzig: Hinrichs, 1919–1923.

Edersheim, Alfred, *The Temple: Its Ministry and Services*. Updated Edition; Peabody, MA: Hendrickson, 1994.

Edzard, Dietz Otto. *Sumerian Grammar*. Handbook of Oriental Studies/Handbuch Der Orientalistik. Leiden: Brill, 2003.

Eichrodt, Walther. *Ezekiel: A Commentary*. Translated by Cosslett Quin. OTL. Philadelphia: Westminster, 1970.

Enns, Peter. *Inspiration and Incarnation: Evangelicals and the Problem of the Old Testament*. Grand Rapids: Baker Academic, 2005.

Even-Shosan, Abraham. *A New Concordance of the Old Testament*. Hebrew edition. Grand Rapids: Baker, 1983.

Faulkner, Raymond O. *A Concise Dictionary of Middle Egyptian*. Oxford: Oxford University Press, 1962.

Fischer-Elfert, H. W. *Die Vision von der Statue im Stein: Studien zum altägyptischen Mundöffnungsritual*. Schriften der Philosophisch-historichen Klasse der HeidelbergerAkademie der Wissenschaften 5. Heidelberg: Carl Winter, 1998.

Fleming, Daniel E. "The Seven-Day Siege of Jericho in Holy War." In *Ki Baruch Hu: Ancient Near Eastern, Biblical, and Judaic Studies in Honor of Baruch A. Levine*, edited by Robert Chazan, et al., 211–28. Winona Lake, IN: Eisenbrauns, 1999.

Eichrodt Walther. *Ezekiel: A Commentary*. Translated by Cosslett Quin. OTL. Philadelphia: Westminster, 1970.

Foster, Benjamin R. *Before the Muses: An Anthology of Akkadian Literature*. 3d edition. Bethesda, MD: CDL, 2005.

Fouts, David. "Selected Lexical and Grammatical Studies in Genesis 1." *AUSS* 42 (2004) 79–90.

Frankfort, Henri, *Kingship and the Gods: A Study of Ancient Near Eastern Religion as the Integration of Society and Nature*. Chicago: University of Chicago Press, 1948.

Freitheim, Terence E. "Were the Days of Creation Twenty-Four Hours Long?" In *The Genesis Debate: Persistent Questions about Creation and the Flood*, edited by Ronald F. Youngblood, 12–30. Grand Rapids: Baker, 1990.

Frymer-Kensky, Tikva. "The Atrahasis Epic and Its Significance for Our Understanding of Genesis 1–9." *BA* 40 (1977) 147–55.

Gardner, Bruce K. *The Genesis Calendar: The Synchronistic Tradition in Genesis 1–11*. Lanham: University Press of America, 2001.

Gelander, Shamai. *The Good Creator: Literature and Theology in Genesis 1–11*. Studies in the History of Judaism 147. Atlanta: Scholars Press, 1997.

Geller, Markham J. *Evil Demons: Canonical Utukkū Lemnūtu Incantations*. State Archives of Assyria Cuneiform Texts V; Helsinki: The Neo-Assyrian Text Corpus Project, 2007.

Gesenius, Wilhelm. *Gesenius' Hebrew Grammar*. 1910 ed. Edited and enlarged by Emil Kautsch. Translated by Arthur Ernest Cowley. 2d English ed. Oxford: Oxford University Press, 2003.

Gibson, J. C. L. *Canaanite Myths and Legends*. 2d ed.; Edinburgh: T. & T. Clark, 1978.

Giere, S. D. *A New Glimpse of Day One: Intertextuality, History of Interpretation, and Genesis 1.1-5*. BZNW 172. Berlin: Walter de Gruyter, 2009.

Grayson, A. K. *Assyrian Royal Inscriptions*. Vol. 2. Wiesbaden: Otto Harrassowitz, 1976.

Greenberg, Moshe. *Ezekiel 1-20: A New Translation with Introduction and Commentary*. Anchor Bible Commentary 22. Garden City, NY: Doubleday, 1983.

Greene-McCreight, K. E. *Ad Litteram: How Augustine, Calvin, and Barth Read the "Plain Sense" of Genesis 1-3*. Issues in Systematic Theology 5. New York: Peter Lang, 1999.

Guillaume, Philippe. *Land and Calendar: The Priestly Document from Genesis 1 to Joshua 18*. LHBOTS 391. New York: T&T Clark, 2009.

Gunkel, Hermann. *Creation and Chaos in the Primeval Era and the Eschaton: A Religio-historical Study of Genesis 1 and Revelation 12*. Translated by William Whitney Jr. Grand Rapids: Eerdmans, 2006.

Gordon, Cyrus. *Ugaritic Textbook: Grammar, Texts in Transliteration, Cuneiform Selections, Glossary, Indices*. Analecta Orientalia 35. Rome: Pontificium Institutum Biblicum, 1955.

Hallo, William H., and K. Lawson Younger Jr. *The Context of Scripture, Volume 1: Canonical Compositions from the Biblical World*. Leiden: Brill, 1997.

———. "The Theogony of Dunnu." In *The Context of Scripture, Volume 1: Canonical Compositions from the Biblical World*, edited by William H. Hallo and K. Lawson Younger Jr., 402-4. Leiden: Brill, 1997.

Hasel, Gerhard F. "The Genealogies of Gen 5 and 11 and Their Alleged Babylonian Background," *Andrew University Seminary Study* 16 (1978) 361-74.

Hayes, John L. *A Manual of Sumerian Grammar and Texts*. 2d rev. and enl. ed. Aids and Research Tools in Ancient Near Eastern Studies 5. Malibu: Undena Publications, 2000.

Hendel, Ronald S. "Genesis." In *ABD* 2:933-41.

———. *The Text of Genesis 1-11: Textual Studies and Critical Edition*. Oxford: Oxford University Press, 1998.

———. "Of Demigods and the Deluge: Toward an Interpretation of Genesis 6:1-4." *JBL* 106 (1987) 13-26.

Herion, Gary A. "Why God Rejected Cain's Offering: The Obvious Answer." In *Fortunate the Eyes that See: Essays in Honor of David Noel Freedman in Celebration of His Seventieth Birthday*, edited by Astrid B. Beck, et al., 52-65. Grand Rapids: Eerdmans, 1995.

Hess, Richard S. *Studies in the Personal Names of Genesis 1-11*. Kevelaer Neukirchen-Vluyn: Verlag Butzon & Bercker; Neukirchener Verlag, 1993.

———, and David Toshio Tsumura. *I Studied Inscriptions from before the Flood: Ancient near Eastern, Literary, and Linguistic Approaches to Genesis 1-11*. Winona Lake, Ind.: Eisenbrauns, 1994.

Hodge, Bryan C. "The Labor of the Gods: Ancient Near Eastern Creation Accounts and the Purpose of Genesis 1." MA Thesis, Trinity Evangelical Divinity School, 2002.

Hodge, Charles. *Systematic Theology*. Grand Rapids: Eerdmans, 1997.

Hoffmeier, James K. "Some Thoughts on Genesis 1 & 2 and Egyptian Cosmology." *JANES* 15 (1983) 39-49.

Hoffner, Harry A., Jr. "A Brief Commentary on the Hittite Illuyanka Myth (CTH 321)." In *Studies Presented to Robert D. Biggs: From the Workshop of the Chicago Assyrian Dictionary*, Vol. 2, edited by Martha Roth, et al., 119–40. Assyriological Studies 27. Chicago: Oriental Institute, 2007.

Hoftijzer, J., and K. Jongeling. *Dictionary of North-West Semitic Inscriptions*. Handbuch der Orientalistik 21. Leiden: Brill, 1995.

Hornung, Erik. *Conceptions of God in Ancient Egypt: The One and the Many*. Translated by J. Baines. Ithaca, NY: Cornell University Press, 1982.

Horowitz, Wayne. *Mesopotamian Cosmic Geography*. Mesopotamian Civilizations 8. Winona Lake, IN: Eisenbrauns, 1998.

Hughes, Jeremy. *Secrets of the Times: Myth and History in Biblical Chronology*. JSOTsup 66. Sheffield: Sheffield Academic Press, 1990.

Hunger, Hermann, and David Pingree. *Astral Sciences in Mesopotamia*. Handbuch der Orientalistik 44. Leiden: Brill, 1999.

Hurowitz, Victor. *I Have Built You an Exalted House*. JSOTsup 115. Sheffield: Sheffield Academic Press, 1992.

Jacobsen, Thorkild. *The Harps That . . .* New Haven: Yale University Press, 1987.

——. *The Treasures of Darkness: A History of Mesopotamian Religion*. New Haven: Yale University Press, 1976.

Jenni, Ernst, and Claus Westermann, eds. *Theological Lexicon of the Old Testament*. 3 vols. Translated by Mark Biddle. Peabody, MA: Hendrickson, 1997.

Jouön, Paul and T. Muraoka. *A Grammar of Biblical Hebrew*. Subsidia Biblica 27. 2d ed. Rome: Biblical Institute Press, 2006.

Judisch, Douglas McC. Lindsay. "The Length of the Days of Creation." *CTQ* 52 (1988) 265–71.

Karenga, Maulana. *Maat, The Moral Ideal in Ancient Egypt: A Study in Classical African Ethics*. New York: Routledge, 2004.

Kearney, P. J. "Creation and Liturgy: The P Redaction of Exod 25–40." *ZAW* 89 (1977) 375–87.

Keil, Carl Friedrich, and F. Delitzsch. *The Pentateuch*. Biblical Commentary on the Old Testament, Vol. 1. Peabody, MA: Hendrickson, 1996.

Keel, Othmar, and Christoph Uehlinger, *Gods, Goddesses, and Images of God in Ancient Israel*. Translated by Thomas H. Trapp. Minneapolis: Fortress, 1998.

Kidner, Derek. *Genesis: An Introduction and Commentary*. Tyndale Old Testament Commentary 1. Downer's Grove, IL: Intervarsity, 1967.

Kikawada, Isaac M., and Arthur Quinn. *Before Abraham Was*. Nashville: Abingdon, 1985.

Kim, Yoon Kyung. *Augustine's Changing Interpretations of Genesis 1–3: From De Genesi contra Manichaeos to De Genesi ad litteram*. Lewiston: Edwin Mellen, 2006.

Koehler, Ludwig, and Walter Baumgartner. *The Hebrew and Aramaic Lexicon of the Old Testament*. Study Edition. Translated by M. E. J. Richardson. Leiden: Brill, 2002.

Kramer, Samuel Noah. "Sumerische Litteraire Teksten uit Ur." *Phoenix* 10 (1964) 99–108.

——. "The Temple in Sumerian Literature." In *Temple in Society*, edited by Michael V. Fox, 1–16. Winona Lake: Eisenbrauns, 1988.

Kovacs, Maureen G. *The Epic of Gilgamesh: Translated with an Introduction*. Stanford: Stanford University Press, 1989.

Kugel, James L. *The Bible As It Was*. Cambridge, MA: Harvard University Press, 1997.

———. *The Idea of Biblical Poetry: Parallelism and Its History*. New Haven: Yale University Press, 1981.
———. *Traditions of the Bible: A Guide to the Bible as It Was at the Start of the Common Era*. Cambridge, MA: Harvard University Press, 1998.
Kutsko, John F. *Between Heaven and Earth: Divine Presence and Absence in the Book of Ezekiel*. Biblical and Judaic Studies 7. Winona Lake, IN: Eisenbrauns, 2000.
Lambert, W. G., and A. R. Millard. *Atra-Ḫasīs: The Babylonian Story of the Flood*. Winona Lake: Eisenbrauns, 1999.
———. "Three Unpublished Fragments of the Tukulti-Ninurta Epic." *AfO* 18 (1957) 38–51.
Landsberger, B., and J. V. Kinnier Wilson. "The Fifth Tablet of 'Enuma Elish.'" *Journal of Near Eastern Studies* 20 (1961) 172
Lapinkivi, Pirjo. *The Neo-Assyrian Myth of Ishtar's Descent and Resurrection*. State Archives of Assyria Cuneiform Texts 6. Helsinki: Neo-Assyrian Text Corpus Project, 2010.
Leick, Gwendolyn. *A Dictionary of Ancient Near Eastern Architecture*. New York:Routledge, 1988.
Leitz, C. *Magical and Medical Papyri of the New Kingdom*. Hieratic Papyri in the British Museum 6. London: British Museum Press, 1999.
Levenson, Jon D. *Creation and the Persistence of Evil: The Jewish Drama of Divine Omnipotence*. Princeton, NJ: Princeton University Press, 1988.
———. "The Temple and the World," *JR* 64 (1984) 275–98.
Lewis, Jack P. *A Study of the Interpretation of Noah and the Flood in Jewish and Christian Literature*. Leiden: Brill, 1968.
Lichtheim, Miriam. "The Shipwrecked Sailor." In *The Context of Scripture, Volume 1: Canonical Compositions from the Biblical World*, edited by William H. Hallo and K. Lawson Younger Jr., 83–85. Leiden: Brill, 1997.
———. *Ancient Egyptian Literature: A Book of Readings*. 3 vols. Berkeley: University of California Press, 1975–1980.
Link, Christian. "Providence: An Unsolved Problem of the Doctrine of Creation." In *Creation in Jewish and Christian Tradition*, edited by Henning Graf Reventlow and Yair Hoffman, 266–76. JSOTsup 319. London: Sheffield Academic Press, 2002.
Livingstone, David N., and Mark A. Noll. "B.B. Warfield (1851–1921): A Biblical Inerrantist as Evolutionist." *Isis* 91 (2000) 283–94.
Lorton, David. "The Theology of Cult Statues in Ancient Egypt." In *Born in Heaven, Made on Earth: The Making of the Cult Image in the Ancient Near East*, edited by Michael B. Dick, 123–210. Winona Lake, IN: Eisenbrauns, 1999.
Louth, Andrew. *Genesis 1–11*. Ancient Christian Commentary on Scripture: Old Testament, Vol. 1. Downers Grove, IL: Intervarsity, 2001.
Luckenbill, Daniel D. *Ancient Records of Assyria and Babylonia*. Part 2. London: Histories and Mysteries of Man, 1989.
Lundbom, Jack R. *Jeremiah 1–20*. Anchor Bible 21A; New York: Doubleday, 1999.
Lundquist, John M. "What Is a Temple? A Preliminary Typology." In *The Quest for the Kingdom of God: Studies in Honor of George E. Mendenhall*, edited by H. B. Huffmon, 205–20. Winona Lake, IN: Eisenbrauns, 1983.
Machinist, Peter. "Literature as Politics: The Tukulti-Ninurta Epic and the Bible." *CBQ* 38 (1976) 455–82.

———. *The Epic of Tukulti-Ninurta I: A Study in Middle Assyrian Literature*. PhD diss., Yale University, 1978.

Maimonides, Moses. *The Guide of the Perplexed*. Abridged with Introduction and Commentary by Julius Guttmann. Translated by Chaim Rabin. New Introduction by Daniel H. Frank. Indianapolis, IN: Hackett, 1985.

Martínez, Florentino García, and Eibert J. C. Tigchelaar. *The Dead Sea Scrolls: Study Edition*. 2 vols. Leiden: Brill, 2000.

Martínez, Florentino García, and Gerard P. Luttikhuizen. *Interpretations of the Flood*. Themes in Biblical Narrative. Leiden: Brill, 1999.

McKane, William. *A Critical and Exegetical Commentary on Jeremiah*, revised ed. Edinburgh: T&T Clark, 1999.

Mettinger, Tryggve N. D. *The Eden Narrative: A Literary and Religio-historical Study of Genesis 2–3*. Winona Lake, IN: Eisenbrauns, 2007.

Meyers, Carol. *The Tabernacle Menorah*. Missoula: Scholars Press, 1976.

Migne, Jacques Paul, ed. *Patrologiae Cursus Completus: Series Graeca*. 161 vols. Paris: Imprimerie Catholique, 1857–68.

———. *Patrologiae Cursus Completus: Series Latine*. 217 vols. Paris: Imprimerie Catholique, 1844–55.

Milgrom, Jacob. *Leviticus 1–16: A New Translation with Introduction and Commentary*. Anchor Bible 3. New York: Doubleday, 1991.

Miller, Cynthia L. *The Representation of Speech in Biblical Hebrew Narrative: A Linguistic Analysis*. Harvard Semitic Monographs 75. Winona Lake, IN: Eisenbrauns, 2003.

Moberly, R. W. L. *The Theology of the Book of Genesis*. Old Testament Theology. Cambridge University Press: Cambridge, 2009.

Morris, P., and D. Sawyer, eds. *A Walk in the Garden: Biblical, Iconographical and Literary Images of Eden*. JSOTsup 136. Sheffield: Sheffield Academic Press, 1992.

Nickelsburg, George W. E. *Jewish Literature between the Bible and the Mishnah*. Minneapolis: Fortress, 2005.

Niditch, Susan. *Chaos to Cosmos: Studies in Biblical Patterns of Creation*. Scholars Press Study in Humanities. Duke University Press, 1985.

Noll, Mark, ed. *The Princeton Theology, 1812–1921*. Phillipsburg, NJ: Presbyterian and Reformed Publishing, 1983.

Ockinga, Boyo. *Die Gottebenbildlichkeit im Alten Ägypten und im Alten Testament*. Wiesbaden: Harrassowitz, 1984.

Oppenheim, A. Leo. "Babylonian and Assyrian Historical Texts." In *Ancient Near Eastern Texts Relating to the Old Testament*, 3d ed., edited by James B. Pritchard, 265–6. Princeton: Princeton University Press, 1969.

Oswalt, John. *The Bible among the Myths: Unique Revelation or Just Ancient Literature?* Grand Rapids: Zondervan, 2009.

Philo. "On the Creation (*De Opificio Mundi*)." In *The Works of Philo: New Updated Edition*. Translated by C. D. Yonge, 3–24. Peabody, MA: Hendrickson, 1993.

Paas, Stefan. *Creation and Judgement: Creation Texts in Some Eighth Century Prophets*. Oudtestamentische Studiën XLVII. Leiden: Brill, 2003.

Pardee, Dennis. "The Ba'lu Myth." In *The Context of Scripture, Volume 1: Canonical Compositions from the Biblical World*, edited by William H. Hallo and K. Lawson Younger Jr., 241–74. Leiden: Brill, 1997.

Parpola, Simon, ed. *The Standard Babylonian Epic of Gilgamesh*. State Archives of Assyria Cuneiform Texts 1. Helsinki: Neo-Assyrian Text Corpus Project, 1977.

Peckham, Brian. "History and Time." In *Ki Baruch Hu: Ancient Near Eastern, Biblical, and Judaic Studies in Honor of Baruch A. Levine*, edited by Robert Chazan, et al., 295–314. Winona Lake, IN: Eisenbrauns, 1999.

Pelikan, Jaroslav, ed. *Luther's Works, Volume 1: Lectures on Genesis, Chapters 1–5*. St. Louis: Concordia, 1958.

Pettinato, G. *Das altorientalische Menschenbild und die sumerischen und akkadischen Schöpfungsmythen*. Heidelberg: Carl Winter Universitätsverlag, 1971.

Polak, Frank H. "Poetic Style and Parallelism in the Creation Account (Genesis 1.1–2.3)." In *Creation in Jewish and Christian Tradition*, edited by Henning Graf Reventlow and Yair Hoffman, 2–31. JSOTsup 319. London: Sheffield Academic Press, 2002.

Pope, Marvin H. *Song of Songs: A New Translation with Introduction and Commentary*. Anchor Bible 7c. Garden City, NY: 1977.

Pritchard, James B. *Ancient Near Eastern Texts Relating to the Old Testament*. 3d ed. Princeton: Princeton University, 1969.

Propp, William C. *Exodus 19–40: A New Translation with Introduction and Commentary*. Anchor Bible 2a. New York: Doubleday, 2006.

Reiner, E., and D. Pingree, *Babylonian Planetary Omens: 1–2*. Bibliotheca Mesopotamica. Malibu: Udena Publications, 1975.

Roaf, Michael, "Palaces and Temples in Ancient Mesopotamia." In *Civilizations of the Ancient Near East*, edited by Jack M. Sasson, 423–42. Peabody, MA: Hendrickson, 2000.

Roberts, Alexander, and James Donaldson. *Ante-Nicene Fathers*. Volumes 1–10. Peabody, MA: Hendrickson, 1995.

Robins, Gay, "Cult Statues in Ancient Egypt." In *Cult Image and Divine Representation in the Ancient Near East*, edited by Neal H. Walls, 1–12. ASOR 10. Boston, MA: American Schools for Oriental Research, 2005.

Rochberg-Halton, F. "TCL 6 13: Mixed Traditions in Late Babylonian Assyriology." ZA 77 (1987) 207–228.

Roth, Martha, et al. *The Assyrian Dictionary of the Oriental Institute of the University of Chicago. 21 vols. in 26 parts*. Chicago: University of Chicago Press, 1956–2006.

Rudolph, David J. "Festivals in Genesis 1:14." *TynBul* 54.2 (2003) 23–40.

Sæbø, M. "יוֹם yôm." In *Theological Dictionary of the Old Testament*, Vol. 6, edited by Johannes Botterweck and Helmer Ringgren, 7–32. Translated by David E. Green. Grand Rapids: Eerdmans, 1990.

Sarna, Nahum. *Genesis: The Traditional Hebrew Text with the New JPS Translation*. JPS Torah Commentary; Philadelphia: Jewish Publication Society, 1989.

Schaff, Philip. *The Creeds of Christendom*. Grand Rapids: Baker, 1996.

Schaff, Philip, and Henry Wace, *Nicene and Post-Nicene Fathers*. Series 2. Volumes 1–14. A Select Library of the Christian Church. Peabody, MA: Hendrickson, 1999.

Schmidt, W.H. *Die Schöpfungsgeschichte der Priestershrift. Zur Überlieferungsgeschichte von Genesis 1,1–2,4a und 2,4b–3,24*. 2d ed. Wissenschaftliche Monographien zum Alten und Neuen Testament 17. Neukirchen-Vluyn: Neukirchener Verlag, 1967.

Schmutzer, Andrew J. *Be Fruitful and Multiply: A Crux of Thematic Repetition in Genesis 1–11*. Eugene, OR: Wipf & Stock, 2009.

Schüle, Andreas. "Made in the Image of God: The Concepts of Divine Images in Gen 1–3." *ZAW* 117 (2005) 1–20.

Segert, Stanislav. *A Basic Grammar of the Ugaritic Language with Selected Texts and Glossary*. Berkeley: University of California Press, 1984.

Shaffer, Aaron. "Sumerian Sources of Tablet XII of the Epic of Gilgamesh." PhD diss., University of Pennsylvania, 1963.

Shedd, William G.T. *Dogmatic Theology.* Vol. 1. Edinburgh: T.& T. Clark, 1889.

Shimon Bar-Efrat. *Narrative Art in the Bible.* Translated by Dorothea Shefer-Vanson. Bible and Literature 17/JSOTsup 70. Sheffield: Almond, 1989.

Silberman, Rabbi A. M., trans. *Chumash with Targum Onkelos, Haphtaroth and Rashi's Commentary: Bereshith.* Jerusalem: Silberman Family, 1934.

Sivan, Daniel. *A Grammar of the Ugaritic Language.* 2d impression with corrections. Handbook of Oriental Studies 28. Atlanta: Society of Biblical Literature, 2001.

Skinner, John. *A Critical and Exegetical Commentary on Genesis.* 2d ed. Edinburgh: T&T Clark, 1969.

Smick, Elmer. "Another Look at the Mythological Elements in the Book of Job." *WTJ* 40 (1978) 213–28.

Smith, Mark S. "Like Deities, Like Temples (Like People)." In *Temple and Worship in Biblical Israel*, edited by John Day, 3–27. Library of Hebrew Bible/Old Testament Studies 422. London/New York: T&T Clark, 2005.

———. *The Priestly Vision of Genesis 1.* Minneapolis: Fortress, 2010.

Speiser, E. A. *Genesis: Translated with an Introduction and Notes.* Anchor Bible 1; Garden City, NY: Doubleday, 1964.

Spicq, Ceslas. *Theological Lexicon of the New Testament.* Translated and edited by James D. Ernest. 3 vols. Peabody, MA: Hendrickson, 1994.

Stager, L. E. "Jerusalem and the Garden of Eden," *ErIsr* 26 (1999)183–94.

Stadelmann, Luis I. J. *The Hebrew Conception of the World: A Philological and Literary Study.* Analecta Biblica 39. Rome: Pontifical Biblical Institute, 1970.

Sternberg, Meir. *The Poetics of Biblical Narrative.* Indiana Literary Biblical Series. Bloomington, IN: Indiana University Press, 1985.

Stordalen, Terje. "Genesis 2, 4. Restudying a Locus Classicus." *ZAW* 104.2 (1992) 163–76.

———. "Man, Soil, Garden: Basic Plot in Genesis 2–3 Reconsidered." *JSOT* 53 (1992) 3–26.

———. *Echoes of Eden: Genesis 2–3 and Symbolism of the Eden Garden in Biblical Hebrew Literature.* Leuven, Belgium: Peeters, 2000.

Strassmaier, J. N. *Alphabetisches Verzeichnis der assyrischen und akkadischen Wörter der Cuneiform Inscriptions of Western Asia, Vol. 2: sowie anderer meist unveröffentlichter Inschriften.* Leipzig, 1886.

Talon, Philippe. *The Standard Babylonian Creation Myth: Enuma Elish: Introduction, Cuneiform Text, Transliteration, and Sign List with a Translation and Glossary in French.* State Archives of Assyria 4; Finland: The Neo-Assyrian Text Corpus Project, 2005.

Tappert, Theodore G., ed., and trans. "Table Talk," Luther's Works, Vol. 54. Edited by Helmut T. Lehmann. Philadelphia: Fortress, 1967.

Tigchelaar, Eibert. "'Lights Serving as Signs for Festivals' (Genesis 1:14b) in Enūma Eliš and Early Judaism." In *The Creation of Heaven and Earth: Re-interpretations of Genesis I in the Context of Judaism, Ancient Philosophy, Christianity, and Modern Physics*, edited by George H. van Kooten, 31–48. Leiden: Brill, 2005.

Tsumura, David T. *The Earth and the Waters in Genesis 1 and 2: A Linguistic Investigation.* JSOTsup 83. Sheffield: Sheffield Academic Press, 1989.

van der Toorn, Karel, et al. *Dictionary of Deities and Demons in the Bible*. 2d ed. Grand Rapids: Eerdmans, 1999.
van Ruiten, J.T.A.G.M. *Primaeval History Interpreted: The Rewriting of Genesis 1–11 in the book of Jubilees*. Journal for the Study of Judaism 66. Leiden: Brill, 2000.
van Seters, John. *Prologue to History: The Yahwist as Historian in Genesis*. Louisville, KY: Westminster John Knox, 1992.
Vanderkam, James C. *The Book of Jubilees*. Guides to the Apocrypha and Pseudepigrapha. Sheffield: Sheffield Academic Press, 2001.
VanGemeren, Willem A., ed. *New International Dictionary of Old Testament Theology and Exegesis*. 5 vols. Grand Rapids: Zondervan, 1997.
Vanstiphout, H. L. J. "The Mesopotamian Debate Poems: A General Presentation (Part 1)." *Acta Sumerologica* 12 (1990) 271–318.
———. "The Mesopotamian Debate Poems: A General Presentation. Part II. The Subject." *Acta Sumerologica* 14 (1992) 347–48.
———. "A Note on the Format of 'Bird and Fish.'" *NABU* (1991) No. 104.
Vogels, Walter, "The Cultic and Civil Calendars of the Fourth Day of Creation." *SJOT* 11 (1997) 163–80.
———. "'Like One of Us, Knowing ṬOB and RAʿ'" In *Thinking in Signs: Semiotics and Biblical Studies . . . Thirty Years After*, edited by Daniel Patte, 145–57. Semeia 81. Atlanta: Scholars Press, 1989.
Volk, Konrad. *A Sumerian Reader*. 2d revised ed. Studia Pohl: Series Maior 18. Rome: Editrice Pontificio Instituto Biblico, 1999.
von Rad, Gerhard. *Genesis*. Revised ed. OTL. Philadelphia: Westminster, 1972.
von Soden, W. *Akkadisches Handwörterbuch*. 3 vols. Wiesbaden: Harrassowitz Verlag, 1985.
Wallace, Howard N. *The Eden Narrative*. Harvard Semitic Monographs 32. Missoula, MT: Scholars Press, 1985.
Waltke, Bruce K., and M. O'Connor. *An Introduction to Biblical Hebrew Syntax*. Winona Lake, IN: Eisenbrauns, 1990.
Walton, John H., "Equilibrium and the Sacred Compass: The Structure of Leviticus." *BBR* 11 (2001) 293–304.
———. *The Lost World of Genesis 1: Ancient Chronology and the Origins Debate*. Downers Grove, IL: IVP Academic, 2009.
Weinfeld, Moshe. "Sabbath, Temple and the Enthronement of the Lord: The Problem of the Sitz im Leben of Genesis 1:1–2:3." In *Mélanges bibliques et orientaux en l'honneur de M. Henri Cazelles*, edited by A. Caquot and M. Delcor, 501–12. AOAT 212. Kevelaer: Butzon & Bercker / Neukirchen-Vluyn: Neukirchener Verlag, 1981.
Wenham, Gordon J. *Genesis 1–15*. Word Biblical Commentary. Waco, TX: Word, 1987.
———. "The Coherence of the Flood Narrative." In *I Studied Inscriptions from before the Flood: Ancient Near Eastern, Literary, and Linguistic Approaches to Genesis 1–11*, edited by Richard S. Hess and David T. Tsumura, 436–47. Sources for Biblical and Theological Study 4. Winona Lake, IN: Eisenbrauns, 1994.
———. "Sanctuary Symbolism in the Garden of Eden Story." In *I Studied Inscriptions from before the Flood: Ancient Near Eastern, Literary, and Linguistic Approaches to Genesis 1–11*, edited by Richard S. Hess and David T. Tsumura, 399–404. Sources for Biblical and Theological Study 4. Winona Lake, IN: Eisenbrauns, 1994.
Westermann, Claus. *Genesis 1–11: A Continental Commentary*. Translated by John J. Scullion S. J. Continental Commentaries. Minneapolis: Fortress, 1994.

Wevers, John W., ed. *Notes on the Greek Text of Genesis*. Septuagint and Cognate Studies Series 35. Atlanta: Scholars Press, 1993.

White, Hugh C. *Narration and Discourse in the Book of Genesis*. Cambridge: Cambridge University Press, 2008.

Widengren, Geo. *The King and the Tree of Life in Ancient Near Eastern religion: (King and Saviour IV)*. Uppsala universitets aÌšrsskrift: Lundequistska bokhandeln, 1951.

Wilch, John R. *Time and Event: An Exegetical Study of the Use of ʿēth in the Old Testament in Comparison to Other Temporal Expressions in Clarification of the Concept of Time*. Leiden: Brill, 1969.

Williams, Ronald J. *Hebrew Syntax: An Outline*. 2d ed. Toronto: University of Toronto Press, 1976.

Wilson, Robert R. "The Old Testament Genealogies in Recent Research." In *I Studied Inscriptions from before the Flood: Ancient Near Eastern, Literary, and Linguistic Approaches to Genesis 1–11*, edited by Richard S. Hess and David T. Tsumura, 200–23. Sources for Biblical and Theological Study 4. Winona Lake, IN: Eisenbrauns, 1994.

Wintermute O. S. "Jubilees: A New Translation." In *The Old Testament Pseudepigrapha*, Volume 2. Edited by James H. Charlesworth. New York: Doubleday, 1985.

Wiseman, P. J. *Creation Revealed in Six Days: The Evidence of Scripture Confirmed by Archaeology*. 3d ed. London: Marshall, Morgan & Scott, 1958.

Wyatt, N. "The Mythic Mind." *SJOT* 15 (2001) 3–56.

———. *Religious Texts from Ugarit*. 2d ed. The Biblical Seminar 53. London: Sheffield Academic Press, 2003.

Yoshikawa, M. "Spatial Deictic System in Sumerian." *Acta Sumerologica* 15 (1993) 185–92.

Zadok, Tikva. "The Use of Subordinating Particles *Inūmī/Inu/Inūma* 'When' in Old Babylonian Royal Inscriptions." In *Past Links: Studies in the Languages and Cultures of the Ancient Near East*, edited by Shlomo Isreʾel, et al., 19–32. Israel Oriental Studies XVIII. Winona Lake, Eisenbrauns, 1998.

www.ingramcontent.com/pod-product-compliance
Lightning Source LLC
Chambersburg PA
CBHW062000220426
43662CB00011B/1764